ARNHEM
Myth and Reality

About the Author

Sebastian Ritchie is an official historian at the Air Historical Branch (RAF) of the Ministry of Defence. He has a PhD from King's College, London, and he lectured for three years at the University of Manchester before joining the Air Historical Branch. He is the author of numerous official narratives covering RAF operations in Iraq and the Former Yugoslavia, and he has also lectured and published widely on aspects of air power and air operations, as well as airborne operations and special operations in the Second World War.

ARNHEM
Myth and Reality

Airborne Warfare, Air Power and the
Failure of Operation Market Garden

Sebastian Ritchie

ROBERT HALE

First published in 2011 by Robert Hale, an imprint of
The Crowood Press Ltd, Ramsbury, Marlborough Wiltshire SN8 2HR

www.crowood.com

Paperback edition 2019

British Library Cataloguing-in-Publication Data
A catalogue record for this book is available from the British Library.

ISBN 978 0 7198 2921 5

Typeset by e-type, Liverpool
Printed and bound in India by Replika Press Pvt Ltd

To Jacqueline, with love

Contents

Acknowledgements

Arnhem: Myth and Reality is an entirely private project, and is not related in any way to my work as an official historian at the Ministry of Defence (MOD). It was researched and written in my own time and the historical judgements contained within its pages are mine alone and in no way reflect the views of the RAF or the MOD.

Having said that, I cannot deny that this book had its origins in the MOD's Directorate of Equipment Capability (Deep Target Attack) staff ride to Arnhem in 2004. I am grateful to the officers who staffed the directorate at that time for inviting me along, and to Bill McQuade for introducing me to the Market Garden area, which I have explored on many occasions since. I am also indebted to the numerous British military personnel who have accompanied me for their many constructive questions and comments. They have played an invaluable part in helping me to rethink the events of September 1944.

My basic thesis was first published in rudimentary form in the *Royal Air Force Air Power Review* in 2005 and first presented at the Society of Military History's annual conference at Kansas State University in 2006; further presentations then followed at the RAF College, Cranwell, in 2008 and at Birmingham University in 2009. These opportunities to publicize my position proved immensely useful, and my views were in some cases substantially refined as a result. I must therefore thank all of those involved, particularly Air Commodore Neville Parton, formerly (as Group Captain) Director of Defence Studies, RAF, Dr Joel Hayward and Air Commodore Peter Grey. I also owe an immense debt of gratitude to my colleagues at the Air Historical Branch, particularly Sebastian Cox, Steve Lloyd, Clive Richards, Mary Hudson and Lee Barton, for help and encouragement and for alerting me to a number of valuable sources I had previously ignored or failed to identify. At the RAF museum, Peter Elliot's assistance with Hollinghurst papers was likewise very valuable, and immensely appreciated.

Beyond this, *Arnhem: Myth and Reality* owes much to the many historians who have tackled Market Garden before me. Although I argue in this book that a substantial reassessment of the operation is long overdue, this is not in any way to deny the historical value of earlier studies, and the extent to which they have helped to shape my perspective. Finally I am grateful to my family for tolerating extended periods of research and writing when I undoubtedly neglected my duties as a husband and father.

This book is primarily a study of military planning. Operation plans (especially airborne plans) have a tendency to become highly complex. The records they generate for historians are often contradictory or deficient, while the recollections of those involved may not always answer outstanding questions or resolve discrepancies. I have sought to make the following chapters as accurate and well-documented as possible but if, despite my efforts, any factual errors have gone undetected, I am of course solely responsible.

Abbreviations

ADGB	Air Defence Great Britain
AEAF	Allied Expeditionary Air Force
AHB	Air Historical Branch
CIGS	Chief of the Imperial General Staff
DZ	Drop Zone
GCI	Ground Control Intercept
LZ	Landing Zone
MGAF	Major General Airborne Forces
MOD	Ministry of Defence
PARA	Battalion, the Parachute Regiment
PIR	Parachute Infantry Regiment
POW	Prisoner of War
RAF	Royal Air Force
SAS	Special Air Service Brigade
SHAEF	Supreme Headquarters Allied Expeditionary Force
TAF	Tactical Air Force
TCC	Troop Carrier Command
USAAF	United States Army Air Force
VCP	Visual Control Post

General Introduction

O PERATION MARKET GARDEN, launched on 17 September 1944, is often depicted as one of the most decisive military actions of the Allied campaign to liberate Western Europe. After finally breaking out of Normandy in August, Allied forces had quickly crossed northern and eastern France, raising hopes that the European war might be brought to a successful conclusion by the end of the year. But Hitler's armies were not yet defeated; early in September their chaotic retreat from Normandy was halted, units and formations were reorganized, and reserves were deployed to points of particular vulnerability. Through an extraordinary combination of resourcefulness, improvisation and administrative skill, a defensive line was re-established from the North Sea to Switzerland; the Allied advance – already jeopardized by mounting logistical problems – was finally stopped in its tracks. More than any other action, Market Garden has come to symbolize this so-called 'check in the west'. To its proponents it offered an opportunity to cross the River Rhine and seize the Ruhr – Germany's industrial heartland. But its failure ended any realistic chance of securing a Rhine bridgehead before 1945.

Aside from the Normandy landings and perhaps the German offensive in the Ardennes, no other large-scale operation mounted in Western Europe in the final year of the war has so captured the popular imagination. With its dramatic mass airborne landings, heroic tactical actions like the defence of the Arnhem road bridge and the Waal assault river crossing, alleged command failures and planning and intelligence blunders, Market Garden has generated an enduring fascination and consequently an enormous literature. Thus it was never the intention that this book should be just another history of the operation. Readers seeking one more narrative of 1st Airborne Division's epic struggle at Arnhem or of XXX Corps' ill-fated efforts to relieve them will search these pages in vain.

Rather, the aim of this account is to place Market Garden in its correct historical context and to survey a number of major themes in its historiography. It was written for two principal reasons. First, it is contended that many critical aspects of the operation have consistently been misunderstood or misrepresented in past histories. Second (and from the perspective of a historian who works closely with the modern military), it is clear that until we have a more accurate understanding of these issues the most valuable and enduring lessons of Market Garden's failure simply cannot be learnt.

The existing literature on Market Garden suffers from one particular drawback. Considering its scale the operation is one of the worst documented of the Second World War, chiefly because it was initiated at only four days' notice; it was originally sanctioned on 10 September with D-Day envisaged as the 14th; on the 12th it was postponed until 17 September. Official records certainly survive, but detailed planning papers – minutes of meetings, records of decisions – from the 10 to 17 September period are few and far between. Presumably, given the lack of time, much of this planning activity was conducted verbally or was at least never recorded in a form deemed worthy of long-term preservation. Unfortunately the well-known scarcity of such documents has led historians to ignore even the relatively limited quantity of official papers still available. Instead they have tended to rely heavily for source material on the memoirs and recorded testimonies of those involved. Of course, these accounts are of immense value but they also suffer from predictable problems of bias, parochialism and selective recollection. As is typical in the aftermath of any failed military endeavour, many of the participants later claimed to have strenuously promoted alternative courses of action which (they alleged) would have produced more successful outcomes than those actually adopted. Yet invariably such arguments gain credibility only with the advantage of hindsight – an asset at the time unavailable to the actual decision-makers.

Another consequence of this limited source base has been a disproportionate focus among historians on the more emotive aspects of the operation. The five Victoria Cross awards and the innumerable stories of heroism, sacrifice and achievement in the face of extreme adversity naturally have an important place in the Market Garden saga, but they have not encouraged careful and dispassionate scholarly investigation. Equally, the strenuous efforts devoted over many years to portraying 1st Airborne Division as the blameless victims of misguided 'actions taken by others' serve no useful historical purpose.[1] They merely ensure that research on the operation is confined within narrow boundaries and that, to this day, many aspects of 1st Airborne's experience at Arnhem are wrongly described and imperfectly grasped.

Yet the most acute problem lies not so much in the inherent weaknesses of anecdotal source material but in the fact that so much of it is drawn from only one of the armed services involved in Market Garden, namely the airborne forces. This focus reflects an elementary misconception among historians concerning the very nature of airborne operations: all too often they are viewed simply as an extension of conventional land warfare. Yet the very concept of airborne warfare actually grew out of the application of air power, that is, out of the exploitation of air power's inherent flexibility and reach to deliver a particular load (airborne troops) to a defined objective. Air power should therefore be central to any study of airborne warfare. And yet invariably it is regarded as a peripheral element – a minor detail compared with the fighting on the ground. Hence no major study of Market Garden published in recent years has attempted to describe the planning or execution of the airlifts in any detail.[2] Typically, histories of the operation devote only pages to the air plan and dwell largely on its alleged failings. Another important reason for this bias is that the history of airborne operations – and especially of Market Garden – has predominantly been written by scholars of land warfare, former army personnel or 'generalists' who have only a limited understanding of air issues.

Cornelius Ryan's *A Bridge Too Far*, which is still one of the most widely read and influential books on Market Garden, provides a perfect illustration. In preparing *A Bridge Too Far*, Ryan claimed to have followed 'certain strict guidelines'. Each statement or quotation in the book was allegedly reinforced by documentary evidence or by the corroboration of others who heard or witnessed the event described. 'Hearsay, rumour or third-party accounts could not be included.'[3] But Ryan did not maintain that his sources were notable for their objectivity. In point of fact, the contributors who he 'singled out for special thanks' were:

Major General Roy Urquhart: commander of 1st Airborne Division at Arnhem
General Charles Mackenzie: formerly Lieutenant Colonel, Urquhart's chief of staff
Major General John D. Frost: formerly Lieutenant Colonel, commander of 2nd Parachute Battalion at Arnhem
Colonel Eric M. Mackay: formerly Captain, with the Royal Engineers at Arnhem
Major General Philip H.W. Hicks: formerly Brigadier, commander of 1 Airlanding Brigade at Arnhem
General Sir John Hackett: formerly Brigadier, commander of 4 Parachute Brigade at Arnhem
Brigadier George Chatterton: formerly Colonel, commander of the Glider Pilot Regiment at Arnhem
Brigadier Gordon Walch: I Airborne Corps chief of staff during Market Garden

Other notable contributors were General (formerly Brigadier General) James Gavin, commander of 82nd Airborne Division during Market Garden; General (formerly Major General) Maxwell Taylor, commander of 101st Airborne Division during Market Garden; Major General Stanislaw Sosabowski, commander of 1 Polish Parachute Brigade during Market Garden; and Daphne du Maurier, wife of the commander of I Airborne Corps, Lieutenant General F.A.M. (later Sir Frederick) 'Boy' Browning.[4] It is difficult to imagine how anyone could expect such a one-dimensional array of sources to provide a remotely balanced or comprehensive view of a joint operation.

Equally, the published memoirs cited in so many histories of Market Garden almost all provide the perspective of airborne or army officers. Urquhart, Hackett, Chatterton and Frost are among the most commonly quoted, although key figures from XXX Corps such as Lieutenant General Brian (later Sir Brian) Horrocks and Lieutenant Colonel (later Brigadier) Joe Vandeleur also wrote accounts of the operation. Other regularly cited memoirs include those of Gavin, Eisenhower and of course Field Marshal Bernard Law Montgomery, commander of British and Canadian forces in northwest Europe (21st Army Group). By contrast, of the air officers who held senior command appointments during Market Garden, only Air Chief Marshal Sir Arthur (later Marshal of the Royal Air Force Lord) Tedder would later produce memoirs. But Tedder (as Eisenhower's deputy) had no responsibility for planning the supporting air effort.

For all of these reasons, then, there are good grounds for reconsidering Market Garden. It is particularly important that its history should be based as far as possible on such official sources as survive rather than on personal accounts of the operation, that we should not attach undue weight to the more emotive aspects of the story, and that we should to some extent reorient our attention away from the airborne divisions and towards the Allied air forces. After all, without them Market Garden would not have been possible. It is only through this means that the numerous myths and legends that have clouded our perceptions of the operation for so long will ultimately be dispelled.

Three of these myths form the central focus of this study. The first is that airborne warfare had proved an effective and successful means of conducting operations before September 1944. This belief has been bolstered by the failure of many published accounts of Market Garden to place the operation in historical context by considering the German and Allied airborne record earlier in the war.[5] Historians merely assume or imply that the airborne medium did not differ fundamentally from any other means of applying military force. The contention here, on the other hand, is that the operation cannot properly be understood unless past airborne experience is examined in some detail. The first three chapters of this book thus break completely with established tradition by surveying all the large-scale airborne operations mounted in the European theatre by both the Germans and the Allies between 1940 and 1944. Only some such survey can provide an accurate foundation for assessing the events that culminated in the launch of Market Garden, the basis upon which it was planned, and its prospects of success.

The second myth is that Market Garden was a brilliant conceptual plan at the military-strategic level, which only failed because of flawed operational-tactical level execution.[6] In other words, responsibility for Market Garden's failure rests not with the British Army commander who initiated it – Montgomery – but with the Allied airborne headquarters that was required to turn the concept into a detailed plan. The prevailing assumption is that, although the airborne planners had a variety of practicable options at their disposal, they consistently chose the wrong ones; allegedly they let Montgomery down.[7] This depiction of events has appeared both plausible and convenient to the majority of authors, especially in the United Kingdom, yet it is unsatisfactory on a number of counts. In particular, it has left little scope for careful investigation of the relationship between conceptual and detailed planning. Chapters 2.1, 2.2 and 2.3 seek to rectify this imbalance in the historiography by tracing the emergence and development of the conceptual plan for staging an airborne Rhine crossing at Arnhem, and by critically assessing its feasibility. The influence of higher command levels upon the process of operational-tactical level planning is also considered in the context of intelligence analysis and exploitation.

The third and most enduring myth of all is that the Allied air forces – the Royal Air Force (RAF) and the United States Army Air Force (USAAF) – bore a particular responsibility for Market Garden's failure. At a time when other large-scale air operations were being mounted in support of 21st Army Group, both the RAF and the USAAF lent their backing to Market Garden on an immense scale. In a period of nine days some 14,751 air sorties and 2,598 glider sorties were flown in support of the operation.[8] If it is considered that the most intensive air operations were required during the first few days of the offensive, and that poor weather grounded the majority of Allied aircraft on at least two days in this period (19 and 20 September), the true extent of the air effort will be appreciated. The air forces also went to quite extraordinary and unprecedented lengths to ensure that the airborne troops were delivered accurately and safely to their drop zones and landing zones. It is nevertheless now common to read that senior air commanders – Lieutenant General Lewis Brereton of First Allied Airborne Army and his subordinates, Major General Paul Williams of 9th Troop Carrier Command (9th TCC), and Air Vice-Marshal Leslie Hollinghurst of 38 Group, RAF – are primarily to blame for the Allied defeat.[9]

This line of argument can be traced all the way back to an after-action report signed off by the commanding officer of 1st Airborne Division, Major General Urquhart, on 10 January 1945. Urquhart's report did not overtly criticize the

Allied air forces, but his basic message would not have been lost on any reader with a knowledge of how Allied airborne operations were planned and executed. Urquhart identified three basic lessons from 'Market' – the airborne phase of Market Garden.* The first concerned the staging of the airlifts, the second the location of the drop zones and landing zones at Arnhem and the third the availability or otherwise of close air support. His words have had such a profound impact on historians that they deserve to be quoted in detail.

Planning

An Airborne Division is designed to fight as a whole. If the Division is split and committed to a 2nd lift some 24 hrs later then, owing to the necessity of allotting part of the first lift to protect the DZs and LZs of the following troops, the effective strength for immediate offensive action of the Div[ision] is reduced to that of a B[riga]de.

It is considered that we must be prepared to take more risks during the initial stages of an Airborne operation. When the balance sheet of casualties at Arnhem is made, it would appear a reasonable risk to have landed the Div much closer to the objective chosen, even in the face of some enemy flak. It has always been the rule when planning that the maximum distance from the DZ or LZ to the objective should not exceed 5 miles. In the ARNHEM operation the distance was 7 miles and in some cases 8 miles. An extra two minutes flying time in the face of flak, if not too severe, would have put the Div – always supposing the ground was suitable – much nearer its objective. Initial surprise in this operation was obtained, but the effect of the surprise was lost owing to the time lag of some 4 hrs before the troops could arrive at the objective chosen.

A whole B[riga]de dropped near the bridge site at ARNHEM might have been a major factor in the outcome of the battle ... The forecast of the photographic interpretation and of the 'I' [intelligence] appreciation both RAF and Army, of the flak defences to be met in the area proved very pessimistic....

Air support

Close air support during the first afternoon of the operation would have been invaluable. If there had been a 'cab rank'** available then and on subsequent days, the effect on the enemy would have been considerable. Close air

---

* The airborne operation was simply named 'Market', while the ground operation was named 'Garden'. For the sake of simplicity, as both operations are referred to, the combined operation name 'Market Garden' is employed throughout this book.
** Tactical support aircraft, normally fighter-bombers, maintaining a presence over ground troops by operating in relays, and receiving requests for support from those troops by ground-to-air radio or pre-arranged signals.

support during the period when troops were in movement might easily have turned the scale and allowed the whole of 1 Para B[riga]de to have concentrated near the main ARNHEM Bridge…[10]

Urquhart did not of course maintain that these were the only lessons to be learnt from the Arnhem debacle. Later in the report he acknowledged that his communications infrastructure had failed, although he devoted only four lines to this subject, and he accepted that his forces had sometimes been held up by only small numbers of Germans equipped with light weapons. He also hinted at disciplinary problems, at 'stickiness' among less experienced troops, at deficient training for low-level decision-making, and at tactical failings that prevented infiltration and manoeuvre during the Arnhem battle.[11] Nevertheless, his fundamental argument was that 1st Airborne Division fell victim to a series of extraneous factors completely beyond its control. The division should have been infiltrated more rapidly into Arnhem, it should have been dropped closer to the road bridge and it should have received far more offensive air support. In such circumstances – in his view – the outcome of the battle might have been very different.

Historians have since been almost unanimous in their backing for Urquhart's position. Indeed, his arguments about planning were repeated by William Buckingham in a study published as recently as 2002. For Buckingham, 'the lion's share of responsibility [for the Allied defeat at Arnhem] has to go the airmen involved, whose decisions significantly tilted the odds against the airborne soldiers before they left the UK'. The air forces' allegedly excessive influence over the Market Garden plan not only caused the airlift to be unnecessarily protracted, but also lumbered 1st Airborne Division with landing areas that were too far from their primary objectives.

This compounded the effects of delivering 1st Airborne over a three-day period, it flew in the face of all airborne experience, and the professional opinion of the airborne soldiers involved. The location of the landing zones was thus the single most important factor in the failure at Arnhem. The Arnhem portion of Market Garden failed … because the bulk of 1st Airborne's first lift did not manage to reach the Arnhem road bridge at all, and the major reason for this was the distance between the landing areas and that bridge.[12]

Writing in 1994, Martin Middlebrook was no less critical of the Allied air forces. He described as 'the cardinal, fundamental errors' their 'refusal to consider a night drop or to land at least parts of the force as *coup-de-main* parties closer to the two bridges, and their failure to land any part of the force at both

17

ends of the bridge objectives'. Similarly, he deplored 'the refusal to fly two lifts on the first day, which resulted in the prolonged dispersal of the division and its failure to achieve concentration of effort'. To Middlebrook, a major factor in the Allied defeat at Arnhem was what he termed 'the failure of the air plan'.[13]

In another 50th anniversary study, Peter Harclerode drew similarly damning conclusions. He wrote that:

The major flaws in Major General Roy Urquhart's plan were the distance between his division's objectives and its dropping and landing zones, and their location west of Arnhem and north of the Lower Rhine. But Urquhart had little choice. The RAF vetoed his initial selections on grounds of the threat from enemy flak defences in the vicinity of Arnhem itself and the air base at Deelen to the north. His idea of a glider-borne *coup-de-main* force had to be discarded because of an RAF veto on the use of terrain south of the river despite the spectacular success of the Orne Bridge attack in Normandy: this was reported as being unsuitable for parachutists or gliders, being heavily defended by flak. In both instances, the intelligence proved incorrect.[14]

Urquhart's 1945 critique of offensive air support at Arnhem likewise retains a prominent position in the published literature. Thus in 2001 A.D. Harvey argued that 'the fighting round Arnhem provided ideal opportunities for fighter-bomber intervention'.

The British had a few small Bren carriers but nothing that could be mistaken from the air for a German tank or self-propelled gun or even a half-track, and the British 75mm howitzers and anti-tank guns had much less high and bulky profiles than the German 88mm flak guns; the Luftwaffe carried out ground-strafing missions ... and Allied fighter-bombers could have done the same. Of all the battles in Europe in the Second World War this was the one where the equipment of the two sides was most easily distinguishable from the air; but it was also the battle where the Allies' vast superiority in ground attack aircraft had least significance.[15]

Similarly, both Middlebrook and Harclerode maintain that the absence of close air support at Arnhem contributed much to 1st Airborne's defeat. Middlebrook echoed Urquhart's complaint about 'the failure to employ fighter-bomber units of the Second Tactical Air Force in the "cab-rank" ground-support role'.[16] It has also been argued that deficient air support seriously delayed the northward advance of XXX Corps – the formation tasked with relieving 1st Airborne at Arnhem. One of the most widely read battle-field tour guides of the Market Garden area devotes considerable space to unsubstantiated claims to the effect that XXX Corps were the victims of a major 'friendly fire' incident involving RAF Typhoons on 17 September.[17] Elsewhere it is implied that they were for no good reason denied air support south of Eindhoven the following day.[18] And, moving north of Nijmegen on 21 September, XXX Corps were again allegedly unable to obtain tactical air power at a critical stage of the battle.[19]

Thus some 60 years of scholarship has not substantially altered our understanding of the fundamental reasons for Market Garden's failure; historians have been unable to move far beyond the main parameters established by 1st Airborne's post-operation report barely four months after the shattered remnants of the division withdrew across the Lower Rhine. The restrictive nature of this discourse inevitably means that many important questions concerning air operations in support of Market Garden have yet to be posed, let alone satisfactorily answered, and little or no attempt has been made to view the key air planning decisions from the air forces' perspective. Instead, their senior officers are invariably accused of acting either through ignorance or self-interest. Critical influences upon the highly complex and technical air planning process are either neglected or (if acknowledged at all) incorrectly portrayed. The second half of this book therefore seeks to challenge the existing orthodoxy by reconsidering the three specific issues first raised in Urquhart's after-action report, i.e., the selection of the airborne landing areas, the airlift plan and the provision of offensive air support.

By surveying the past record of airborne warfare, by investigating the origins and development of the Market Garden concept, and by explaining (and not merely criticizing) the role of the air forces in the Allied defeat, this book provides a radically different view of the events of September 1944. While the conclusions ultimately reached do not in any sense belittle the remarkable achievements of some of the servicemen involved, *Arnhem: Myth and Reality* does ride roughshod across hallowed airborne ground and its perspective may thus not be palatable to all. But if it persuades at least some readers that the reality of Market Garden contains much more important lessons than the popular but deeply flawed mythology, it will have been worth writing.

Notes

1. Martin Middlebrook, *Arnhem 1944: The Airborne Battle, 17–26 September* (Penguin, London, 1995) p. 442.
2. The most recent detailed study of air power in Market Garden was Sebastian Cox's 'Air Power in Operation Market Garden', *Air Clues* (April, May and June 1985).

3. Cornelius Ryan, *A Bridge Too Far* (Wordsworth Editions, Ware, 1999), p. 460.
4. Ibid., pp. 462–463.
5. This basic failure is common to Middlebrook, *Arnhem*, Ryan, *A Bridge Too Far*, Peter Harclerode, *Arnhem: A Tragedy of Errors* (Caxton Editions, London, 2000) and A.D. Harvey, *Arnhem* (Cassell, London, 2001), to name but a few. William Buckingham, *Arnhem 1944* (Tempus, Stroud, 2004), considers earlier operations involving 1st Airborne Division but otherwise also avoids comparing or contrasting Market Garden with previous airborne ventures.
6. Chester Wilmot, *The Struggle for Europe* (Reprint Society, London, 1954), p. 585; Middlebrook, *Arnhem*, p. 442.
7. Richard Lamb, *Montgomery in Europe 1943–45: Success or Failure* (Buchan & Enright, London, 1983), p. 226.
8. First Allied Airborne Army, Operations in Holland, September to November 1944, 22 December 1944 (held at Air Historical Branch – AHB); AIR 25/698, 83 Group F.540, September 1944. The figure of 14,751 comprises the 12,996 sorties recorded by First Allied Airborne Army and 1,755 fighter sorties mounted by 83 Group, Second Tactical Air Force, which were excluded from the First Allied Airborne Army totals.
9. Buckingham, *Arnhem*, pp. 231–232; Harvey, *Arnhem*, pp. 37–39, 180.
10. 1st Airborne Division Report on Operation Market, 10 January 1945 (held at AHB).
11. Ibid.
12. Buckingham, *Arnhem*, p. 231.
13. Middlebrook, *Arnhem* p. 443.
14. Harclerode, *Arnhem*, p. 161.
15. Harvey, *Arnhem*, p. 185.
16. Middlebrook, *Arnhem*, p. 444, Harclerode, *Arnhem*, pp. 168–169.
17. Major & Mrs Holt's Battlefield Guide, *Operation Market Garden* (Leo Cooper, Barnsley, 2001), pp. 59–60.
18. Ryan, *A Bridge Too Far*, p. 253.
19. Harvey, *Arnhem*, p. 126; Harclerode, *Arnhem*, p. 135.

PART ONE

Airborne Warfare in Historical Context

Introduction

O F ALL THE weaknesses in the published history of Market Garden, the most fundamental is the absence of historical context; all too often the events of September 1944 are considered in near-total isolation, and accounts of Market Garden are still regularly published that contain no discussion whatsoever of the development of airborne warfare. A.D. Harvey's recent study is typical. Harvey ostensibly 'tried to show how the battle appeared to those in positions of command'.[1] Yet he offers no examination of earlier airborne ventures and his analysis is therefore bereft of any discussion of how they might have influenced commanders' views and actions. At best, historians tend to offer vague contentions to the effect that early German airborne experience, such as the capture of Fort Eben-Emael, illustrated the critical importance of shock effect and surprise – fundamentals supposedly ignored during the planning and implementation of Market Garden.

Another common but equally simplistic approach is to contrast the Allies' failure in Holland in September 1944 with 6th Airborne Division's success in capturing the Orne River and Caen Canal bridges in Normandy on 6 June. Readers are invited to conclude that the two operations are readily comparable merely because bridge objectives were involved. In actual fact, they could hardly have been more different. In short, then, the tendency is to imply that these two outstandingly successful airborne operations typified the employment of airborne forces prior to Market Garden. Occasionally, historians also acknowledge that acute risks are inherent in airborne warfare, but their true severity is rarely described in detail. To place Market Garden in historical context, the course of previous airborne operations must first be thoroughly investigated. We need to keep in mind the fact that past experience is one of the most fundamental determinants of human action. And from the following analysis it will quickly be appreciated that the accumulated experience of airborne operations before September 1944 was far from positive.

Notes

1. Harvey, *Arnhem*, p. 11.

1.1. Airborne Warfare: The German Experience, 1939–41

AIRBORNE WARFARE WAS pioneered by Italy and the Soviet Union during the 1930s, but it was in Germany that the concept advanced furthest before the outbreak of the Second World War, and it was the apparent success of early German airborne operations that persuaded Britain and America to create their own airborne arms. German airborne doctrine was at this time very different from Allied practice as it evolved in the later years of hostilities. First, the airborne forces themselves were part of the Luftwaffe rather than the Wehrmacht. Second, early German operations were directed against countries not known for their military prowess – countries which did not possess large or modern air forces or extensive ground-based air defences. Third, these operations were not mass ventures but were for the most part company-sized drops aimed at specific objectives – fortifications, bridges or airfields. The troops involved carried very few weapons heavier than machine guns and light mortars; they had virtually no ground transportation and little air-portable equipment.

The appearance of mass airborne landings came from the German tactic of using a vanguard of genuinely 'airborne' troops (i.e., paratroops or glider-borne infantry) to seize airfields before much larger numbers of air landing troops were flown in by powered transport aircraft. Light assault gliders were only employed in small numbers. Operations were planned to ensure that the airborne had only to hold their objectives for limited periods before they were reinforced or relieved by conventional forces, and they were always scheduled in daylight. Finally, as both Hitler and Goering took a very strong personal interest in the airborne, their commander, General Kurt Student, found himself in 'a certain privileged position which he seized with both hands'.[1] He could always be certain that the interests of his troops would not be neglected by other branches of the German armed forces – by the ground units tasked to link up with them, or by the air formations that provided the fire support they otherwise lacked.

The main tenets of German airborne doctrine are clearly visible in their operations in Denmark and Norway in April 1940. Less than one company of paratroops captured the two-mile Vordingborg bridge linking the Danish islands of Falster and Seeland, while only one platoon took the two airfields at Aalborg in northern Denmark. Similarly the seizure of airfields near Stavanger and Oslo in Norway was assigned to single companies. Despite poor weather conditions, which complicated air navigation over Norway, all the objectives were taken and such Danish and Norwegian troops as were encountered were completely overawed by what was, at that time, an entirely new medium of warfare. Within hours of the initial assaults, the airborne units were being reinforced either by ground forces or by troops landed by Junkers JU 52 transports.

This first ever employment of airborne forces in live combat thus appears to have been an outstanding success. Yet German airborne actions in Scandinavia also illustrate another feature of early airborne warfare: virtually any flaw in the planning or execution of operations usually resulted in heavy losses of personnel and/or equipment, and in mission failure. A few days after their initial offensive the Germans dropped another company of paratroops at Dombas, on the Lägen river northwest of Oslo, to block a route being used by retreating Norwegian forces. The operation was a disastrous failure. The landings were widely dispersed and many paratroops were captured before they could assemble into a cohesive force; others were killed or injured in the drop, which was executed at too low an altitude. From a broader perspective even the limited operations conducted in Denmark and Norway proved extremely expensive in transport aircraft. Some 100 JU 52s were lost – primarily through the hazardous tactic of air-landing reinforcements onto enemy airfields. Many of these aircraft were required by the Luftwaffe for bomber crew training, blind flying training and navigational training, and their destruction therefore served to lower the output of new aircrew.[2]

The German airborne operations mounted in the Low Countries on 10 May 1940 were in many respects similar to those conducted in Scandinavia. The opening attacks on Fort Eben-Emael and the Albert Canal bridges involved a single company and a platoon of engineers conveyed in 42 DFS 230 gliders, although these were to be reinforced by paratroops. These objectives were only around 20 miles from the German frontier and hence the German airborne forces were quickly relieved by ground troops. The other goals assigned to 7th Air Division and the air landing division – 22nd Infantry Division – were mostly airfields and bridges and were largely divided between companies. Full battalions were used in but two instances to take the bridge across the Holland Deep at Moerdijk and the Waalhaven airfield southwest of Rotterdam.

Of the various operations, Eben-Emael has predictably attracted by far the most attention from historians. It is portrayed as perhaps the classic example of how to stage a *coup-de-main* attack of the type that some authors claim should have been employed by British forces at Arnhem. The comparison is completely misleading, however, for the assault on Eben-Emael was always far more likely than Market Garden to secure absolute tactical surprise and to encounter relatively weak opposition: it effectively initiated hostilities by one of the world's strongest military powers against a small and uncommitted nation. Unlike Arnhem, Eben-Emael was not a deep objective, and the troops sent to capture the fortress and the Albert Canal bridges had been training for these specific tasks since the previous November, whereas in Market Garden there was no opportunity at all for preparatory exercises or rehearsals. Even then, it is worth noting that the Germans did not succeed in capturing all three Albert Canal bridges intact.[3]

Historians have been slow to contrast other German airborne operations in the Low Countries with Market Garden, and yet in many ways the German actions between Moerdijk and The Hague offer far greater scope for meaningful comparisons to be drawn than Eben-Emael. Indeed, they virtually involved a 'Market Garden in reverse' in so far as they required 7th Air Division and part of 22nd Infantry Division to secure crossings over the Maas and the Rhine delta so that German ground forces could advance through Rotterdam to link up with the remainder of 22nd Infantry Division, which was responsible for capturing the Dutch capital.

A number of problems confronted the German airborne. To begin with, airborne warfare was no longer the total novelty that it had been in April, so there was a greater likelihood that the Dutch would be anticipating an assault by parachute or glider-borne forces. To make matters worse, they would be able to observe the approaching airborne formations, which had to fly from German airfields all the way across Holland to reach their objectives, and they would be on the alert because operations along the frontier would already have commenced. Finally, as the various landing areas were located 70 to 90 miles from the nearest German territory, the two airborne divisions would be dangerously exposed until the arrival of the first ground units.

But offsetting these disadvantages was the fact that Holland possessed neither a capable air force nor strong anti-aircraft defences. Moreover, the importance attached to the airborne missions at the most senior levels of the National Socialist hierarchy made their success the top priority of both the Luftwaffe and the German army. The responsible air commander, Field Marshal Albert Kesselring, later recalled how he visited his army counterpart, General Von Bock, and insisted 'that on the third day of the offensive the Panzer forces would have to join up with Student's air landing parties in or near Rotterdam'.

Von Bock was not by any means sure that he could keep to the Rotterdam time-table, but when I made no bones about it that the fate of the air landing group, and indeed of the Army Group's operation, hung on the punctual arrival of the mechanized army units, he assured me that he would do everything humanly possible. I made it easier for him to give me this promise by guaranteeing him the fullest air support.[4]

One of Kesselring's *fliegerkorps* (Air Corps) was also specifically earmarked for the airborne forces, not only to provide them with direct air support but also to impede Dutch troop movements and counter-attacks.[5]

Broadly speaking, 7th Air Division's operations went according to plan. The one significant failure – to take the Dordrecht bridge over the Oude Maas – occurred because too few paratroops were assigned to the task, and because Dutch resistance was underestimated. There was heavy fighting around all the bridge objectives, and 7th Air Division could well have found themselves in severe difficulties given their lack of logistical support and heavy weaponry. But fortunately for the Germans the successful capture of Waalhaven airfield once more allowed reinforcements to be flown in and used to secure the all-important crossing. The German airborne afterwards had little difficulty holding out until the arrival of ground forces on the 12th.

But the fact that an extra 2,000 air landing troops were available to strengthen 7th Air Division 's hold on the Dordrecht-Rotterdam sector was a reflection of the disastrous failure of the German airborne missions further north. The ambitious role assigned to 22nd Infantry Division again involved

German paratroops in Holland, May 1940

the tactic of using small parachute teams to seize airfields – this time around The Hague – where JU 52s could land and offload the main air landing force. But only one slightly enlarged parachute battalion was made available for the capture of three separate airfields – again, too few troops assigned to too many objectives – and the Dutch had strengthened their airfield defences to confront the airborne threat. Long before the airfields had been secured the air landing units began to arrive, their JU 52s coming under intense fire as they sought to land. Eleven out of thirteen aircraft carrying one assault company to Ypenburg airfield were shot down. The grass strips themselves proved unable to support the heavy transport aircraft and many became stuck in the soft soil. Soon the airfields were so littered with wrecked JU 52s that further landings became impossible. In all, of the 9,300 personnel who were originally to land around the Dutch capital on 10 May, only around 3,800 succeeded in doing so, and they soon found themselves dispersed into small and vulnerable pockets.[6] They were eventually ordered south to Rotterdam and the attack on The Hague was abandoned. By the time they were withdrawn some 40 per cent of their officers and 28 per cent of their other ranks had become casualties.[7] But the worst losses were again sustained by the Luftwaffe's air transport fleet: during the course of the airborne attacks on both the Albert Canal and western Holland, as many as 280 JU 52s may have been destroyed and many others were damaged.

The losses sustained in these operations should have given the Germans ample understanding of the potential hazards inherent in airborne warfare – particularly when conducted in broad daylight. But instead they were dazzled by the success of their actions in the Albert Canal and Rotterdam areas, and the critical role played by conventional land forces in rapidly linking up with the airborne was largely overlooked. Their paratroops were showered with medals, the airborne formations were enlarged, and ambitious plans were drawn up for their employment in the invasion of Great Britain – Operation Sea Lion. But on 17 September Sea Lion was indefinitely postponed and a new factor came into play, which would also exert a profound influence on Allied planning exactly four years later. Airborne troops are expensive: they require large amounts of air transport, specialized training and equipment, and dedicated logistical provisions. And yet the role for which they are prepared is necessarily an intermittent one. Hence, when unused, they appear to tie up substantial resources that are often required urgently elsewhere. This in turn creates pressure to deploy them in further operations and, as the pressure builds, there is an inevitable tendency for new operation plans to become conceptually more optimistic, and more detached from reality. Student later recalled how, in January 1941, Hitler proposed a scheme for an airborne operation on the Devon-Cornwall peninsula that bore no relation to any other German plan

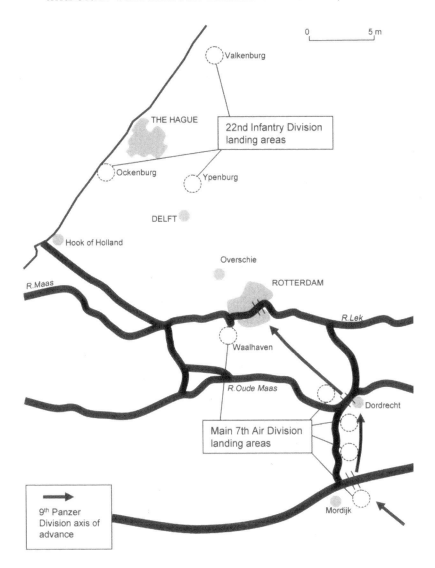

Map 1: The German airborne plan in western Holland, 1940

for an invasion of Britain. But Student himself then went on to suggest a diversionary airborne assault on Northern Ireland.[8]

In the event, this pressure to employ the airborne would ultimately find an outlet in an entirely different theatre – the Balkans. German airborne operations in Greece began with a regiment assault on the Corinth Canal Bridge – another lightly defended pinpoint objective. At the operational level this action was completely unnecessary, as German ground forces had already crossed the Gulf of Corinth further west; moreover, although the German paratroops and a three-glider engineer unit were dropped immediately next to the bridge, they were unable to capture it intact. Historically, the operation has been justified not on the basis that it achieved its primary goals but because it produced the collateral effect of trapping a few thousand Greek and Yugoslav troops north of the gulf.[9] Yet the Corinth Canal bridge action also produced more negative consequences by reinforcing overconfidence among German airborne commanders and the expectation that future operations would be no more difficult.

In September 1944 Montgomery provided the primary impetus behind Operation Market Garden, selling one of the most ambitious airborne plans of the Second World War to Eisenhower in the hope of winning the race across the German frontier. In April 1941, in a very similar fashion, Student and Goering successfully promoted the invasion of Crete (Operation Mercury), believing that the Luftwaffe could play a more prominent role in a forward Mediterranean strategy than in the planned invasion of the Soviet Union. The operation had very little to do with strategic necessity and a great deal to do with finding more employment – and more glory – for the German airborne. Student produced a far-fetched scheme for using Crete and Cyprus as stepping stones across the Mediterranean, but Hitler never accepted this proposal and would have preferred to halt Germany's southward advance at the Peloponnese. According to his Operation Directive, he envisaged that Crete would become an important air base; historians also speculate without much supporting evidence that he saw the island as a natural defensive barrier that could block any hostile penetration of his southern flank.[10] The fact is that the strategic rationale for Mercury was always vague in the extreme.

By the time Operation Mercury was being planned the Germans had largely exhausted the surprise factor that had played such a vital part in their airborne operations in Scandinavia and the Low Countries. During the preparations for Sea Lion the previous summer the British had been observed erecting obstacles in a number of the areas chosen as drop zones, and in all the likely alternative locations.[11] And as early as November 1940 Brigadier Tidbury, then commander of British forces on Crete, correctly identified every German objective and their four main dropping zones on the island; this was six and a half months before Mercury was launched. By May 1941 Tidbury's successor, Major General Bernard Freyberg VC, had additionally been supplied with high-grade signals intelligence – so-called 'Ultra' – on the German invasion plans.[12]

Student's concept of operations in Crete represented a marked departure from earlier German airborne ventures. It is true that the landings were primarily focused on airfields with the aim of airlifting 5th Mountain Division onto the island as soon as they had been secured. It is also a fact that the airborne element of the operation overwhelmingly involved parachute rather than glider landings (only 80 gliders were employed), and that air support was assigned a critically important role. To that extent Mercury did conform to established German airborne doctrine. Yet there were also certain clear differences. To begin with, the plan envisaged not only attacks on pinpoint targets, but also area domination of such locations as Canea, Suda Bay, the Akrotiri, Retimo and Heraklion. This was, to say the least, a very optimistic agenda given the inherent limitations of airborne forces at the time – no heavy weapons, no mechanized transport and minimal logistical support.

Secondly, in so far as the operation was launched against an island, there was of course no scope for the all-important link-up with conventional ground forces that had rescued 7th Air Division around Rotterdam in the previous year. The only planned role for surface forces (scheduled for the third day of the operation) involved a high-risk crossing of the Aegean by two battalions of mountain troops. To all intents and purposes, Mercury would be an independent airborne operation: Crete was to be seized by airborne forces, and by airlifted troops brought into captured airfields in their wake.[13] Finally, whereas German operations in the Low Countries were preceded by months of intensive planning activity, including thorough exercises and rehearsals, no equivalent preparations preceded Mercury as virtually no time was available; indeed, the final operation plan was not settled until 16 May, only four days before the assault. This was all the more unfortunate as the German airborne had since been enlarged by a substantial influx of new and inexperienced personnel.[14]

Mercury should be of particular interest to scholars of Market Garden for it illustrates the critical importance of intelligence in determining the success or failure of airborne operations. German intelligence on the defending forces in Crete was abysmal. On the eve of Operation Mercury they assessed that the British garrison on the island numbered no more than 5,000. Only 400 troops were allegedly based at Heraklion, while Retimo was believed to be entirely undefended. In fact, the island was held by some 40,000 British, Commonwealth and Greek troops.[15] This mistaken assessment provided the foundation for the German battle plan, with its ambitious objectives and its far-flung and dispersed landing areas, strung out across an eighty-mile stretch of coast so that no one airborne force could support another. Not surprisingly, the landings were a near-total disaster. In a number of instances, defending units were literally waiting to ambush the airborne troops from high ground overlooking the drop zones.[16]

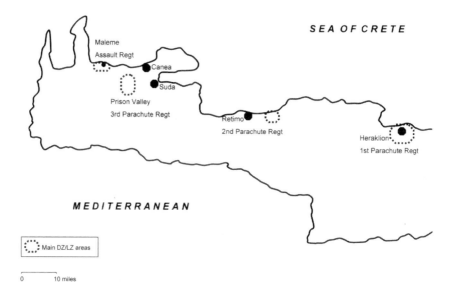

Map 2: The main German landing areas on western Crete; their objectives spanned 80 miles of the island's northern coast

In planning Operation Mercury the Germans confronted one particular problem that also faced the Allied planners before Market Garden: due to the heavy losses they had suffered in Holland the previous year they possessed insufficient transport aircraft to infiltrate all their airborne troops in a single lift.[17] In Market Garden the Allies quickly concluded that it would be too difficult to organize two lifts on one day and opted instead to stage their principal landings on 17 and 18 September 1944. As we have noted, this decision (which is considered in more detail elsewhere in this book) has since proved highly controversial; many historians argue that a second lift should have been staged on 17 September.

In Mercury the Germans opted to attempt two lifts on the first day of the operation. The first succeeded in establishing only a very tenuous foothold in the Maleme and Prison Valley areas. The plan was that the second lift would follow on as soon as possible after the first, on the afternoon of 20 May 1941, to convey airborne units to Heraklion and Retimo. However, as events turned out, the second lift was late, partly because of delays in the departure of the first lift and partly because the German plan assigned insufficient time for the maintenance, repair and refuelling of the JU 52s. Chaos ensued as the original starting order was abandoned in a misconceived effort to make up for lost time.

In the meantime, preliminary bombing attacks around the DZs were executed in accordance with the original timetable, more than an hour before the airborne drops actually commenced. Hence there was ample time for the defenders to recover before the first transport aircraft appeared. Instead of the lift being concentrated into a short period, it was extended over two hours; some units reached Crete in the wrong tactical order, and some did not take off at all. At Retimo many paratroops were inaccurately dropped, with some coming down in the sea and drowning under the weight of their equipment.[18] Both landings were complete failures. When the slaughter was over the two severely depleted parachute regiments dug themselves into defensive positions and awaited relief from the west.[19]

How, then, did the Germans snatch victory from the jaws of defeat? They were primarily rescued by two factors. The first was the manifest incompetence of their adversaries. Freyberg famously misinterpreted the Ultra, deployed his forces primarily to meet a German amphibious landing and left the critically important Maleme airfield area defended by only a single battalion.[20] No less catastrophic was the voluntary withdrawal of Allied infantry from Hill 107 (which dominated the airfield) on the night of 20–21 May and the subsequent protracted delay in mounting a counter-attack into the area, in stark contrast to the near-immediate counter-attacks launched by the Germans around Arnhem and Nijmegen in 1944. The second factor was that (unlike 1st Airborne Division at Arnhem) the German airborne on Crete succeeded in establishing at least some functional communications with their headquarters on the Greek mainland. Via this means, they were able to provide guidance to the Luftwaffe on how best to exploit their crushing air superiority. Most of all, however, the availability of timely and accurate intelligence on the tactical situation on the island allowed Student to alter his plans and send 5th Mountain Division to Maleme.[21]

And so ultimately Crete was largely captured not by the German airborne but by mountain troops airlifted into a location which was (by that time) behind German lines; there were no Allied units west of Maleme so Mercury can hardly be described as a triumph of vertical envelopment. And even 5th Mountain Division's infiltration was achieved through a medium that was clearly unsustainable and could never have been built into any deliberate plan. JU 52s had to be crammed onto the small Maleme runway, which was under Allied artillery fire, and many were destroyed or damaged; others, to get down at all, had to be crash-landed into whatever space remained available to them. In its entirety, the capture of Crete cost the Germans some 350 aircraft, of which at least 151 were JU 52s. The German aircraft industry afterwards proved unable to make good these losses and provide for other wastage, predominantly on the eastern front, and the

German dead by a DFS 230 glider during Operation Mercury

Luftwaffe's transport forces were still suffering from the effects at the time of the Stalingrad airlift.[22]*

The German airborne incurred appalling casualties. Killed, wounded and missing 7th Air Division and Air Assault Regiment losses totalled 4,522 personnel – a rate of 56 per cent.[23] The divisional commander, Generalleutnant Sussman, died when his assault glider crashed during take-off on the first day of the operation; the commander of the Air Assault Regiment was severely wounded; the commanders of his first and third battalions became casualties – wounded and killed respectively; all of the officers of one company dropped near Retimo were killed, and all three brothers from the Von Blucher family perished in the fighting around Heraklion.[24]

From the German perspective this sacrifice was in no way offset by the fact

---

* When in November 1942 the entire German Sixth Army was encircled by Soviet forces at Stalingrad, Hitler sought to hold the city by supplying his beleaguered troops by air. But whereas in May 1941 it had been possible to commit more than 500 JU 52s to Operation Mercury, the formation tasked with the Stalingrad airlift (Luftflotte 4) never controlled more than 300 transport aircraft, a force that included not only dedicated JU 52 units but also converted bombers and JU 86s of limited utility; aircraft had also to be transferred to Luftflotte 4 from western theatres and stripped from training units. Not surprisingly, the airlift was a total failure.

that Mercury ended in victory. Crete was of no particular strategic value and was never used either as a stepping stone across the Mediterranean or as a major air base. Hitler probably only sanctioned the operation on the understanding that it could be executed at minimal cost, and he was therefore horrified by the losses. 'We shall never do another airborne operation', he told Student afterwards. 'Crete proved that the days of parachute troops are over. The parachute arm is one that relies entirely on surprise. In the meantime the surprise factor has exhausted itself.'[25]

Although undoubtedly true, this was not the only question that the operation raised about the viability of German airborne tactics. Mercury also suggested that the practice of dropping airborne troops straight onto their objectives might be far too hazardous, and that the concept of directly seizing airfields in enemy territory so that reinforcements could be air-landed in powered aircraft was impracticable against all but the very weakest opposition. As Luftflotte 4's post-operation report stated, 'a repetition of an attack under such circumstances will not be possible; future attacks will probably have to be made in a locality free from the enemy.'[26] Hence the German airborne simultaneously lost Hitler's patronage and certain fundamental tenets of their

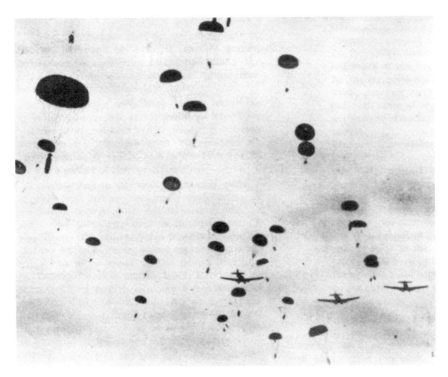

Crete: paratroops and canisters fill the air

tactical doctrine. It was a disaster from which they never recovered. Although the Germans maintained a substantial airborne capability for the rest of the war, they subsequently attempted only a limited number of small-scale operations, and the vast majority of their paratroops were employed as conventional infantry in theatres such as Italy and indeed Holland.

* * *

The following conclusions can be drawn from this brief survey of the German airborne experience from 1940 to 1941. First, the airborne medium was at its most effective in fairly small-scale operations against clearly identified and limited tactical objectives, such as bridges. The Germans certainly did not establish a clear case for the creation of *strategic* airborne forces. Second, airborne warfare was best employed against militarily weak adversaries. Third, as air navigation was still a very uncertain science, airborne lifts were best scheduled in daylight; however, daylight operations against even limited opposition could be very costly, especially in terms of lost or damaged aircraft. Fourth, it was inadvisable to infiltrate airborne troops into locations where they could not promptly be relieved or reinforced by conventional ground forces. In addition, preliminary exercises and rehearsals were at the very least immensely important, if not operationally essential; equally vital were robust communications, accurate intelligence and pre-arranged tactical air support.

Finally, it is worth noting that the German airborne never achieved absolute mission success. Although they secured their primary objectives in Denmark and Norway, the Dombas operation was a farcical failure; in Belgium they secured only two out of the three Albert Canal bridges; in Holland their operations around The Hague went disastrously wrong; and in Crete only one of their three objectives was captured – at an exceptionally high cost in both manpower and aircraft. In the earlier operations, there was inevitably a great deal of trial and error, given the experimental nature of airborne warfare. But the disaster that befell the German airborne on Crete resulted in large part from poor conceptual planning, which in turn set the parameters within which detailed operation plans were formulated. The flawed conceptual plans were the responsibility of particularly ambitious personalities – primarily Student and Goering – and were also encouraged by the ever-present need to justify the existence of airborne forces by finding employment for them.

Notes

1. Field Marshal Albert Kesselring, *The Memoirs of Field Marshal Kesselring* (William Kimber, London, 1953), p. 55.
2. Chris Chant, 'Denmark and Norway', in Philip de Ste. Croix (ed.), *Airborne*

Operations: An Illustrated History of the Battles, Tactics and Equipment of the World's Airborne Forces (Salamander, London, 1982), pp. 33–38.

3. Chris Chant, 'Eben-Emael and Holland', in Ste. Croix (ed.), *Airborne Operations*, pp. 42–43; I.H. Lyall Grant, 'The German Airborne Attack on Belgium in May 1940', *Journal of the Royal United Services Institution*, Vol. CIII, February 1958, pp. 94–102.

4. Kesselring, *Memoirs*, p. 53.

5. Ibid, pp. 53–54.

6. Jean Paul Pallud, *Blitzkrieg in the West Then and Now* (After The Battle, London, 1991), pp. 113, 118, 128.

7. Maurice Tugwell, *Airborne to Battle: A History of Airborne Warfare* (William Kimber, London, 1971), pp. 48, 50, 59–61.

8. Tugwell, *Airborne to Battle*, pp. 72–73.

9. Ibid., p. 78; Shelford Bidwell, 'Operation Mercury – The Invasion of Crete', in Ste. Croix (ed.), *Airborne Operations*, p. 52.

10. Anthony Beevor, *Crete: The Battle and the Resistance* (Penguin, London, 1991), pp. 73–74.

11. Tugwell, *Airborne to Battle*, p. 72.

12. Beevor, *Crete*, pp. 72, 88.

13. Report by Luftflotte 4, The Invasion of Crete, 28 November 1941 (held at AHB).

14. D.W. Pissin, *The Battle of Crete* (USAF Historical Study 162, 1956), http://afhra.maxwell.af.mil., pp. 8, 64.

15. Tugwell, *Airborne to Battle*, pp. 84–87.

16. Beevor, *Crete*, pp. 111–112, 132–133, 136–137, 152–153.

17. Brongers, *The Battle for the Hague*, p. 270.

18. Beevor, *Crete*, pp. 130–132; report by Luftflotte 4, The Invasion of Crete, 28 November 1941.

19. Lieutenant Colonel T.B.H. Otway, *Airborne Forces* (War Office official monograph, 1951), p. 12.

20. Beevor, *Crete*, pp. 87–94.

21. Tugwell, *Airborne to Battle*, pp. 102–103.

22. Beevor, *Crete*, pp. 154–155; 229–230; some sources record a figure of 170 lost transport aircraft. On the Stalingrad airlift, see Williamson Murray, *Strategy for Defeat: The Luftwaffe, 1933–1945* (Air University Press, Alabama, 1983), pp. 150–155.

23. Bidwell, 'Operation Mercury', p. 61.

24. Tugwell, *Airborne to Battle*, pp. 92, 95, 101; information obtained from the German military cemetery at Maleme.

25. Beevor, *Crete*, pp. 229–230.

26. Report by Luftflotte 4, The Invasion of Crete, 28 November 1941.

1.2. Airborne Warfare: The Allied Experience, 1940–43

The history of the creation of the Allied airborne forces has been told many times and there is no need to re-tell it here. But it is worth considering certain aspects of Allied airborne development in the light of German experience in the early years of the war. First, the Allies' understanding of what the Germans achieved in the Low Countries in 1940 – and how they achieved it – was vague in the extreme. Ironically, although far less successful, Mercury provided a much greater stimulus to both British and American action to generate airborne capabilities.[1] The mistaken perception that Mercury represented a 'model' strategic airborne assault diverted the Allies' attention from the more limited and successful operations that preceded it and contributed significantly to their failure to formulate clear doctrine on how airborne forces could best be employed.

Second, it seems to have escaped Allied attention that, whereas the German airborne victories were achieved against such relatively weak opposition as Denmark, Norway, Belgium and Holland, Allied airborne forces would have to prevail against the world's finest army, its most potent ground-based air defences and what was arguably in 1941 still the world's best trained and equipped air force. Against such an adversary it would prove far more difficult for the Allies to exploit the airborne medium. Indeed, the German military machine would have to be heavily degraded before the Allied airborne could be usefully employed in large-scale operations. In the interim, they would require substantial resources merely to provide for their recruitment, training, equipment and then maintenance at a state approximating to operational readiness.

The relative strength of their opposition raised two particular problems for the Allies. The first was that, for the foreseeable future, airborne assaults on German-held territory would be very difficult to conduct safely in daylight due to the inherent vulnerability of transport aircraft – low speed, lack of defence, low altitude and straight and level flight during parachute drops. This posed the question of whether such operations could practicably be launched under cover of darkness. The second problem was the manifest impossibility of seizing enemy airfields for use as 'air heads' by powered transport aircraft in the manner employed by the Germans; both air and ground defences were likely to be far too strong. Mass parachute drops would ultimately prove to be the main alternative, together with the employment of assault gliders on a scale substantially greater than had been witnessed in any German operation in 1940–41. Initially, however, it was very difficult to see how airborne forces could usefully be employed against the Axis.

To be fair, the obvious difficulties involved in exploiting the airborne medium effectively in the early years of the war were acknowledged in Britain in both the War Office and the Air Ministry as early as 1940, when Churchill first demanded the creation of a paratroop force. Indeed, their response to his directive was distinctly half-hearted partly because they could see no very obvious role for airborne troops. As the War Office's official historian later recorded,

> There was no clear idea as to how airborne forces would fit into the developing picture and therefore how they should be organized. Throughout 1940, and most of 1941, ideas on their employment were by no means definite and were not agreed either in principle or in detail by the two main organizations – the War Office and the Air Ministry. This was probably the main factor in the delay that ensued.[2]

Crete would ultimately compel both the British War Office and the US War Department to grasp the airborne nettle more firmly. Yet the task confronting them did not then merely involve the generation of airborne formations. It was also essential to co-ordinate the development of the airborne with the expansion of air transport forces, and both British and American policy left much to be desired in this respect.

In Britain in mid-1941 there were no purpose-built military transport aircraft, and there was little prospect that wartime air transport demands would be met by the British aircraft industry, as several years would have been required to bring a new design from the drawing board into front-line service. For airlift then, the British airborne would always be dependent on limited numbers of converted RAF bombers, on such troop carriers as could be bought or coaxed from the Americans and on the USAAF. Logically, these constraints should have directly influenced both the structure and employment of the airborne forces. A force tailored to the airlift available (or likely to become available in the foreseeable future) would have been small (perhaps two brigades) and lightly equipped; it would not have been suitable for use in deep operations or for area domination, but it could have been tasked very effectively with seizing limited and clearly defined tactical objectives a short distance behind enemy lines – objectives that could easily and quickly be reached by a simultaneous ground offensive. The airborne's lack of heavier weapons could have been offset by the exploitation of tactical air support, mimicking German practice.

Unfortunately, however, the War Office pursued an entirely different strategy. They simply embarked on the construction of the largest possible airborne force, paying little heed to airlift considerations. At the end of October 1941 they decided to create 1st Airborne Division; in the spring of 1943, after a protracted struggle with the Air Ministry, they obtained authority to form a second division – 6th Airborne Division. Other units such as the Independent Polish Parachute Brigade and the Special Air Service Brigade (SAS) also emerged. Fully established, the two airborne divisions alone would comprise more than 20,000 men in total, whereas Churchill had originally proposed a force of only 5,000. Moreover, the War Office originally intended that one of the divisions should be based in an overseas theatre – a concept with truly daunting airlift implications.

Beyond this, the extensive use of heavy assault gliders with significant cargo-carrying capacity soon led the British airborne to procure of all manner of air-portable equipment, ranging from jeeps to artillery pieces. Compared to their German counterparts they were far more heavily equipped, and they showed a pronounced tendency to become heavier as the war progressed.[3] This may well have enhanced their combat capability for limited periods but it inevitably increased their air transport requirements still further, as a growing proportion of airlift capacity came to be used for transporting equipment rather than combat troops, as well as support personnel and expendables such as fuel, ammunition and spare parts.[4] No consideration whatsoever was given to the subject of tactical air support, despite its crucial role in German airborne operations and its steady development in support of the mainstream British Army between 1941 and 1943.[5]

With far more resources at their disposal, it might be thought that the Americans would have enjoyed greater freedom to develop their airborne forces along similar lines, and to some extent this was indeed the case. Yet a reluctance to co-ordinate the growth of the airborne with the expansion of the air transport fleet would have serious consequences in the US too. Between 1940 and mid-1942 the US airborne arm was steadily enlarged from a single experimental platoon to a four-regiment force (roughly equivalent to four British brigades), and the decision was taken in August 1942 to form two airborne divisions. Each division would be somewhat larger than a British airborne division and again far more heavily equipped than the German airborne.

And yet the airlift available in the US was for some time not nearly large enough to support such a force. In 1940 no transport aircraft suitable for airborne forces were in service with the USAAF. Only five transports were delivered in the second half of 1940 and only 133 throughout 1941. In June 1941 the USAAF were unable to spare twelve aircraft for paratroop training and had to strain their resources to provide 39 for airborne exercises that year. Unlike the RAF, they did at least possess an acceptable troop carrier proto- type in the converted DC-3 airliner – the Douglas C-47 (or Dakota to the British). But it took time to organize large-scale production arrangements for the C-47, and deliveries only began in September 1941. Output was slow to expand in the following year and remained completely inadequate in relation to USAAF (and indeed RAF) air transport requirements. It was not until the summer of 1943 that deliveries came close to satisfying demand. If the avail- ability of aircraft alone had been the issue this timetable would have been problematic enough, but of course aircraft do not operate themselves. They must be flown by qualified personnel, and America's airborne plans left completely inadequate time for aircrew training.

In June 1942, shortly before their deployment to Britain, the first and best of the US troop carrier groups – 60th Group – possessed a nucleus of experi- enced pilots but only 36 out of 60 authorized navigators. With a single exception, all of the navigators were 'fresh out of school with about 50 hours'.[6] It should perhaps be added here that this limited instruction would have been very largely confined to daylight hours: the US transport crews were provided with little night-time flying or navigation training.[7]

Of the other formations, 64th Group, which began deploying in July, 'did not compare with the 60th', while 62nd Group had even less experience. Held in the US until September,

> The delay was needed to provide its men with a minimum of unit training. Most of its pilots had graduated in midsummer from TCC's [Troop Carrier Command's] five-week transition training course, a course in which the students did not [fly] solo until the next-to-last week.[8]

At this stage of the war, then, the Americans provided their airborne troops with a substantial troop carrier fleet only by curtailing aircrew training to a wholly unacceptable degree. It would have been better to generate a smaller airborne force, thereby imposing less pressure on TCC's training infrastruc- ture and ensuring that crews were more thoroughly schooled before they became involved in live operations. In the event, both the American and the British airborne would pay a high price in return for committing of such woefully unprepared men to battle.

The uncertainty which at first characterized Allied thinking on the employment of airborne forces was replaced by a somewhat clearer vision during this period. For a time, only a small-scale raiding role was envisaged for the British airborne; later it was suggested that they could usefully target enemy communications centres, attack enemy field formations in the rear (in conjunction with an advance by conventional ground forces), seize Axis airfields or possibly undertake subsidiary operations in support of seaborne expeditions.[9] However, by the later months of 1942 it was broadly accepted that the airborne would be required to spearhead the re-entry of Allied forces into enemy-occupied Europe. As the Chief of the Imperial General Staff (CIGS) put it:

> We are all agreed that for the defeat of Germany it will sooner or later be necessary for our armies to invade the Continent. To do this we shall first be confronted with the attack of strongly defended beaches. The employment of the Airborne Division in the rear may offer the only means of obtaining a footing on these beaches.[10]

The airborne forces were thus to be deployed in set-piece operations in conjunction with amphibious landing forces. But what did this very general concept mean in terms of detailed tactical planning? As yet, no answers were forthcoming, and events were soon to demonstrate the enormous difficulties that would be involved in translating theory into practice.

The first opportunity to test airborne capabilities at battalion strength in a venture of this type presented itself on 8 November 1942, when the Allies launched Operation Torch – the invasion of North Africa – and American paratroops were tasked to seize airfields near Oran in Algeria. Their mission could hardly illustrate more clearly the Allies' very limited grasp of the airborne medium at this time. As in Germany, there was clearly strong pressure at higher command levels to find a use for the airborne arm merely because it existed and the result, mirroring German experience in Operation Mercury, was a conceptually flawed plan. The senior member of Eisenhower's air staff for Torch, Air Marshal Welsh, described the proposed operation as 'harebrained' (as it undoubtedly was) and recommended conserving the troop carriers involved for subsequent action in Tunisia, but he was overruled.[11]

Oran was a bizarre affair involving a 1,100-mile direct and unescorted transit from Cornwall across neutral Spain to North Africa and then two potential courses of action, depending on whether or not French forces around Oran seemed likely to offer resistance. If resistance was anticipated, the airborne would stage a night drop to capture the Tafaraoui airfield for future use by the Allied air forces – an utterly unrealistic concept as there was not the slightest likelihood of the troop carriers being able to find their way to Tafaraoui in darkness. If no resistance was expected, the transit would be delayed four hours, and the troop carriers would then conduct an overnight flight to reach North Africa after daybreak, landing at the second of Oran's airfields, La Senia. In this case, the aim would simply be to move troop carriers and airborne forces into theatre, where they would stand ready for drops around Bône or Tunis. This deployment could quite easily have taken place in conditions of complete safety over the following 48 hours. Instead, in their determination to commit at least some paratroops to the initial Torch assault, the Allies elected to gamble on the French response. It was to prove a costly error.

Planning for the operation was amateurish in the extreme. It was preceded by no rehearsals or exercises, and by precious little joint training between the participating formations – the USAAF's 60th Group and 2nd Battalion, 503rd Parachute Infantry Regiment (PIR). Preparatory briefings were hopelessly inadequate and 14 pilots received virtually no briefing at all. Aircrew were given little in the way of mapping, charts and topographical information on North Africa, and only 11 out of their 39 aircraft boasted US night navigation instruments, the remainder being fitted with British equipment unfamiliar to the Americans.[12]

On the afternoon of 7 November – with the aircraft loaded and ready for take-off for the Tafaraoui mission – word was received to the effect that French resistance was not expected. Take-off was therefore postponed until the evening. Needless to say, the subsequent transit to La Senia went badly wrong. Darkness and bad weather combined with inadequate aircrew training and preparation to ensure that the C-47s quickly became dispersed, and a number lost their way. Six aircraft never reached the Oran area and a seventh was forced to offload its cargo of airborne troops in Spanish Morocco to conserve the fuel necessary to reach Oran. The remaining C-47s, after a variety of adventures, largely found themselves in French or Spanish Moroccan airspace and, after eventually recovering their bearings, flew east to reach the Oran area in dribs and drabs. There it quickly became clear that, contrary to Allied intelligence, the French were determined to resist, and a number of aircraft came under attack from French fighters or were fired on by anti-aircraft guns. Unable to get down at La Senia and with near-empty fuel tanks, the C-47s began landing on a dry lake, the Sebkra D'Oran, where some of the more isolated personnel were taken prisoner by the French.

The main body attempted to taxi their aircraft across the Sebkra for an assault on Tafaraoui, but the C-47s soon began to bog down in muddy ground. The airborne troops continued the journey on foot until word was received that their objective had already been captured by Allied ground forces; they then decided to pool resources into three aircraft to fly troops into Tafaraoui to garrison the airfield. But, after taking off successfully, all three C-47s were forced down by French fighters, sustaining damage beyond repair along with a number of casualties, including five fatalities. Those still capable of marching eventually reached Tafaraoui on foot, and trucks were afterwards sent out to pick up the main body of the battalion from the Sebkra. By 10 November, only 25 of the original 39 aircraft had reached Tafaraoui and, of those, only 14 were operational. Of the 39 officers and 492 men of 2nd Battalion 503rd PIR that had taken off from Cornwall, only 150 were judged fit for another mission within three days.[13]

After the initial Torch landings there were, of course, no further opportunities for the airborne to be used in support of amphibious operations, so alternative tasking had to be identified for them. In essence, they were to find themselves employed in a reconnaissance role, ahead of the ground forces advancing into Tunisia. The first such mission was launched in daylight on 12 November, when the British 3rd Parachute Battalion (3 PARA), recently arrived at Maison Blanche in Algiers, targeted Bône airfield. The delivery of 3 PARA was accurate by Second World War standards but the airfield was found to be undefended. The next two drops followed a similar pattern: 2nd Battalion 503rd PIR landed on Youks les Bains airfield on 15 November only to be

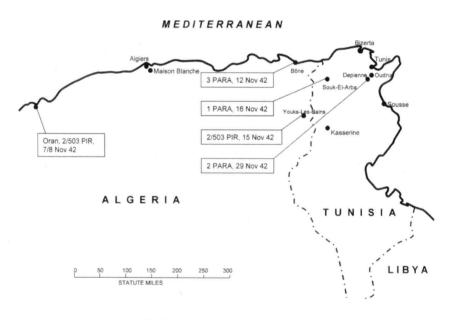

Map 3: Allied airborne operations in North Africa,
November–December 1942

44

warmly welcomed by the local French commander; on the 16th the British 1st Parachute Battalion (1 PARA) received an equally hospitable reception at Souk el Arba. The troops involved would acquit themselves well in subsequent fighting in Tunisia, but effectively as conventional infantry. It is not clear whether the Allies secured any tangible military advantage from the use of airborne forces at Bône, Youks les Bains or Souk el Arba.

The three airborne operations conducted by the Allies between 8 and 16 November were again conceptually weak. If the airborne objectives tended to be vague, the precise relationship between airborne and conventional ground operations was no more clearly defined. The selection of Youks les Bains as an objective remains shrouded in mystery, as the US airborne were originally tasked to capture the airfield and crossroads at Tebessa, ten miles east.[14] At Souk el Arba, 1 PARA were assigned a multiplicity of tasks: they were to drop on the airfield, contact local French forces, hold the crossroads and patrol east to harass the enemy, resorting to guerrilla warfare if necessary.[15] No thought appears to have been given to the provision of tactical air support for the airborne, and there is no record that the airborne forces requested it. But their most serious handicap, as at Oran, was a chronic shortage of reliable intelligence. In the various landings the airborne escaped severe casualties more through luck than judgement. Of the assault on Youks les Bains, the official USAAF historian wrote:

Never had an airborne mission been ordered and launched with less information to guide it. Some maps given to the pilots and paratroops were on a scale of 1:50,000, but there was only one detailed map of Tebessa. No aerial photographs were available, and no weather reports. The Germans had been reported within a few miles of Tebessa, but no one knew whether they had taken it, or whether, assuming the French still held it, they would resist the allies.[16]

In the event, the US paratroops dropped right on top of a very capable French unit – the 3rd Zouaves. 'As they drifted down, the troops could see beneath them entrenchments filled with armed men ... well supplied with machine guns and mortars and supported by 75mm guns.'[17] Had they proved hostile the Americans would have been annihilated.

But the Allies' luck then ran out. After the cancellation of several operations involving the British 2nd Parachute Battalion (2 PARA – under the recently promoted Lieutenant Colonel John Frost), a plan was finally concocted involving a deep airborne attack on German airfields at Pont du Fahs, Depienne and Oudna on 29 November, the initial drop taking place at Pont du Fahs. This would be the only deep airborne mission mounted by the Allies before Market Garden – their only prior opportunity to gauge the severity of the risks involved in such ventures. At the airfields, 2 PARA were to destroy enemy aircraft and stores. In the meantime, the Allied First Army would launch an offensive towards Tunis and Bizerta. The airborne objectives were some 50 miles in advance of First Army and it would therefore take up to five days for the ground forces to relieve 2 PARA, but the risks were deemed acceptable because the paratroops were only expected to encounter light opposition.

The operation was on the very point of being launched when it was discovered that the Germans had abandoned both Pont du Fahs and Depienne, and 2 PARA's task was therefore confined to Oudna alone. But for reasons that remain obscure they were ordered to drop at Depienne, which was about 15 miles to the southwest. Hence, given their total lack of mechanized transport, the plan at the very least required the battalion to undertake a fifteen-hour march across harsh desert terrain before they reached their objective. Furthermore, there was insufficient time to brief all the airborne troops on the change of plan, and many personnel therefore landed at Depienne, erroneously believing it to be Pont du Fahs. Equally, there was no opportunity for DZ selection before the troop carriers took off: Frost had to identify an appropriate area visually from the lead aircraft. When he jumped, the rest of the battalion were to follow. It is hardly surprising in these circumstances that the drop should have been quite widely dispersed, and that 2 PARA's subsequent assembly should have been both protracted and incomplete.

At Oudna, 2 PARA quickly overcame such German forces as were located in the area, but no aircraft or stores were found at the landing ground. Like Depienne, Oudna was no longer in use; the entire airborne mission thus proved to be completely futile. To make matters worse, 2 PARA soon found themselves under attack by German tanks, mechanized infantry and aircraft. Frost therefore decided to move west to accelerate the link-up with First Army but unfortunately, on the morning of 1 December, he received a wireless message that the British ground offensive had been postponed. Therefore, 2 PARA had to retreat on foot across miles of desert while under repeated attack from vastly superior German forces. By 5 December 200 troops had reached Allied lines (some of whom were wounded) and 50 more had rejoined the battalion by the 11th, but this still left 210 (or 45 per cent) killed or missing.

The Depienne/Oudna fiasco perfectly illustrates everything that was wrong with the Allied application of airborne warfare in North Africa. Launched at the very last moment, 2 PARA's mission was preceded by virtually no proper planning or preparation, and the decision that they should drop at Depienne when Oudna was the objective represents a blunder of truly epic proportions. Allied intelligence proved hopelessly flawed, both on the status of Oudna airfield and on the strength of German forces in the area, and no proper consideration was given to the battalion's subsequent link-up with First Army; no airborne force could reasonably have been expected to operate in such a hostile environment without relief or re-supply for so long a period as five days. Frost's troops should never have been committed unless it was certain that First Army's offensive would proceed as planned.[18]

There were many lessons that the Allies might have learned from their experiences in North Africa. At the very least it should have been recognized that, without extremely careful planning based on sound intelligence, airborne operations could be exceptionally hazardous. The importance of rehearsals and exercises should also have become more readily apparent, and the Oran mission should have demonstrated the exceptional difficulties likely to arise from attempts to stage airborne actions in darkness. Yet although there was some consideration of intelligence and air navigation in the relevant Allied after-action documents, none of the other issues received significant attention. For example, the key British report (which was prepared by Browning, then a Major General and commander of the British 1st Airborne Division) was predominantly concerned with administrative matters and with equipment problems, such as the difficulty involved in using American troop carriers to transport British paratroops.[19]

Behind these specific issues far more fundamental doctrinal questions remained unanswered. As Frost himself put it, 'the fact of the matter was that the British Army had no idea how or when the new airborne capability should be used'.[20] Yet in the absence of robust doctrine it would inevitably be very difficult to formulate effective operation plans. Browning's report did identify a need for the appointment of 'an expert in airborne matters at either Allied Force Headquarters or First Army',[21] and the creation of such a post made obvious sense given the chronic lack of airborne expertise within the Allied high command in North Africa. But Browning's recommendation must also be seen for what it was, namely the transparent attempt of a very ambitious officer to secure his own appointment to the new position; for much of the war Browning succeeded in linking his personal career advancement to the expansion of the airborne forces. In truth, the novelty of airborne warfare was such that there were few if any British or American officers who could mean-ingfully have been considered 'experts in airborne matters' at the end of 1942.

The Allies' failure to identify and apply the most important lessons from the North African campaign would have truly disastrous consequences in their next large-scale airborne ventures, which were staged during Operation Husky – the invasion of Sicily. Although Husky began in July 1943, the Allies were producing plans as early as April to mount the accompanying airborne assault after nightfall, albeit in moonlit conditions. The determining factor here was that the Allied amphibious landings on Sicily were to be executed at dawn so that shipping convoys from North Africa could transit to Sicily under cover of darkness. It was considered that the airborne forces, which were originally to be employed to neutralize beach defences, would require several hours to complete their tasks.[22] At the same time, as the Allies lacked full control of the air over Sicily, night operations would provide valuable protection for their transport aircraft.

By the spring Browning had duly secured the position of senior Allied airborne adviser in the Mediterranean, but theatre airborne command and control provisions were otherwise chaotically divided between several widely dispersed headquarters.[23] In this environment Browning was easily outmanoeuvred by the no less career-minded Major General G.F. 'Hoppy' Hopkinson, former commander of the British Air Landing Brigade and Browning's successor as commander of 1st Airborne Division. Seeking to raise the profile of assault glider operations, Hopkinson bypassed Browning and managed to secure direct access to General Montgomery, who was to command British forces in Husky. Montgomery had no knowledge of airborne warfare, nor was he familiar with the structure or capabilities of the Allied airborne forces. 'All he knew was that there was an airborne force – therefore by all means let us use it.'[24] On this basis he accepted Hopkinson's proposals for three brigade assaults on inland objectives. The first of these would be a mass glider landing to capture the Ponte Grande – a key river bridge on the road from the British beaches to Syracuse – while the second would be a combined parachute and glider mission near Augusta. A subsequent British assault by 1 Parachute Brigade had as its objective the Primasole Bridge over the Simento river, on the road from Syracuse to Catania.[25]

At roughly the same time the commander of the US 82nd Airborne Division, then Brigadier General Maxwell Taylor, similarly persuaded General Patton (US commander in Husky) to accept changes in the American airborne plans. Again, instead of directly supporting the beach landings, the US airborne were to seize an inland objective – an area of high ground known as the Piano Lupo. By dominating the Piano Lupo the airborne troops could block Axis counter-attacks towards the beaches from the north or east. Follow-up operations were also proposed in support of the Allied advance from the coast.

A number of very serious constraints on the proposed glider assault were largely ignored. Both the glider and the glider tug pilots were inexperienced, and were especially unfamiliar with night formation flying, night navigation and (where the glider pilots were concerned) night landing. There had been literally no training in remote glider release by night without a flare path for guidance. Furthermore, the British glider pilots and air-landing troops had not previously used the American Waco gliders they were predominantly to

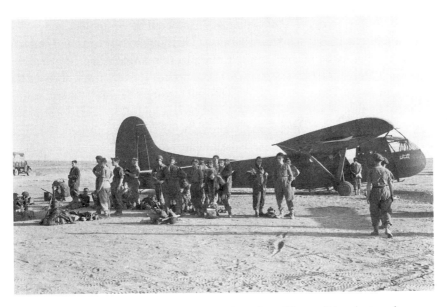

*British airborne troops next to an American Waco glider during the
preparations for Operation Husky*

employ in the operation (as few British Horsas were as yet available).[26] The
areas chosen as landing zones around the Ponte Grande were also entirely
unsuitable, being obstructed by large boulders, stone walls and olive groves. All
of these potential problems were brought to the attention of Montgomery and
Hopkinson but were dismissed out of hand.[27] Hopkinson allegedly warned the
commander of the Glider Pilot Regiment that he would be replaced if he
continued to object to the plan.[28]

Glider training for the operation progressed very slowly because of the
delayed arrival of Wacos and Horsas in North Africa. Ultimately it was not
until June that the glider pilots began training with the USAAF's 51st Wing on
even a limited scale. When the training period ended the British glider pilots
had received an average of only four and half hours of flying on the Waco,
including an average of 1.2 hours of night flying. As one British observer
remarked, 'Practically none of our glider pilots have sufficient training, and it
is too late to rectify this omission now.'[29]

Where parachute training was concerned the situation was not much better.
For the 51st Wing opportunities were limited after the end of May because
priority was then assigned to the belated glider training effort. Before that the
wing undertook only one significant night exercise, which did not give cause
for much optimism. However, two further practice missions flown in the
evening (on 16 June) and at night (on 18 June) are said to have achieved 'fair

success'. The progress of 52nd Wing was hampered by equipment and infra-structure deficiencies and by 82nd Airborne Division's focus on ground combat training rather than practice jumps. In the end, the wing conducted two night parachute drops: one became badly dispersed, while the other was deceptively successful. According to the USAAF's official history, 'the wing was still insuf-ficiently trained in formation flying, navigation, and drop-zone location at night'.[30] A later report on airborne training before Husky recorded: 'Neither the parachute nor the glider exercises simulated the conditions of the coming operations closely enough to give any very definite indication of their probable results'.[31] There had been no mass release of gliders over water or at night and very little practice in landing gliders under simulated combat conditions. From 20 June the various participating air and airborne formations were moved to forward airfields in Tunisia. Hence between 20 June and 9 July – when the first aircraft took off for Sicily – no training was possible at all.[32]

The inexperience and limited training of Allied aircrew might have been less significant had they been required to follow a reasonably direct course from Tunisia to Sicily, but unfortunately this was not the case. Instead, to avoid over-flight of naval convoys moving towards the landing beaches and the accompanying threat posed by their anti-aircraft fire, the airborne were routed east to Malta and then north to the Sicilian coast. For the first 82nd Airborne Division mission it was then necessary to turn west to a point just short of the American landing beaches, and then finally north to the drop zones – three sharp turns over water on a dimly moonlit night. The routing assigned to the next US airlift was not much easier.[33]

The precise details of individual airborne missions on Sicily do not concern us here. Suffice it to say that a number of factors – aircrew inexperience and inadequate training, complex routing, darkness, enemy and 'friendly' anti-aircraft fire and a strong offshore wind – combined to produce one of the most depressing chapters in the troubled history of Second World War airborne oper-ations. The first mission was the glider landing near the Ponte Grande – Operation Ladbroke. Of the 144 gliders involved, 69 landed in the sea and a further 10 were completely unaccounted for; 54 came down somewhere in Sicily but in many cases at a considerable distance from their objectives, and some of these were wrecked by obstacles on landing.[34] Only four gliders landed on their designated LZs. Major General Hopkinson, who was primarily responsible for the disaster, was found that night clinging to the water-logged wreckage of his glider and cursing the aircrew of 51st Wing with every breath in his body.[35]

Only 73 personnel reached the Ponte Grande that night. A few reinforce-ments arrived later, but there was no prospect of holding the bridge for long.[36] After a desperate struggle, they surrendered to Italian troops on the following afternoon. However, the bridge had by that time been stripped of explosive charges and the Italians were unable to destroy it before the arrival of British ground forces from the beaches. To that extent, Ladbroke could be described as successful. Yet the Allied victory was bought at an appalling cost. The Air Landing Brigade left Tunisia with 148 officers and 1,927 other ranks. A total of 61 men were killed in action while 133 were wounded; it is not clear whether these figures include all casualties incurred on landing. In addition, 44 personnel were listed as missing and it was firmly established that 252 had drowned. 'Original reports of over 500 probably drowned were reduced, as many survivors clinging to floating gliders were rescued by passing ships and subsequently landed all over the Mediterranean seaboard.'[37]

The US 505th PIR, destined for the Piano Lupo, were dropped all over southern Sicily. Some paratroops landed as far as 65 miles from their drop zones and only small groups could be assembled around their objectives. The 200 who reached the Piano Lupo (out of 3,405 in the regiment) played some part in slowing the advance of the Herman Goering Division towards the landing beaches, incurring a 66 per cent casualty rate in the process. But the Germans were ultimately halted not by the airborne but by naval gunfire and by Allied ground forces moving inland from the coast.[38] On 11 July the Americans launched a second mission involving 82nd Airborne Division's 504th PIR; this should have been a straightforward reinforcement drop behind Allied lines onto an abandoned airfield three miles east of Gela. However, to avoid German-occupied territory, the mission required over-flight of Allied naval forces and the landing beaches. Protracted efforts were made to protect the troop carriers from friendly anti-aircraft guns, and naval commanders offered suitable assurances. But as they neared southern Sicily the transport formations came under heavy fire and 23 of their 144 aircraft were ultimately shot down. Inevitably the drop itself was widely scattered and in the first 24 hours only 37 officers and 518 other ranks could be assembled.[39] During the drop and afterwards, the airborne came under fire from American ground forces, who mistook them for Germans. Of their 400 or so casualties, it is possible that more than 300 were incurred from friendly fire on the ground.

In the meantime, the planned British mission to Augusta was cancelled after Montgomery's troops overran the proposed objectives. So it was not until 13 July that the troop carriers again took off to convey 1 Parachute Brigade to the Ponte Primasole. Another complex route (five over-water turns in moonlight) had been devised around the Allied naval convoys but the airborne still came under naval anti-aircraft fire as they neared Sicily, and this was followed by an intense barrage of enemy flak. A total of 14 aircraft were shot down and many more were damaged, while 25 turned back towards Tunisia with their paratroops still onboard. Only 39 parachute aircraft dropped their troops on or within half a mile of the DZs; 48 more dropped them at distances of between half a mile and twenty miles away.[40] Four out of eight gliders that landed intact were accurately put down, but nine others either crashed on landing or were lost at sea.[41] At first, the Brigade could muster only 12 officers and 283 other ranks out of a total of 1,856 personnel who left North Africa.[42] They held the bridge for a day but were compelled to withdraw on the evening of the 14th. British ground forces recaptured the Ponte Primasole early on the 16th, but the Germans had in the meantime consolidated their defences around Catania and the town did not fall until 5 August.[43]

The airborne missions staged during Operation Husky were mounted at immense cost but to very little positive tactical effect. Only the Ladbroke mission achieved a significant measure of success but through a grossly inefficient level of resource expenditure, given the limited number of troops that actually reached the Ponte Grande. The operations were effectively managed by enthusiastic amateurs as there was still no real airborne expertise within the Allied armed forces: as one of Browning's subsequent reports put it, 'airborne forces had been used in strength for the first time under Army and RAF

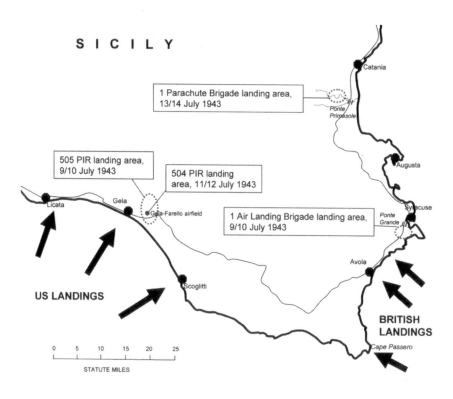

Map 4: Allied airborne operations in Sicily, July 1943

commanders who had no experience of them, and with headquarters staffs who had had no chance of learning their problems and requirements.'[44]

Not surprisingly, Husky was followed by an outpouring of airborne lessons and doctrine papers, as the Allies sought to ensure that the mistakes of the operation were not repeated. The main British inquest into the fiasco conducted jointly by the War Office and the Air Ministry produced a veritable raft of recommendations. It was stated that 'airborne operations must be planned sufficiently far in advance to allow for the necessary training and rehearsals', that 'airborne troops should not be landed in an area where they are immediately faced with opposition' and that, because of their limited supplies of food and ammunition, 'they should not … normally be used in a role requiring their separation from the main [ground] force except for a short period'.[45] All three of these eminently sensible proposals would be ignored during the planning of Market Garden in September 1944, and yet historians have preferred to focus their attention on one further post-Husky recommendation, which supposedly contributed to the Allied defeat at Arnhem. This was the stipulation that future airborne operations should be the responsibility of the theatre air commander-in-chief. Although he was to be 'assisted by a joint staff',[46] it is nevertheless often alleged that this arrangement gave the Allied air forces too much control over airborne planning.

Such arguments depend on selective quotation, and misrepresent both the meaning and context of the joint War Office and Air Ministry ruling. Of course, there was no suggestion that theatre air commanders should be made responsible for the planning and execution of airborne operations in their entirety. The decision to employ airborne troops, the manner in which they would contribute to ground operations and the tasks they were expected to fulfil were matters solely for senior land commanders to determine. What the War Office and Air Ministry sought to achieve was greater air influence over the planning and execution of the accompanying *airlifts*. Moreover, it was argued that airborne lifts should be 'planned integrally' with broader air activity and 'controlled tactically by the same formation that is controlling other air operations in the same area'.[47] There were of course very good reasons for all of this. Allied experience in both North Africa and Sicily had shown that airlift planning represented by far the greatest challenge in mounting successful airborne missions; this was where the critical problems seemed most likely to occur. Army officers inevitably lacked the necessary professional and technical qualifications required to plan airlifts and the lifts had in any case to be carefully co-ordinated with other air operations – a task that could only be performed by the air commander.

As the US armed forces were structured differently, the USAAF being part of the US Army, the Americans inevitably expressed the problem in rather different terms.

The principal airborne doctrine paper to emerge from the US War Department after Husky decreed:

> Airborne and troop carrier units are theater of operations forces. Plans for their combined employment must be prepared by the agency having authority to direct the necessary co-ordinated action of all land, and air forces in the areas involved. This responsibility should not be delegated to lower headquarters since positive co-ordination can be ensured only by the one agency in control of all elements.[48]

Properly observed, this call for the status of airborne plans to be elevated would have had broadly the same effect on the command and control of airlifts as the War Office and Air Ministry were seeking – i.e., their subordination to the theatre air commander. But in practice ample scope remained for airmen to be overruled, bypassed or ignored during the planning process – just as they had been before Torch and Husky. This issue is addressed in later chapters.

Husky brutally exposed the fundamental contradiction that lay behind Allied airborne strategy in Europe in the Second World War. While broader planning considerations and the threat posed by enemy air defences would effectively confine airborne landings to the hours of darkness, the task of accurate night navigation in live operational conditions was beyond a substantial proportion of the Allied air transport fleet. The issue was clear at the time and the Sicilian debacle was not surprisingly followed by recommendations in some quarters – notably in the United States – for curbing the expansion of the airborne arm.[49] Yet it was all too easy to claim that the airborne actions during Husky had been successful simply because they had contributed to a broader campaign from which the Allies emerged victorious. Hence Eisenhower himself performed a monumental act of self-deception by recording in his report on Sicily that the outstanding tactical lesson of the whole campaign was the potential value of airborne operations.[50] US and British expansion plans proceeded, and in response to both airborne demands and more general military requirements for airlift the USAAF continued mass-producing dangerously under-trained aircrew.[51]

Notes

1. Tugwell, *Airborne to Battle*, p. 122.
2. Otway, *Airborne Forces*, p. 25.
3. Ibid., pp. 21, 37–39, 45–48, 94–95. According to Otway, the glider-borne air landing troops were the most heavily armed infantry in the British Army.
4. Tugwell, *Airborne to Battle*, pp. 233–234.

5. Ian Gooderson, *Air Power at the Battlefront: Allied Close Air Support in Europe, 1943–45* (Frank Cass, London, 1998), pp. 94–96.

6. John C. Warren, *Airborne Missions in the Mediterranean 1942–1945* (United States Air Force Historical Division Research Studies Institute, Air University, 1955), pp. 1–3.

7. Otway, *Airborne Forces*, p. 81.

8. Warren, *Airborne Missions in the Mediterranean, 1942–1945*, p. 3.

9. Otway, *Airborne Forces*, pp. 22, 37.

10. Air Publication (AP) 3231, *The Second World War 1939–1945, Royal Air Force, Airborne Forces* (Air Ministry official monograph, 1951), p. 48.

11. Warren, *Airborne Missions in the Mediterranean, 1942–1945*, p. 5.

12. Ibid., pp. 6–9.

13. Ibid., pp. 9–13.

14. Ibid., pp. 14–17.

15. Otway, *Airborne Forces*, p. 75.

16. Warren, *Airborne Missions in the Mediterranean, 1942–1945*, pp. 14–16.

17. Ibid., p. 16.

18. Otway, *Airborne Forces*, pp. 78–81; Major General John Frost, *A Drop Too Many* (Cassell, London, 1980), pp. 74–100.

19. Otway, *Airborne Forces*, pp. 81–82.

20. Frost, *A Drop Too Many*, p. 103.

21. Otway, *Airborne Forces*, p. 81.

22. Warren, *Airborne Missions in the Mediterranean, 1942–1945*, p. 21.

23. Otway, *Airborne Forces*, p. 118. Headquarters nodes with at least some influence over airborne matters included Allied Forces Headquarters, 15th Army Group, Eighth Army, Seventh Army, Mediterranean Air Command, 12th US Troop Carrier Command, Browning and his staff and the airborne divisional headquarters.

24. Brigadier George Chatterton, *The Wings of Pegasus: The Story of the Glider Pilot Regiment* (Battery Press, Nashville, 1982), p. 64.

25. Otway, *Airborne Forces*, p. 115.

26. Warren, *Airborne Missions in the Mediterranean*, pp. 22, 26.

27. Ibid., p. 23. 'In vain did the British Airborne Forces adviser, Group Capt. T.B. Cooper, RAF, protest that a glider assault on a dark night with inexperienced crews was not practicable. The decision stood.' See also AP 3231, *Airborne Forces*, p. 95.

28. Chatterton, *Wings of Pegasus*, p. 42.

29. Warren, *Airborne Missions in the Mediterranean*, p. 28

30. Ibid., pp. 26–28.

31. 38 Wing RAF Report on Training and Operations in North Africa and Sicily, May/July 1943 (held at AHB).

32. Warren, *Airborne Missions in the Mediterranean*, pp. 27–28. A meeting of British airborne and RAF commanders in August 1943 noted that 'few [glider] crews had carried out night landings for several weeks prior to the operation, which probably accounted for some of the casualties'. See Royal Air Force Airborne Assault Operations, 1940–45, Vol. 1 (held at AHB), minutes of a meeting held at Norfolk House on 10 August 1943 to discuss future policy relating to the employment of airborne forces.

33. Warren, *Airborne Missions in the Mediterranean*, p. 25.

34. 38 Wing RAF Report on Training and Operations in North Africa and Sicily, May/July 1943.

35. Warren, *Airborne Missions in the Mediterranean*, p. 46.

36. AP 3231, *Airborne Forces*, p. 90.

37. Otway, *Airborne Forces*, pp. 120, 123.

38. Warren, *Airborne Missions in the Mediterranean*, pp. 33–36; Tugwell, *Airborne to Battle*, pp. 165–166.

39. Ste. Croix (ed.), *Airborne Operations*, pp. 85–86.

40. Warren, *Airborne Missions in the Mediterranean*, pp. 40–41, 51–52.

41. Tugwell, *Airborne to Battle*, p. 164.

42. Otway, *Airborne Forces*, p. 127.

43. Tugwell, *Airborne to Battle*, p. 165.

44. Otway, *Airborne Forces*, p. 137.

45. Extract from Joint War Office/Air Ministry Report on the Employment of Airborne Forces, Part A, Lessons of Airborne Operations in Sicily, Appendix D to Appendix V/19, Wing Commander W.D. Macpherson to SASO, 27 November 1943, Notes on the Planning and Preparation of the Allied Expeditionary Air Force for the Invasion of North West France in June 1944, appendices (held at AHB). Other post-Husky doctrine papers included US War Department Training Circular 113, an un-numbered SHAEF memorandum dated 19 January 1944, and Combined Chiefs of Staff Paper 496. See also US Army Air Forces Board Project (T) 27, Long Range Study of Airborne Operations, 29 April 1944 (held at AHB).

46. Extract from Joint War Office/Air Ministry Report on the Employment of Airborne Forces, Part A, Lessons of Airborne Operations in Sicily, Appendix D to Appendix V/19, Wing Commander W.D. Macpherson to SASO, 27 November 1943, Notes on the Planning and Preparation of the Allied Expeditionary Air Force for the Invasion of North West France in June 1944, appendices.

47. Ibid.

48. US War Department Training Circular 113, 9 October 1943.

49. Tugwell, *Airborne to Battle*, p. 166.

50. AP 3231, *Airborne Forces*, p. 96.

51. Tugwell, *Airborne to Battle*, p. 166.

1.3. Airborne Warfare: Normandy and Beyond

GIVEN THE DISASTERS that accompanied Husky, the Allies' decision to stage their next major airborne venture in darkness might ostensibly appear to rank as one of the most outstanding examples in military history of a failure to apply the lessons of past operations.[1] Yet such a judgement would not be entirely fair. The Allies did of course recognize after Sicily that night operations were likely to present very serious difficulties, but before the commencement of Operation Neptune (the landing phase of Operation Overlord) in Normandy in June 1944 they persuaded themselves that the problems could be rectified in two ways. The first was through better aircrew training, including intensive rehearsals and realistic exercises. The joint War Office and Air Ministry report on the employment of airborne forces produced after Husky pointed out that airborne operations were highly complex.

> Aircraft crews participating must therefore be trained to an operational standard. In particular, pilots require intensive training in low flying, navigation over sea, and in judging distances by moonlight. All the aircraft crews must have some preliminary operational experience and be able to drop human bodies as accurately as bomber crews drop their loads.[2]

American doctrine similarly stressed the critical importance of accurate troop carrier navigation and its dependence upon thorough training. 'Troop carrier units must be qualified for both day and night operations. This in turn dictates a high order of training requirements.'[3]

Otherwise, the Allies pinned their hopes on the employment of navigational aids and so-called 'pathfinder' troops. The pathfinders would act as the vanguard of larger airborne formations, arriving a short time before them, marking or illuminating landing areas and setting up radar homing beacons such as the Rebecca/Eureka system.* It was believed that these measures would give aircrew a far better chance of finding their objectives after nightfall.[4]

* Rebecca/Eureka was a transponder system used as a radio homing beacon by means of a Eureka ground emitter responding to queries from an airborne Rebecca interrogator.

The Allies' faith in the potential of night operations may have been bolstered by the relative success of smaller-scale airborne missions around Salerno in Italy in September 1943. The only drop made inside enemy territory, involving the 2nd Battalion of the US 509th Parachute Combat Team at Avellino, was another failure. Only 15 of the 40 aircraft involved placed their paratroops within five miles of the drop zone, and nearly 20 per cent of those who made the jump were still listed as dead, wounded or missing in October. But two other reinforcement landings behind Allied lines, both of which were guided by pathfinders, were far more accurate. This may have given credence to arguments that some such achievement could be repeated in Normandy.[5] Yet the Allies probably had little alternative but to opt for a further night operation in June 1944 once it had been decided that airborne troops should be employed, both to assist the advance inland and to hinder German counterattacks towards the coast. Again, the Allied shipping convoys had to cross the channel under cover of darkness, which in turn dictated that the amphibious landings would be made at dawn. Again, the main airborne task was to support the landings, which meant that the paratroops and air landing forces had to arrive in Normandy several hours in advance. If they arrived before nightfall on the previous evening they would warn the Germans of the impending amphibious assault, and they would in any case be far more vulnerable to German air defences.

The decision to launch a further night-time airborne operation in Normandy after the experience of Sicily can therefore be rationalized, yet this does not mean that the concept was very much more likely to prove successful. In the months before the Normandy landings the Allies mounted an intense programme of night training for their troop carrier and airborne formations; they created pathfinder units and trained aircrew in the use of a range of navigational aids. But their efforts to confront the challenges of night navigation and night formation flying by the troop carriers were hampered by three basic obstacles. The first was the phenomenal scale of the forthcoming operation. In February 1944, the Allies decided that it would be necessary to mount the largest airborne assault of the war to date, involving the deployment of three airborne divisions into Normandy; moreover, it was eventually determined that the preponderance of this colossal force should be infiltrated in a single lift. The task required the creation of substantially larger American and British air transport forces in a period of just four months.

The inevitable consequence was that on the night of 5/6 June the Allied troop carrier and glider forces that set off for Normandy still contained significant numbers of under-trained and very inexperienced aircrew.[6] At the end of March (just over two months before D-Day) 9th TCC possessed 760 crews; by D-Day this figure had somehow been raised to 1,116. Of the 915

*British Horsa gliders and their tugs awaiting take-off for
Normandy in June 1944*

glider crews in the command on the eve of Neptune, 595 had arrived in
Britain since 'late March', following unspecified but 'drastic steps ... taken to
step up the rate of advanced glider training'.[7] As before, many American
crews received only the most rudimentary instruction in night navigation,
9th TCC instead having little option but to place all their faith in formation
flying, with the untrained mass attempting to follow a few trained leaders.[8]
The RAF's 46 Group, the second of two air transport groups committed to
Neptune, only formed in January 1944 and did not begin converting to
Dakotas until March.[9]

The second problem was the difficulty of replicating operational conditions
in exercises. Most of the Allied air transport crews committed to Neptune were
capable of delivering airborne troops accurately to their objectives on a still
moonlit night without enemy interference, but to achieve such a feat in adverse
weather conditions and under even limited anti-aircraft fire was an entirely
different proposition. Only a minority of the aircrew had faced German flak
before Neptune. Unfortunately the Allies appear to have interpreted the relatively good results achieved in favourable weather as being representative of
what would be accomplished during the actual operation. There was a

tendency to assume that exercises spoiled by cloud or haze did not provide a fair reflection of aircrew capabilities. Indeed, while the field orders for the main airborne command rehearsal (code-named 'Eagle') on 11–12 May contained full and specific precautionary instructions that were to be followed in the event of bad weather, no equivalent advice was included in the field orders for Neptune.[10] It was presumably doubted that the operation would be sanctioned in anything other than clear and calm conditions. This was not unreasonable, however, for Allied doctrine was by this time emphasizing that airborne warfare was weather-dependent. Therefore, if the airborne objectives were considered to be vital to the success of a far broader venture (such as Neptune itself), this might have to be delayed until suitable weather conditions prevailed.[11] This argument appears to have been accepted by the Allied high command before the landings in Normandy but, when poor weather actually struck early in June, the airborne perspective was forgotten. Eisenhower's ultimate decision to launch Neptune on the 6th was based overwhelmingly on maritime considerations.

As for Exercise Eagle itself, the air plan was designed 'to be, so far as practicable, exactly similar to that for the operation, i.e., the same pathfinder procedure, the same number of aircraft, the same length of flight, the same landing times and relative position of dropping zones etc., to be adopted'. But on 27 May the American lift plan was thrown into disarray by a revised 21st Army Group intelligence assessment of enemy strength around their landing areas. This necessitated extensive last-minute changes to both the air routing and drop zone locations of 82nd Airborne Division, so that at least half the final 9th TCC plan for D-Day diverged considerably from the arrangements prepared for the exercise.[12]

The third problem related to the troop carrier formations responsible for carrying one particular division – the US 101st Airborne. As early as 18 April the divisional commander repeated the error made by 82nd Airborne Division before Husky and opted to cease jump training.[13] No doubt there appeared to be good reasons for this from the paratroops' perspective, but the decision perfectly illustrates how ignorant most airborne commanders were of air matters in the Second World War, and how difficult it was for them to grasp that the air represented a different and infinitely more complex means of delivering troops to the battlefield than surface transportation. The result was that, with the exception of Exercise Eagle, the aircrew responsible for conveying 101st Airborne to Normandy on D-Day had not undertaken any training with the division for a period of more than six weeks. The competence of less experienced personnel would very probably have declined during this hiatus.

If the Allies were unjustifiably confident about their pre-Neptune parachute training programme, there were clearly far more doubts regarding the viability of night glider landings. The potential problem where the gliders were concerned centred not merely on night navigation but on the nature of the terrain in the proposed landing areas. In the east – the British sector – there were numerous flat, open fields. But the terrain in western Normandy where the American airborne objectives were located could hardly have been less suitable for glider operations: the area was so-called bocage, typified by small fields enclosed by high hedgerows. It was always clear that the difficulties of landing heavily laden assault gliders safely in such territory would be significant even in daylight; after dark the challenge would be a daunting one.

Hopes of finding a solution by scheduling mass landings at dawn were ultimately abandoned after an unsuccessful rehearsal on 18 April and the appearance of numerous anti-glider obstacles on the intended LZs in Normandy. Instead, the Allies decided to devote most of the initial D-Day lift to the paratroops, who were (among other things) charged with removing the obstacles. The main glider landings would be delayed until the evening of 6 June – before nightfall. However, more limited glider operations were eventually still scheduled for dawn on 6 June in both the British and American sectors, and these plans exerted a direct influence on the glider training programme conducted by 9th TCC. As no night landings were envisaged, the command's training logically enough focused on day and night formation flying and on dawn and dusk landings. Such were the parameters of their glider aircrew instruction when, at the end of May, the broader revision of US airlift arrangements caused the glider landings to be rescheduled before daybreak.[14] This decision was taken against the explicit advice of Brigadier General Paul Williams, commander of 9th TCC, but once again the senior army officers were unable to comprehend the issues involved. When informed that Williams 'did not think the gliders could operate by night', Montgomery simply replied that they should be ordered to do so.[15]

On the night of 5/6 June the American parachute drops in western Normandy went disastrously wrong. This was not in any sense the fault of 9th TCC. Rather, it was again the result of failures in conceptual planning, which caused Williams' aircrew to be assigned a task that they were manifestly unable to perform. In the most favourable conditions possible the story might have been different, but circumstances were sadly very far from favourable. Thus, although most of the pathfinders provided at least some marking on or near the drop zones, a combination of factors – the late routing changes, poor visibility, a lack of distinctive DZ features, a strong northwest wind, German flak and consequent evasive action by the troop carriers – caused both 82nd and 101st Airborne Division to be widely scattered. Many paratroops were dropped far from their zones; many more lost

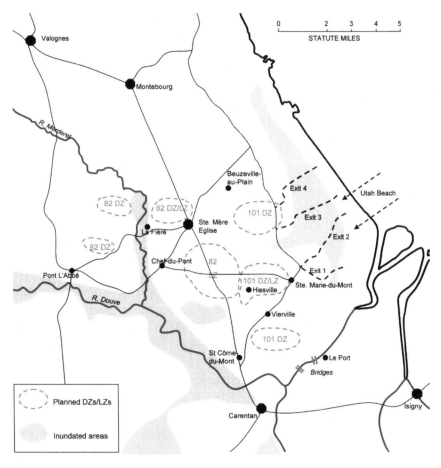

Map 5: The American landing areas in western Normandy

their weapons and equipment. Unable to establish proper command and control arrangements, they suffered a massive loss of force cohesion.[16] Only 10 per cent actually landed on their drop zones, and 45 per cent landed anything from 2 to 25 miles away. The full breakdown was:

10% on DZ
Between 25% and 30% within a mile of DZ or pathfinder beacon
Between 15% and 20% from 1 to 2 miles
25% from 2 to 5 miles
10% from 5 to 10 miles
4% from 10 to 25 miles
6% unaccounted for[17]

The impact of this dispersion was massively increased by the enclosed bocage terrain, by obstacles such as waterways and flooded areas, by darkness and by the airborne troops' unfamiliarity with their surroundings. Despite all the planning, training and exercises that preceded Neptune, elementary problems involved in landing airborne troops in darkness in an entirely unfamiliar environment had not been properly evaluated. Many troops who did not land directly on their drop zones were left with virtually no means of orientating themselves until daybreak, at the very earliest. Only then, if they were lucky, were they able to establish whether they were a mile or 25 miles from their DZs.

And then of course there were the Germans. To begin with, while Utah Beach proved less heavily defended than expected, Allied intelligence clearly underestimated the strength of enemy forces inland. The presence of elements of such formations as the 1,058th Regiment and the 191st Artillery Regiment appears to have caught the Americans by surprise.[18] Secondly, by 1944, the Germans were fully appraised of the Allies' airborne capability and with typical Teutonic efficiency had formulated effective counter-airborne doctrine and training programmes for their forces in France.[19] Coastal areas were carefully studied and potential DZs and LZs were flooded or blocked by obstacles. Thus while some German troops in Normandy clearly succumbed to the 'shock effect and surprise' that airborne landings are often said to instil among opposing forces, others did not. Take, for example, the experience of the 3rd Battalion 506th PIR (101st Airborne Division). The battalion 'had been given a good drop'.

> Unfortunately the Germans were ready and waiting and had converted the drop area into a deathtrap. The moment the jump began an oil-soaked building burst into flame, and by its light machine guns and mortars mowed down the paratroops before they could get clear of their chutes. Both the battalion commander and his executive were among the slain. The survivors had all they could do to assemble and maintain themselves.[20]

If the US parachute drops were chaotic, sadly it cannot be maintained that the glider landings undertaken in support of 101st and 82nd Airborne were much more successful. Here again the combination of darkness and enclosed terrain was the fundamental problem. The 'Chicago' mission was flown by elements of 101st Airborne. As the gliders lost altitude during their descent to the LZ, the markers guiding them disappeared behind the high Normandy hedgerows, causing many aircraft to miss the zone completely and to land in nearby fields that were not sufficiently long. The hedges themselves contained trees averaging 40 feet in height; prior warnings of their presence had gone unheeded. Many pilots found that they had insufficient space to clear the trees at the near end of the selected landing field without crashing into the boundary at the far end. Of 49 gliders, only 6 landed on the LZ, the rest making crash landings in the surrounding area.

> It took time to pry equipment out of smashed gliders and more time to assemble, with occasional interruptions by rifle fire or mortar shells. A detachment sent out at dawn by the 101st Division to meet the mission at the LZ and guide the reinforcements to Hiesville [which was within the LZ perimeter] did not return until noon.

They brought with them only 6 out of the 16 57mm anti-tank guns that had been loaded into the gliders in England and, from a total of 25 vehicles, just 3 jeeps.[21]

The fate of 82nd Airborne's 'Detroit' glider mission was no happier. Cloud and enemy fire scattered the 52-glider formation, and many of the pilots who remained on course afterwards lost sight of the LZ. The number that landed 'on or near' the zone is estimated at between 17 and 23, although it should be noted that at least 9 of these aircraft put down around Ste. Mère Eglise, which was outside the LZ. Of the gliders that at least landed somewhere in Normandy, 22 were destroyed on landing and all but 12 were badly damaged. The bocage terrain was again the main cause but other hazards, including marshland and German anti-glider obstacles, also took their toll, and one glider ran into a herd of cattle. Only 8 of the 16 anti-tank guns carried by the mission were recovered from gliders in the LZ area, and at least 11 out of the 22 jeeps were rendered unusable by crash landings.

The follow-up glider operations on the evening of 6 June also ran into difficulties. 'Keokuk' mission, flown for 101st Airborne, carried equipment, supplies and 157 personnel, 44 of whom became casualties from enemy fire or accidents during the landings. Only 5 out of a total of 32 gliders dispatched actually landed on their designated LZ. 'Elmira' mission for 82nd Airborne ran into many of the problems encountered by 'Detroit' – small fields bordered by high trees, flooded terrain, anti-glider obstacles and enemy fire. To make matters worse, 82nd Airborne had failed to secure full control of the LZ and part of it was in German hands. Around half of the 76 gliders in the first echelon missed their LZ by more than a mile, some mistakenly landing on the zone illuminated for Keokuk. Crash landings and enemy fire destroyed 3 Wacos and 21 Horsas, but many more sustained extensive damage. Personnel casualties were surprisingly light, but it is not clear how much of the gliders' cargo could afterwards be usefully employed.[22] The second echelon suffered an even worse fate, presumably because the Germans had been fully alerted by the initial landings.

Counting some damage done after landing by enemy fire, only 13 of 84 Horsas were left intact, and 56 of them were totally destroyed … None of the 14 Wacos which were sent survived intact and 8 of them were destroyed. Of 196 glider pilots 10 were killed, 29 or more were wounded or injured and 7 were still missing at the end of the month. The airborne had 28 killed and 106 wounded or injured.

This amounted to 32 per cent of the airborne personnel who participated in the mission. Of their 59 jeeps 17 were lost, together with 9 of their 24 howitzers. Of the equipment that remained serviceable, much could not be collected or used immediately.[23]

Ultimately, then, the effects of dispersion, darkness, enclosed or flooded terrain, disorientation and German resistance combined to produce chaos. Although the US airlift of 5/6 June involved some 13,000 personnel, only around 4,500 were under divisional control after 24 hours.[24] The two US divisions also suffered an estimated 2,500 casualties on the first day of the operation alone.[25]

Typically the impression conveyed by historians of the Normandy landings is that despite the immense difficulties caused by their inaccurate and dispersed drops, by crash landings and by stronger than expected opposition, the US airborne ultimately secured their objectives. The airborne operations are held to have been successful because Neptune as a whole was successful. Yet in fact, when the airborne missions are analysed in detail, it soon becomes clear that many vital objectives set for D-Day were not achieved.

Of the four causeways running inland from Utah Beach that were assigned to 101st Airborne Division, only one was captured outright by airborne troops within the timetable originally set. Another fell to a combined assault by the airborne and by elements of US VII Corps arriving from Utah, but not until the early afternoon of 6 June; the third fell to troops advancing from the beach before the airborne reached it and the fourth was so effectively covered by nearby German guns that it proved unusable. To the north of 101st Airborne's area of responsibility, 1st Battalion 502nd PIR were unable to achieve their objective of securing a firm northern perimeter extending to Beuzeville and linking with 82nd Airborne. To the south, 101st Airborne 'failed in their overall objective, the sealing off of the southern flank of the Utah beachhead. From Carentan to beyond St Côme-du-Mont the north–south highway and its bridges over the Douve remained in German hands.'[26]

Where 82nd Airborne Division were concerned, the crucial objective of Ste. Mère Eglise was captured on the morning of 6 June. But significantly more troops were required to hold the town than the number originally assigned, and this diversion prevented the 2nd Battalion 505th PIR from executing their primary task of establishing a perimeter line on 82nd Airborne's northern flank. The Germans afterwards sought to exploit this gap in American lines which, among other things, left the division's glider landing zone very vulnerable, as we have seen. The 1st Battalion partially fulfilled their mission by seizing one end of the La Fière bridge over the Merderet river but could not capture their second bridge objective at Chef-du-Pont. The 508th PIR were so inaccurately dropped that about half of all regimental personnel were entirely ineffective in the pursuit of their assigned goals. A single battalion, which sought to reach the road bridge across the Douve at Pont l'Abbé, ran into insuperable German opposition and eventually took up position on Hill 30, which overlooked the Merderet between La Fière and Chef-du-Pont. The 507th PIR participated in securing the east end of the La Fière bridge when they had in fact been ordered to take the western end, and also captured the east end of the bridge at Chef-du-Pont. But as, in both cases, the Germans continued to hold the western ends of the bridges, many of the paratroops dropped beyond the Merderet were effectively cut off.[27]

One factor alone prevented the American airborne missions from failing catastrophically – their close proximity to Utah Beach. The furthest objectives were about ten miles from the beach while the nearest were immediately behind it, and therefore most airborne units were relieved by conventional ground forces within 24 hours of the initial drop. 101st Airborne later recorded:

In operation 'NEPTUNE', the 101st Airborne Division could not have maintained itself much over 24 hours without support ... The timely arrival of the 4th Division relieved the airborne troops of concern for their front to the North and East and allowed the elements to reform around Hiesville. The previous conception that an Airborne Division can maintain itself independently for two or three days should be revised downward for action in 'FORTRESS EUROPE'.[28]

Even this frank admission is something of an understatement, as in truth many key objectives would not have been secured at all without relief or reinforcement from Utah. Troops arriving from the beach played a critical role not only in securing a perimeter line to the north of 101st Airborne, but also in fighting south of Vierville to protect the southern flank and in the capture of Ste. Marie-du-Mont and Ste. Mère Eglise.

Their importance is perfectly illustrated by the fate of those 82nd Airborne troops who were unlucky enough to become stranded on the west side of the Merderet river. By 8 June the position of these units had become so desperate that their commanding officer sent out a series of radio messages declaring that the situation was critical and that he could hardly hold out another day unaided. It was not until the 9th that 82nd Airborne finally crossed the Merderet (with armour and fire support from VII Corps), and their hold on the west bank was not secured until the 10th, when elements of the US Army's 90th Division arrived to relieve the airborne.[29] It is very likely that this episode exerted a strong influence on 82nd Airborne's thinking in Market Garden, which again required the division to drop on both sides of a major water obstacle – the Maas-Waal Canal. The supreme irony of this story is that the US airborne assault on western Normandy was specifically promoted by Bradley and Montgomery 'as essential to the success of the landing on the "Utah" beach … General Bradley felt the "Utah" landing was impossible unless the airborne division could neutralize the defending troops'.[30] In the event, the roles were substantially reversed and the US airborne had to be rescued by VII Corps.

In the British sector, 6th Airborne Division's landings were somewhat more concentrated but far from perfect. The story of 38 Group's lift to DZ N reinforces the impression that the Allied airborne did not give nearly enough consideration to the problem of night assembly during their preparations for Neptune. The lift must be judged accurate by the standards set in earlier night operations, and only 4 aircraft out of 95 dropped their paratroops more than 1 mile from the DZ.[31] Yet only 40 per cent of 7th Parachute Battalion (7 PARA) could initially be assembled at the Orne bridges, and the other two component battalions of 5 Parachute Brigade went into action 40 per cent under strength.[32] The lift to DZ K was in the meantime thrown into confusion after pathfinders bound for the zone were dropped in error onto DZ N, which they duly marked incorrectly. Consequently, of the 35 aircraft that were supposed to bring elements of 3 Parachute Brigade to DZ K, only 8 actually dropped their paratroops at the correct location.

But it was the more northerly lift to DZ V that was the most chaotic, and once again a critical influence was the terrain: the zone was located on one side of a marshy river valley interlaced with innumerable minor waterways and drainage ditches. In seeking a DZ close to 3 Parachute Brigade's objectives Allied planners ignored the potentially hazardous nature of this topography, which should have been patently obvious from the available mapping and imagery. All of the equipment carried to the DZ by one of the two pathfinder aircraft was lost or broken on landing, and the second pathfinder contingent came to earth some distance from the zone and could not illuminate it properly before the main lift arrived.[33] As if this were not enough, the DZ was so near to the coast that aircraft making even a marginally inaccurate landfall had hardly any time to correct their course before reaching it. This problem, at least, was appreciated by the RAF but 'had to be accepted in deference to the military plan'.[34] The troop carrier formations also came under fire from anti-aircraft artillery during their approach and the area was affected by dust and haze following a bombing raid on the nearby German gun battery at Merville.[35] Senior airborne planners within the Allied Expeditionary Air Force had voiced concerns about this form of obscuration, but their misgivings were ignored.[36]

It is possible that even the more experienced RAF transport crews of 38 Group would not have executed an accurate drop; few members of a 3 Parachute Brigade advance party carried by 38 Group aircraft landed near DZ V.[37] But bad luck would in any case have it that the main lift was assigned to 46 Group, which had been hastily formed in the months preceding Neptune. Of 71 troop carriers assigned to the DZ V main lift only 17 dropped their paratroops on the zone.[38] Airborne troops conveyed by 29 more aircraft landed at distances from 'within one mile' up to two miles from the DZ but, as in western Normandy, the combination of darkness, disorientation, terrain-related factors and enemy resistance often meant that an error of even a single mile was sufficient to prevent personnel from locating and joining their units before daybreak. Some of the paratroops who came down in flooded areas drowned under the weight of their equipment. Of 750 men assigned to Lieutenant Colonel T.B.H. Otway's 9th Parachute Battalion (9 PARA) to destroy the Merville Battery, he was able to collect together just 150.[39]

Where the British glider landings were concerned, 6th Airborne Division achieved an unprecedented degree of accuracy at LZ N, where 46 out of 72 gliders came down on the landing zone. Yet the inaccuracy of other landings and a significant number of aborted missions served to reduce the overall success rate: of a total of 98 gliders detailed, 40 were either abortive or else landed more than a mile from their intended LZs. The most significant failure again occurred at LZ V, where only 1 out of 11 gliders landed within a mile of the zone. Hardly any of the glider-borne equipment required by 9 PARA reached them before they launched their assault on the Merville Battery.[40]

The brilliant feat of airmanship that brought all three gliders assigned to Pegasus Bridge down onto a tiny LZ (LZ X) was thus by no means representative of the entire 6th Airborne Division assault glider experience. How, then, was it achieved? The answer is that in the two months leading up to D-Day the members of the Glider Pilot Regiment selected for the operation conducted intensive mission-specific training in realistic conditions. In all, they flew no fewer than 43 training sorties, more than half of them at night.[41]. Such was the preparation required to mount a successful glider-borne *coup-de-main*, as Eben-Emael had already demonstrated and as 6th Airborne Division readily

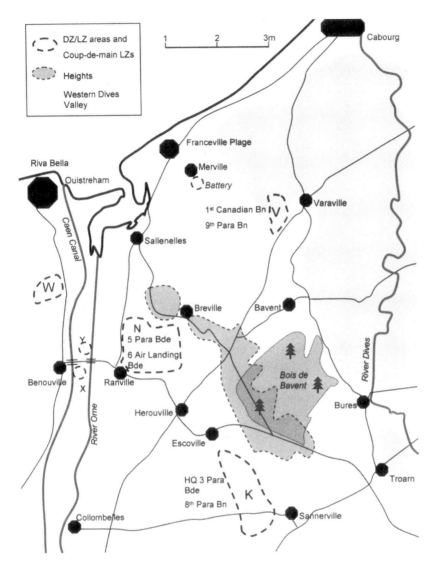

Map 6: 6th Airborne Division's landing areas in eastern Normandy

acknowledged afterwards.[42] Yet even these elaborate preliminaries by no means guaranteed success. Hence, the crews assigned to land three Horsas directly onto the Merville Battery conducted similarly exhaustive training in April and May 1944,[43] but on the night of 5/6 June a broken tow-rope compelled one glider pilot to abort his mission, and the other two missed the battery – one by three miles.[44]

The three Horsa gliders that carried out the coup-de-main
operation at Pegasus Bridge

The relatively accurate lift to DZ/LZ N might be viewed as evidence that there was some genuine scope for the Allies to mount more successful airborne operations by night in the future, but some caution is necessary here. Although 38 Group's achievement at 'N' was indeed exceptional, it should be recalled that they were the most highly trained and experienced of all the Allied air transport units. Hence, while US troop carrier navigation was dependent on the maintenance of close formation flying, 38 Group aircrew were trained to navigate individually. Moreover, all of their aircraft were equipped with the radio-based navigation aid known as GEE,* whereas only a limited number of American aircraft carried the system. 'The Americans simply did not have enough GEE sets to go around.'[45]

The task confronting 38 Group was also a relatively straightforward one. They had only to follow a direct north–south route across the Normandy coast to a landing area that was five miles inland; there was little cloud in the area, they were not exposed to German anti-aircraft fire for very long, and the twin waterways – the Orne river and the Caen canal – were visible throughout the

---

* GEE allowed navigators to calculate the position of their aircraft by observing the time taken to receive pulse signals from three different ground stations.

approach, and were in any case familiar to many aircrew from SAS and Special Operations Executive missions. The area of 'N' could be gauged approximately from the fighting around Pegasus Bridge, and then more precisely from the pathfinder aids. By contrast, US troop carriers were routed west of the Cotentin Peninsula to avoid the Allied invasion fleet, and they had then to fly east across the peninsula for around 20 miles to reach their drop zones. There were few visible ground features to assist navigation, and there was intermittent enemy fire throughout the overland transit.[46] In short, the successful lift to DZ/LZ N resulted from a combination of extremely favourable influences, and it would have been very optimistic for the Allies to plan future operations on the assumption that circumstances might again be so advantageous.

The key lesson for the Allies came not from the initial airlift to DZ/LZ N but from the follow-up mass glider mission flown to zones N andW on the evening of 6 June (OperationMallard).Of the 146 gliders sent to 'N', no fewer than 142 landed on the zone, while only 4 of the 110 gliders dispatched to 'W' failed to put down there successfully.[47] Such levels of accuracy were completely unprecedented in Allied airborne history; Mallard demonstrated that precise and concentrated landings could be achieved if airborne operations were staged in daylight. Yet at the same time it is again important to bear

The second British airlift crosses the Channel on 6 June

in mind that Mallard benefited from a number of advantages compared with the American glider missions that evening. The LZs were in well-marked, open areas that had been brought firmly under British control; anti-glider obstacles had been removed, and the gliders were not targeted by German flak or small arms fire.[48] Daylight may have been important but it was by no means the only factor in Mallard's success.

One of the most enduring airborne legends of the Second World War contends that 6th Airborne Division were completely successful in securing their objectives on D-Day. They captured the Orne bridges and the Merville Battery, destroyed the bridges over the River Dives and prevented German counter-attacks from the east against the landing beaches. Yet the broader goal for the division was to secure an area of high ground between the two rivers that dominated the eastern flank of the landing area, and they were also supposed to gain control of the coast between Sallenelles and Cabourg. Their task was to:

> Mop up and secure the area between the Rivers Orne and Dives, north of the road Colombelles-Sannerville-Troarn. This was to include the capture of the towns of Sallenelles and Franceville Plage, and the clearing of as much as possible of the coastal strip between these places and Cabourg, at the mouth of the River Dives.[49]

This ambitious assignment was at first to be the responsibility of just two parachute brigades. They would be reinforced on the night of 6 June by 6 Air Landing Brigade and by 1 Special Services Brigade advancing inland from Sword Beach. Nevertheless, a perimeter line extending from Collombelles to Cabourg via Troarn would cover around sixteen miles, and would enclose an area between the Orne and the Dives of approximately 60 square miles. It might be concluded that Montgomery and Browning (who was the principal author of the plan) were indulging in pure fantasy if they really expected that a single airborne division stood a realistic chance of capturing and holding such a large area, but a flawed appreciation of the German response to Neptune was probably the decisive factor. In the aftermath of the beach landings the Germans were expected to form their main eastern defensive line to the east of the River Dives,[50] whereas in fact Rommel had identified the high ground west of the Dives as one of the critical areas of the Normandy battlefield.[51] Moreover, the Germans proved exceedingly reluctant to surrender their hold on the coast. To make matters worse, the destruction of the Dives bridges appears to have presented only a limited obstacle to German forces seeking to counter-attack into the area between the two rivers.

Ultimately, 6th Airborne Division did at least establish a secure bridgehead to the east of the Orne, but the story could easily have been very different. In the weeks before D-Day Allied intelligence had warned of the presence of 21st Panzer Division in the Normandy area, although their precise location was not established. In fact, they were based to the south of Caen and were ready to counter-attack with some 120 tanks and 3,000 infantry. Had this formidable force challenged the lightly-armed British paratroops on 6 June it is most unlikely that the Orne bridgehead would have been held but, in the event, the Germans opted to direct their main effort west of the Caen Canal, towards the coast. Only limited opposition therefore confronted 6th Airborne before they were strengthened by conventional ground forces and by the arrival of 6 Air Landing Brigade in the evening.[52]

Even then, instead of extending as far as the Dives, the area secured by 6th Airborne Division eventually had as its eastern boundary the village of Breville, which was finally taken on 12 June with extensive support from 51st (Highland) Division and 4 Special Services Brigade. This achievement cost 6th Airborne the bulk of the 4,500 casualties that they suffered in the Normandy campaign, or nearly half their original strength.[53] The Germans were left in control of much of the all-important high ground and there was afterwards no significant Allied advance to the east until the collapse of German resistance in Normandy in August.[54]

The consequences for Allied progress in eastern Normandy were indeed profound. Montgomery found himself with so little room to manoeuvre on his eastern flank that he was compelled to attack west of Caen, or towards the city itself. Needless to say, this restricted axis of advance made the German defenders' task very much easier. When Montgomery finally decided to strike east of Caen, the small area from which he launched his offensive (Operation Goodwood) became acutely congested as the three armoured divisions of VIII Corps made their way laboriously across the Orne before performing a 90-degree turn and driving south. It was then necessary for each division to advance one by one down a narrow corridor before emerging in more open country southeast of Caen. In the event, between one third and one half of VIII Corps did not even reach this area in time to engage the enemy on a significant scale on the first day of the offensive, when German resistance had largely been suppressed by Allied bombing. By the second day the Germans had recovered sufficiently to halt the British advance.[55]

To the north of the airborne bridgehead, 9 PARA were obliged to relinquish their hold on the Merville Battery soon after the guns had been temporarily put out of commission. The area was strenuously contested during the following days but it was ultimately brought under German control and, again, there was afterwards little change in dispositions until the end of the

Normandy campaign. The whole of the coastal strip from the Orne to the Dives estuaries remained firmly in German hands, leaving their artillery in very close proximity to Sword Beach. Eventually, as one official narrative records, 'during the last two weeks of June the most easterly beaches had to be closed to shipping'.

> What made the Ouistreham beaches untenable was the constant menace from mortars and guns which fired across the Orne from the Franceville area and did considerable execution ... Personnel craft were routed further west after losses on the 15 and 16 June while stores were diverted after the 25 June. The area was finally closed to Allied shipping on the 1 July.[56]

In summary, then, 6th Airborne Division by no means achieved all their objectives in June 1944, and their limited progress east of the Orne had serious operational repercussions later on. This is in no way a reflection on the competence or bravery of 6th Airborne personnel, but it does raise important questions about Montgomery's understanding of the scope and limitations of airborne warfare. Only three months before Market Garden 6th Airborne Division were assigned an unrealistically large area objective by an operation plan that also seriously underestimated German opposition.

The process by which operational and tactical lessons from Neptune were identified with a view to their application in future airborne ventures was evidently very difficult. Many of the airborne troops remained in the front line after Neptune, and thus both officers and other personnel were unavailable for debriefing for weeks or even (in the British case) months. A post-operation report on Neptune and subsequent operations was finally produced by 6th Airborne Division in September, although it was both uninformative and, in certain respects, factually inaccurate. For example, the report did not acknowledge the failure of the pathfinders at DZ V. No account was circulated by 38 Group until 14 November and even this was accompanied by a crucial caveat: 'It is important to note that reports are incomplete.'[57] Neither of these documents would have been available to Allied planners in the lead-up to Market Garden and it is therefore difficult to establish how much formations that did not participate in Neptune, such as 1st Airborne Division, would have been able to learn from the operation. It is entirely possible that they learnt nothing.

Among those who actually participated in Neptune there was clearly broad agreement that the tasks assigned to many of the air transport crews had been far beyond their capabilities, and the commander of 9th TCC, Brigadier General Williams, was among the first to conclude that operations should in future be flown in daylight.[58] For the British the success of Operation Mallard pointed towards the same conclusion, as did the acute difficulties encountered in assembling airborne troops in darkness. But if both Allies concurred on this basic issue, there were nevertheless differences of emphasis. The British attached more importance to the role of pathfinders following their experiences around DZ V, and concluded that similar difficulties might be avoided in future if more pathfinders were infiltrated as an insurance in case some were unable to mark their zones.[59] On the other hand, the Americans do not appear to have accepted that in different circumstances the pathfinder system might have functioned more effectively: 'For the present airborne plans should be drawn to accept a scattered drop pattern.'[60]

There was agreement that flak had played a major part in causing the dispersed drops – particularly in the US sector.[61] Both Allies accepted that it was critically important for ground forces to link up with airborne troops quickly, and Neptune also reinforced the lesson identified in Sicily that airborne operations should always be preceded by realistic exercises and rehearsals.[62] Otherwise, the difficulties that had been imposed by terrain loomed large in both British and American thinking after Neptune. Terrain had been a major influence in the disasters that befell a number of US glider missions and, in the British sector around DZ V, terrain was also a key problem, partly responsible for the failure of the pathfinders as well as for the delay in assembling hundreds of scattered paratroops.[63] One group from 3 Parachute Brigade, which came down in a flooded field, had then to swim the River Dives and cross nine large dykes to reach the DZ – a task that took between five and six hours.[64] In the immediate aftermath of Neptune a projected operation to deploy 1st Airborne Division to reinforce 82nd Airborne was abandoned because the proposed landing areas were found to be completely unsuitable for Horsa gliders.[65] This represented a substantial and very positive shift in Allied thinking.

Beyond this, some thought was given to the issue of fire support. Attention was drawn by 6th Airborne Division to the weakness of their organic artillery support in the early stages of the fighting and to their critical dependence on artillery from outside the division:

> There is no doubt whatsoever that the fire power available within 6 Airborne Division resources was insufficient to break up a really well supported attack by tanks and infantry. It was in fact the artillery of 1 Corps and 3 British Division which enabled the division to carry out its task.[66]

This may well have influenced 1st Airborne Division's decision to bring a very much larger artillery element into Arnhem on the first day of Market Garden. As for air support, the American airborne divisions had by June 1944 developed limited means for requesting air strikes via both radio and signal panels, which could be laid out on the ground.[67] By contrast, the British airborne had made no progress in this area and, although the problem was at least identified after the Normandy landings, no remedial action was initiated until the very eve of Market Garden.[68]

This was unfortunate, not only because of the obvious value of air support to airborne forces but also because the provision of effective close air support requires careful preparation and training, and cannot simply be organized overnight. Moreover, in airborne operations, close air support presents particular problems because the absence of clear delineation between friendly and hostile forces greatly increases the potential for air-to-ground fratricide. In Normandy, 101st Airborne's 506th PIR came under attack from USAAF P-47s, which also destroyed the two bridges that the airborne troops had been ordered to capture.[69] In the British sector, the commander of 3 Parachute Brigade was wounded and several of his staff were killed by an Allied air attack on the morning of D-Day.[70]

There were certainly other conclusions that Allied commanders might have drawn from Neptune about the more general characteristics of airborne warfare. To begin with, it should again have been clear that airborne forces were unlikely to achieve absolute mission success. Neptune also indicated – not for the first time – that airborne troops were best employed against limited and specific goals, such as bridges or gun batteries, rather than more expansive area objectives, and intelligence once more emerged as a critical issue. The strength of German forces was underestimated in both eastern and western Normandy, and both British and US experience demonstrated that determined and rapid counter-attacks could be anticipated in the aftermath of airborne landings. Against such opposition the airborne had once more proved very vulnerable, and casualty rates on D-Day and in the subsequent fighting had been extremely high.

But whether such lessons were in fact identified is another matter. One of the very few documents to acknowledge that Neptune had not been an unqualified success from an airborne perspective was 38 Group's post-operation report, which stated that while 'all the main military tasks were carried out … nevertheless there was a certain proportion of failure'. On this basis it was argued very sensibly that 'no one airborne unit or task should be vital to the whole operation'.[71] Unfortunately, however, this view was not widely shared. Instead there was yet again a tendency to conclude that the airborne had been successful in Neptune because the operation as a whole had succeeded. It was all too easy to overlook the many instances when airborne troops had not fully achieved their goals, or else had secured them only with the support of other forces. Furthermore, to judge from subsequent events, Allied commanders saw no reason after Neptune to narrow the scope of airborne tasking or to show rather more respect to the enemy.

Within a week of Neptune, Montgomery and Browning concocted a plan for employing 1st Airborne Division in an operation entitled Wild Oats in the Evrecy area south of Caen.[72] Had Wild Oats been staged, 1st Airborne would have found themselves in one of the most heavily defended areas of the German line, in close proximity to such formations as the 1st and 12th SS Panzer Divisions. Allied ground troops did not in fact reach Evrecy until the third week of July. Historians are unanimous in their condemnation of Wild Oats and Major General Urquhart himself later expressed relief over its cancellation, remarking with some understatement that 'it would have been a sticky battle'.[73] It was cancelled partly because of the strength of German resistance around Caen, and partly because the Commander-in-Chief of the Allied Expeditionary Air Force (AEAF), Air Chief Marshal Leigh-Mallory, refused to sanction an airlift that would unquestionably have been very problematic.[74] Leigh-Mallory's stance delayed the destruction of 1st Airborne Division by a period of approximately three months. Montgomery was nevertheless furious and famously denounced the Air Commander-in-Chief as a 'gutless bugger'.[75]

In the event, then, 1st Airborne Division did not participate in the Normandy campaign, and there would be no further airborne actions in northern Europe before Market Garden. The only significant operation in this period – Operation Dragoon – involved the equivalent of a single division and was mounted in support of the Allied landings in southern France in August. As Dragoon was launched on 15 August, there would have been minimal time to incorporate any lessons from the operation into planning for Market Garden. Moreover, Dragoon was far more limited in scope, aimed as it was against objectives only a few miles from the Allied landing beaches in an area of only limited German opposition. Nevertheless, as Williams was intimately involved in both operations, it is highly likely that Dragoon to some extent influenced his thinking in September.

As we have seen, Williams concluded after Neptune that, in future, airborne operations should ideally be mounted in daylight; Dragoon would in any case have been impossible to stage at night because 15 August fell within a period of virtually no moon. Not enough transport aircraft were available to allow for a single daylight lift (the bulk were still committed to Normandy) so Williams – facing the same problem that confronted Student before Mercury – scheduled two lifts on 15 August, one arriving over the DZs at first light (before sunrise), while the other reached the zones at the end of the afternoon. Again, the experiment was a failure. Early morning fog over the French coast caused two out of three pathfinder teams to be dropped some distance from their objectives.[76] Consequently, the main troop carrier formations found two of the three DZs unmarked.

At best the six serials without pathfinder assistance dropped less than 110 planeloads, 40 percent of their total, within a mile of their drop zones. The beacons set up on DZ O by the pathfinders made possible much better results, but even there only 73 planes, about 60 percent, made accurate drops.[77]

In addition, one of the two glider missions scheduled that morning was aborted en route to southern France because of the fog. It is hard to believe that these experiences would not have been considered by Williams and his staff when, only a few weeks later, they again faced the task of staging multiple lifts to bring airborne troops to their objectives in Holland.

On the other hand, the afternoon missions flown in Dragoon were extremely accurate. The only significant problems arose when the main glider formation unexpectedly found the intended LZ covered in anti-glider poles. The landings turned into a shambles, with gliders being brought down wherever there was the minimum of open space. There were numerous crashes and many gliders sheared off their wings on the poles or hit other obstacles. Eleven glider pilots were killed and over 30 were injured; about 100 air-landing troops were seriously hurt, though many more presumably suffered minor injuries. Few loads were badly damaged, but 'as usual great difficulty was encountered in getting them out'.[78] The lessons should hardly need repeating. The landings had been planned with insufficient intelligence, and with inadequate scrutiny of the proposed LZs.

Notes

1. Within Allied Expeditionary Air Force Headquarters – the headquarters responsible for planning air operations on D-Day – there were concerns that airborne lessons identified after Husky were being ignored; see Memorandum on the Employment of Airborne Forces in Operation Overlord, April 1944, Appendix V/8, Notes on the Planning and Preparation of the Allied Expeditionary Air Force for the Invasion of North West France in June 1944.
2. Extract from Joint War Office/Air Ministry Report on the Employment of Airborne Forces, Part A, Lessons of Airborne Operations in Sicily, Appendix D to Appendix V/19, Wing Commander W.D. Macpherson to SASO, 27 November 1943, Notes on the Planning and Preparation of the Allied Expeditionary Air Force for the Invasion of North West France in June 1944, appendices.

3. US Army Air Forces Board Project (T) 27, Long Range Study of Airborne Operations, 29 April 1944, pp. 7, 10.

4. AP 3231, *Airborne Forces*, pp. 96–97; John C. Warren, *Airborne Operations in World War II, European Theater* (United States Air Force Historical Division, Research Studies Institute, Air University, 1956), p. 4; Otway, *Airborne Forces*, p. 131.

5. Warren, *Airborne Missions in the Mediterranean, 1942–1945*, pp. 65–69.

6. Warren, *Airborne Operations*, pp. 7–9, 20, 23, 24.

7. Ibid., pp. 18–19.

8. Notes on the Planning and Preparation of the Allied Expeditionary Air Force for the Invasion of North West France in June 1944, by PS to Air C-in-C, AEAF (held at AHB), p. 310.

9. AP 3231, *Airborne Forces*, p. 108.

10. Warren, *Airborne Operations*, pp. 23, 26; AP 3231, *Airborne Forces*, p. 111.

11. See for example Joint War Office/Air Ministry Report on the Employment of Airborne Forces, Part A, Lessons of Airborne Operations in Sicily, Appendix D to Appendix V/19, Wing Commander W.D. Macpherson to SASO, 27 November 1943 and US War Department Training Circular 113, Notes on the Planning and Preparation of the Allied Expeditionary Air Force for the Invasion of North West France in June 1944, appendices.

12. Minutes of the 9th Meeting of the Airborne Air Planning Committee, 28 April 1944, Appendix V/39; Bradley to Montgomery, 26 May 1944, Appendix V/43; Williams to Leigh-Mallory, 27 May 1944, Appendix V/44; notes of a conference held at SHAEF, 27 May 1944, Appendix V/45; all sources contained in Notes on the Planning and Preparation of the Allied Expeditionary Air Force for the Invasion of North West France in June 1944.

13. Warren, *Airborne Operations*, pp. 22, 24.

14. Ibid., pp. 9–10, 22, 61; Notes on the Planning and Preparation of the Allied Expeditionary Air Force for the Invasion of North West France in June 1944, by PS to Air C-in-C, p. 299.

15. Minutes of a Meeting between the Air C-in-C and C-in-C 21st Army Group, 28 May 1944, Appendix V/46, Notes on the Planning and Preparation of the Allied Expeditionary Air Force for the Invasion of North West France in June 1944, appendices.

16. Stephen Ambrose, *D-Day June 6 1944: The Battle for the Normandy Beaches* (Pocket Books, London, 2002), p. 222.

17. Warren, *Airborne Operations*, p. 58.

18. Ibid., pp. 42, 46.

19. Robert J. Kershaw, *It Never Snows in September: The German View of Market Garden and The Battle of Arnhem, September 1944* (Ian Allan, Hersham, 2004), p. 41.

20. Warren, *Airborne Operations*, p. 46.
21. Ibid., pp. 61–64.
22. Ibid., pp. 64–68.
23. Ibid., pp. 68–69.
24. Ibid., p. 58.
25. Shelford Bidwell, 'The Airborne Assault on France', in Ste. Croix (ed.), *Airborne Operations*, p. 105.
26. Warren, *Airborne Operations*, pp. 39, 41, 47, 52.
27. Ibid., pp. 51–56.
28. Notes on the Planning and Preparation of the Allied Expeditionary Air Force for the Invasion of North West France in June 1944, by PS to Air C-in-C, AEAF, p. 316.
29. Warren, *Airborne Operations*, pp. 39, 42, 47–48, 52, 57–58.
30. Notes of a conference at SHAEF, 27 May 1944, to discuss a revision of the plan for the American airborne divisions, Appendix V/45, Notes on the Planning and Preparation of the Allied Expeditionary Air Force for the Invasion of North West France in June 1944, appendices.
31. AP 3231, *Airborne Forces*, p. 132.
32. Otway, *Airborne Forces*, pp. 178–179.
33. AP 3231, *Airborne Forces*, p. 126.
34. Report by 38 and 46 Group RAF on the British Airborne Effort in Operation Neptune, HQ 38 Group, October 1944.
35. AP 3231, *Airborne Forces*, p. 128; Napier Crookenden, *Dropzone Normandy: The Story of the American and British Airborne Assault on D-Day 1944* (Ian Allan, Shepperton, 1976), p. 203.
36. Memorandum on the Employment of Airborne Forces in Operation 'Overlord', by AEAF/S.676/Airborne Plans, April 1944, Appendix V/8, Notes on the Planning and Preparation of the Allied Expeditionary Air Force for the Invasion of North West France in June 1944, appendices.
37. Otway, *Airborne Forces*, p. 179.
38. AP 3231, *Airborne Forces*, pp. 125–128.
39. Ambrose, *D-Day*, p. 228.
40. AP 3231, *Airborne Forces*, pp. 130–131.
41. Stephen Ambrose, *Pegasus Bridge, D-Day: The Daring British Airborne Raid* (Pocket Books, London, 2003), pp. 57–59.
42. 6th Airborne Division Report on Operations in Normandy, 6 June – 27 August 1944.
43. John Golley, *The Big Drop: The Guns of Merville, June 1944* (Jane's, London, 1982), pp. 54–55.
44. AP 3231, *Airborne Forces*, p. 130.
45. Warren, *Airborne Operations*, p. 79.

46. Ibid; Hollinghurst papers, AC 73/23/67, lecture entitled 'Air Aspect of an Airborne Operation', pp. 1–2.
47. AP 3231, *Airborne Forces*, p. 134.
48. Warren, *Airborne Operations*, p. 79.
49. Otway, *Airborne Forces*, p. 173.
50. Ibid., pp. 174–175.
51. Lloyd Clarke, *Orne Bridgehead* (Sutton Publishing, Stroud, 2004), p. 168.
52. Ibid., p. 63.
53. Ibid., pp. 88, 91, 95.
54. The position of the front line is most vividly illustrated in consecutive maps in John Man, *The Penguin Atlas of D-Day and the Normandy Campaign* (Viking, London, 1994).
55. Ian Daglish, *Operation Goodwood* (Pen and Sword, Barnsley, 2004), pp. 34, 167–168.
56. Air Historical Branch, *The Liberation of North West Europe Vol. 4, The Breakout and the Advance to the Lower Rhine, 12 June to 30 September 1944* (unpublished official narrative, first draft), p. 10.
57. 6th Airborne Division Report on Operations in Normandy, 6 June – 27 August 1944; Report by 38 and 46 Group RAF on the British Airborne Effort in Operation Neptune, HQ 38 Group, October 1944.
58. Warren, *Airborne Operations*, p. 61.
59. Otway, *Airborne Forces*, p. 199.
60. Notes on the Planning and Preparation of the Allied Expeditionary Air Force for the Invasion of North West France in June 1944, by PS to Air C-in-C, AEAF, p. 316.
61. Warren, *Airborne Operations*, p. 59.
62. 6th Airborne Division Report on Operations in Normandy, 6 June – 27 August 1944.
63. AP 3231, *Airborne Forces*, pp. 126, 137; Otway, *Airborne Forces*, pp. 198–199, 293.
64. Crookenden, *Dropzone Normandy*, p. 217.
65. Otway, *Airborne Forces*, p. 206.
66. 6th Airborne Division Report on Operations in Normandy, 6 June – 27 August 1944.
67. Warren, *Airborne Operations*, p. 46.
68. AIR 37/1214, Allied Airborne Operations in Holland, September–October 1944, Appendix G, Air Support Notes on Operation Market; Index E, Air Support and Ground-to-Air Signalling.
69. Warren, *Airborne Operations*, p. 46.
70. Crookenden, *Dropzone Normandy*, p. 217.
71. Report by 38 and 46 Group RAF on the British Airborne Effort in Operation Neptune, HQ 38 Group, October 1944.

72. Carlo D'Este, *Decision in Normandy* (Penguin, London, 2001), p. 171.
73. Major General R.E. Urquhart, *Arnhem* (Pan, London, 1958), p. 28.
74. See Warren, *Airborne Operations*, p. 80. The direct route to Evrecy involved over-flight of the invasion fleet, the beaches, the frontline and Caen, and hence the risk of significant anti-aircraft fire from both friendly and enemy forces. The indirect route beyond the western coast of the Cotentin Peninsula required a flight of more than 50 miles over enemy territory, partly beyond the range of navigational aids, on a night when there was hardly any moon. By day, the risks of enemy fire would have been considerable on either route.
75. D'Este, *Decision in Normandy*, pp. 164–166.
76. Warren, *Airborne Missions in the Mediterranean*, p. 95.
77. Ibid., p. 100.
78. Ibid., pp. 101, 107.

Part 1 : Conclusion

B Y LARGELY IGNORING the airborne missions that preceded Market Garden, historians consistently present a view of the operation that is both incomplete and misleading. Market Garden is depicted as being in some way exceptional because it failed. Readers are encouraged to accept a legend of airborne warfare founded on the broader success of the Blitzkrieg, operations like Mercury, Husky and Neptune and dramatic *coup-de-main* actions such as Eben-Emael and Pegasus Bridge. If we agree that the airborne contribution to these ventures was successful, we must also accept that Market Garden was fundamentally different from them all. On this basis the failure of the operation can be explained entirely by reference to specific actions and decisions taken in September 1944.

And yet the legend is wholly at odds with reality. The salient features of airborne warfare in the Second World War can more accurately be summed up as follows. Firstly – perhaps most fundamentally – airborne forces were found to be very expensive to create and to maintain. This expense generated pressure to use them operationally, which often resulted in the promotion of ideas for their employment which were, to say the least, conceptually misguided. Although German thinking on the utility of airborne assault was at first quite coherent, it quickly lost touch with reality. Conceptually, German operation plans for The Hague, Great Britain, Greece and Crete were all highly questionable. The doctrinal basis upon which the Allies committed their new airborne forces to battle was no less suspect, and this contributed directly to the fiascos of the North African campaign and to the Husky disaster. In Normandy, the cards were stacked against the airborne from the outset by the decision to mimic the essentials of the Husky plan. Moreover, the Allies were too optimistic about the objectives that airborne forces could reasonably be expected to achieve. The impact of flawed conceptual planning on the formulation of detailed operation plans should not be underestimated, and is examined more specifically in the context of Market Garden later in this book.

Secondly, against all but the most limited opposition, airborne operations were often characterized by high casualties and by mission failure or, at best, only partial mission success. There is no basis whatsoever for arguing that

Market Garden should somehow have been different. In other words, high casualties and at least some degree of failure were always highly likely in Market Garden merely by virtue of the fact that it was an airborne operation. Past Allied and German experience with *deep* operations furthermore demonstrated that the risks involved in such ventures were particularly high. This inescapable truth should be central to any attempt to explain the Allied defeat in September 1944, yet in the vast majority of histories it is completely overlooked.

Thirdly, a critical problem in Allied airborne operations had been the inaccuracy and dispersion of successive airlifts. The creation of enormous multi-division airborne forces led to economies in aircrew training to secure the required lift. To co-ordinate airborne and amphibious missions, under-trained and inexperienced air transport crews were then committed to a night-flying task that lay far beyond their capabilities – a task magnified by other factors such as ground-to-air fire and adverse weather conditions. Yet behind all this lay a more elementary problem, which was recognized by the Allies but never properly addressed. In all their large-scale airborne undertakings before Market Garden, the airlift was not sufficiently central to operational planning. In Husky, Neptune and Dragoon, airborne operations were subordinated to amphibious landings; the airlifts had consequently to be moulded around the seaborne landings instead of being treated as independent missions of equal importance and status. Such an approach vastly complicated the already very difficult challenge facing the Allied air forces, increasing the probability of failure still further.

The result was that, as late as September 1944, the Allies had yet to mount a large-scale airlift that could be deemed a resounding success. The first Dragoon lift was far from accurate, the American lift in Normandy was very widely dispersed and the British lift also went badly wrong; Husky requires no further comment. Thus when Market Garden was being planned the Allies still did not possess a proven model or established operating procedure upon which to base their lift arrangements. They had only the knowledge that previous airlifts had largely failed. Hence there was every reason to effect a radical departure from past airlift plans, and to employ new ways and means in the hope of somehow delivering a higher proportion of the airborne troops to their objectives.

PART TWO

Market Garden:
The Conceptual Plan

Introduction

THERE IS GENERAL agreement among historians that Market Garden was badly planned, and that poor planning was partly responsible for the operation's failure. Analysis of the plan has largely focused on First Allied Airborne Army and subordinate elements such as I Airborne Corps, the Airborne Divisions and the RAF and USAAF air transport formations. The outstanding problem with this methodology is its failure to acknowledge how detailed planning at these levels was both shaped and constrained by flawed conceptual planning higher up in the command chain – in this case at 21st Army Group and to some extent Second (British) Army. Some accounts imply that First Allied Airborne Army planning was conducted in a vacuum, apparently divorced from higher command and control. Hence Buckingham avoids questioning the basic operational concept of Market Garden and apportions responsibility for the Allied defeat to senior airmen, and to decisions or actions taken at corps and division level.[1] Others quite wrongly maintain that Market Garden was conceptually brilliant but was ruined during the process of detailed planning. Writing only a few years after the war, Chester Wilmot argued that 'if the operation had been as daring in tactical execution as it was in strategic conception, there is little doubt that it would have been a complete triumph'.[2] In a far more recent study Middlebrook maintains that 'the strategic concept of "Market Garden" was sound'.[3]

The reality is very different. In fact, most features of the Market Garden plan, including the vast majority of its failings, can be directly traced back to decisions taken by, or in consultation with, Montgomery and the Second Army commander, Lieutenant General Sir Miles Dempsey. The aim of the following chapters is to address this specific and long-neglected issue by examining the strategic background to the operation, the emergence of the first proposals for employing airborne forces in a Rhine crossing and the evolution of this original concept into Market Garden. Montgomery's position within the Allied high command and his rather idiosyncratic style of leadership are subjected to particularly close scrutiny to illustrate their contribution to the alleged 'planning failures' for which First Allied Airborne Army has so often been held responsible. Finally, and in the light of this analysis, the highly controversial history of Allied intelligence in Market Garden is reappraised.

Notes

1. Buckingham, *Arnhem*, pp. 231–235.
2. Wilmot, *The Struggle for Europe*, p. 585.
3. Middlebrook, *Arnhem*, p. 442.

2.1. The Origins of Market Garden

O PERATION MARKET GARDEN was the product of both 'pull' and 'push' factors. The 'pull' was the seductive lure of an Allied Rhine crossing in September 1944; the 'push' was the need to find a use for a large and very expensive airborne army. In the final week of August 1944 the Allies at last broke out of Normandy and drove rapidly north and east, British and Canadian forces advancing on the more westerly axis, up the coastal plane, while the Americans moved into north-eastern France. Having suffered appalling casualties in the fighting around Falaise, the Germans were at first unable to re-establish a defensive line. But so rapid was the Allied advance that their supply lines back to Normandy became severely strained. The capture of France's Channel ports would have improved the situation, but they remained in enemy hands. On 4 September (with the assistance of local resistance fighters) Second Army seized intact the Belgian port of Antwerp, but unfortunately the mere possession of Antwerp did not alone promise to relieve the pressure on Allied logistics. This is because Antwerp lies at the eastern end of a 50-mile channel – the Scheldt Estuary – which the Germans still held. On the 5th Eisenhower, determined to maintain the Allied advance on a broad front, urged Montgomery to open Antwerp. But Montgomery proved extremely reluctant to embrace the task.

Despite the Allied victory in Normandy the campaign had by no means been an unqualified triumph for Montgomery. His reputation had received a severe and very public battering on both sides of the Atlantic because of his difficulties breaking German resistance around Caen, which contrasted strikingly with the American capture of Cherbourg, their breakout at St Lo, and their subsequent dramatic envelopment of German forces in the Falaise pocket. And although the Allies had agreed months earlier that Eisenhower should assume personal command of land operations in Overlord after the initial assault phase of the campaign was over, Montgomery was incensed when the Supreme Commander formally took up this role, and sought unsuccessfully to dissuade him from doing so.

As it became clear during the advance across northern France that there were insufficient supplies to sustain the progress of both Second Army and

Patton's Third (US) Army towards Germany, Montgomery and Patton predictably enough fought to secure priority in the allocation of logistical support. On 4 September Montgomery famously wrote to Eisenhower of the need for 'one really powerful and full-blooded thrust towards Berlin ... The selected thrust must have all the maintenance resources it needs without any qualification, and any other operation must do the best it can with what is left over ... In my opinion the thrust likely to give the best and quickest results is the northern one via the Ruhr.' Needless to say, Montgomery himself would command this decisive action.[1] Against this background, Eisenhower's actions would increasingly be dictated by the need to sustain what would today be termed 'alliance cohesion'. The tensions that emerged between the British and US Armies in the second half of 1944 opened up an entirely new centre of gravity – the Alliance itself. Eisenhower's broad front strategy of necessity struck a balance between protecting this potential vulnerability and maintaining the advance towards Germany. Historians who castigate him for indecision or compromise fail to grasp this fundamental truth.

During the advance across northern France the Allied airborne forces were formally assigned to 21st Army Group although, as we shall see, this did not necessarily preclude consideration of their partial deployment in support of Bradley's armies. Since Neptune, 6th Airborne Division had remained in the line in Normandy. The two depleted American airborne divisions had eventually been withdrawn to England, where they were patched up with numerous replacements, while 1st Airborne were held on standby for further operations. Soon after the Normandy landings Eisenhower formed a combined Allied command to control the airborne formations and their air transport resources: First Allied Airborne Army. But a British recommendation that Browning be appointed to command First Allied Airborne Army was blocked by American airborne commanders, who were backed by Bradley. The Americans deeply disliked Browning, but their opposition to his candidacy also reflected the fact that both their airborne and troop carrier forces were significantly larger than those of Britain.

In July the USAAF Lieutenant General Lewis Brereton was given the appointment, while Browning became his deputy and commander of I Airborne Corps, which included 1st Airborne Division and the Independent Polish Parachute Brigade; the Americans created an equivalent formation (XVIII Corps) with responsibility for their airborne troops. Brereton had previously commanded the US 9th Air Force, which included 9th TCC, and had therefore played a part in the development of Allied airborne planning in Normandy. But there was in any case a clear logic in the appointment of an air force officer to command First Allied Airborne Army, particularly from a US perspective. The problems that had confronted the US airborne in virtually all their previous operations were felt to have stemmed from a single source – the USAAF's inability to deliver them accurately to their objectives. On taking up his appointment, Brereton received a personal note from Eisenhower specifically asking him to pay particular attention to improving troop carrier navigation.[2] At the same time Eisenhower told the US Chief of Staff, General Marshall, that 'the job is a tough one, and the great reason that I want an American air officer is so I can give him the necessary operational and training control over Troop Carrier Command.'[3] And yet inevitably Brereton's appointment convinced many within the British airborne forces and the Army that the new headquarters was essentially an American institution, and it was therefore viewed with suspicion. The allocation of virtually all the key staff positions to Americans can hardly have helped matters.[4]

Allied thinking on the employment of airborne forces after the Normandy landings was barely more realistic than before. In May Eisenhower's Supreme Headquarters Allied Expeditionary Force (SHAEF) asked both Montgomery's 21st Army Group and Bradley's 1st US Army Group to specify their airborne requirements after D-Day. The reply from 21st Army Group was that there might be a need for no fewer than five airborne divisional operations between D-Day and D+90, and four divisional operations every sixty days after D+90.[5] The hazards involved in the repeated short-notice commitment of airborne troops in this fashion were evidently not appreciated, despite the experience gained in North Africa and the specific lessons identified from the assault on Sicily; nor did Montgomery's headquarters grasp the manifest impossibility of regenerating airborne capabilities at anything like the rate that this implied. Written doctrine envisaged broadly that the airborne would be used to sustain the momentum of the Allied advance from the beachhead,[6] yet it was to prove very difficult to translate this theory into practice. Before the breakout from Normandy enormous risks would have been involved in landing airborne troops behind enemy lines, and the few proposals for doing so came to nothing. After the breakout the pace of the Allied advance effectively rendered the airborne surplus to requirements.

Throughout July and August, one airborne operation after another was proposed and then cancelled. Apart from the problems that this created for the airborne divisions in terms of training, morale and discipline, the implications for the air transport forces were far-reaching. With the logistical position of the Allied land armies deteriorating daily, there was a natural tendency to look on air supply for a solution. Yet the need to keep aircraft and crews at a state of near-immediate readiness for successive airborne ventures had the effect of grounding a large part of the transport fleet. 'No. 46 Group, who had between 175 and 185 serviceable Dakotas, were only able to use small numbers of their aircraft each day for normal transport services between the United

Kingdom and the Normandy landing fields.' The number of USAAF transport aircraft held back for the airborne was of course far greater.[7] Moreover, in August, two US transport wings were diverted to the support of Operation Dragoon.[8] Although on the 25th SHAEF directed that some 400 aircraft per day should be made available for air supply, 'it was understood … that if orders were issued for an airborne mission, the planes needed for that mission would have to be grounded for servicing, loading, and marshalling'.[9]

It is hardly surprising that in these circumstances senior American ground commanders such as Bradley began to argue that all troop carrier aircraft should be withdrawn from airborne commitments and assigned entirely to supply. The corollary – the redeployment of the airborne divisions as conventional infantry – was apparently not confronted at this time, but there would have been no obvious alternative. Needless to say, Brereton voiced the strongest opposition to this diversion of his troop carriers, as the training task for which he had primarily been appointed would have been impossible in such circumstances; Eisenhower was, as usual, left to mediate between the warring factions.[10] But it is easy to understand why, by the end of August 1944, he was so desperate to use First Allied Airborne Army. The episode once again illustrates how the enormous cost of maintaining the airborne could generate intense pressure for their employment; effectively they were burning a hole in Eisenhower's pocket.

Between the last week of August and 10 September, when Eisenhower sanctioned Market Garden, First Allied Airborne Army became something of a political football. It remains difficult to fathom the precise motives of the key players, but at the very least it is clear that mounting tensions within the Western alliance were impacting on Brereton's command. To begin with, on 24 August, Eisenhower advised Montgomery that he could not expect his proposed thrust into Germany to be given priority before the airborne divisions then held in England had been deployed. Responding to Montgomery's request that American ground forces be used in support of a single British-led offensive to the north, Eisenhower wrote:

> We must prepare definite plans for the employment of the entire airborne force so as to speed up the accomplishment of the missions that you must attain rapidly in the north-east. Unless we use the Airborne Army … we will not be using all available assets and there would be no excuse for insisting upon the deployment of the major part of Bradley's strength on his extreme left.[11]

Bradley's extreme left was Montgomery's right flank.

Although Montgomery then gave some limited consideration to an operation plan code-named 'Boxer', which focused on the Boulogne area, the first airborne venture devised partly in response to Eisenhower's stipulation was entitled 'Linnet' and envisaged the deployment of 1st, 82nd and 101st Airborne Divisions, the Polish Parachute Brigade and several other formations. It would have been a completely pointless undertaking. Linnet's largely intangible and unquantifiable objectives were:

a. To present a major threat to the enemy's lines of communication, and hence
b. To cause the enemy to divert, from the main battle, forces which he can ill afford, and thereby
c. Create opportunities for enveloping and destroying the maximum enemy force by the combined action of airborne and ground forces.[12]

Linnet 'offered nothing decisive, nothing not quickly obtainable by ground action, only a few miles more ground, a few thousand more prisoners and an unimportant river crossing'.[13] Ultimately it was cancelled on 2 September, when American and British ground forces reached Tournai – the primary airborne objective.[14] Bradley would later claim that he had deliberately diverted troops to Tournai (which lay inside the British sector) to ensure that Linnet was halted.[15] On the same day, Eisenhower met Bradley and Patton and gave Patton permission to cross the Moselle River – an action that effectively ensured that Montgomery would not obtain the resources he required for his 'narrow thrust'.[16]

The decision to deploy First Allied Airborne Army in support of 21st Army Group had predictably been unwelcome to the American airborne and played a significant part in generating counter-proposals for an alternative operation to Linnet (sometimes referred to as Linnet 2) to secure crossings over the Meuse north of Liège ahead of Bradley's advance. Brereton submitted the scheme to SHAEF on the afternoon of 2 September, when it became clear that the original Linnet operation would probably be cancelled.[17] At almost exactly the same time, the Chief of Staff at 21st Army Group headquarters, Major General de Guingand, signalled to Montgomery:

In view of delay and uncertain weather feel we should dispense with LINNET if possible and prepare similar operation to suit your future plans.[18]

Linnet 2 appeared likely to frustrate this proposal and, from the British perspective, seemed deliberately designed to divert airborne resources away from their axis of advance. Browning was so unhappy with the plan that he threatened resignation.[19] But Montgomery was inclined to agree with de Guingand and the records show that, by the evening, 'the new plan was being worked on' at 21st Army Group.[20] In its essentials, this scheme involved using airborne troops to help Second Army cross the only two major water obstacles still blocking their advance into Germany – the Meuse (or, in Dutch, 'Maas') and the Rhine. As the most forward elements of Second Army were then positioned in Belgium, the proposed airborne landings would be of quite exceptional depth.

On the 3rd – with this broad concept already clear in his mind – Montgomery met Bradley and learnt that he was not interested in Linnet 2. Bradley's preference was 'that all available aircraft should go on to transport work so that we can maintain momentum of the advance'. To this Montgomery expressed his wholehearted agreement, even though it was already his intention to use airborne forces in an operation to cross the Rhine.[21] However, in the aftermath of the Linnet 2 episode, it was still uncertain whether the American elements within First Allied Airborne Army would be available for the venture he had in mind. Consequently, although the operation would be far more ambitious than Linnet, Montgomery decided that it should be restricted to British airborne forces alone (along with the Poles, who were under British command). Immediately after the meeting (where it was agreed that Second Army would be responsible for capturing the Ruhr) Montgomery signalled 21st Army Group headquarters that 'Second Army will advance from line Brussels-Antwerp on 6 Sep directed on Wesel and Arnhem and passing round north side of Ruhr. Require airborne operation of One British Division and Poles on evening 6 Sep or morning 7 Sep to secure bridges over Rhine between Wesel and Arnhem.' Montgomery then issued instructions that de Guingand and Browning were to visit him the following day to discuss the plan – soon to be christened 'Comet'.[22]

Thus did the race for Germany give rise to a process of Anglo-US bidding and counter-bidding which paid woefully inadequate attention to the complex realities of airborne operational planning. Yet it would be wrong to suppose that such issues were forgotten entirely. At First Allied Airborne Army Headquarters, Brereton's staff were in this period considering the potential for staging operations further east than the Linnet/Linnet 2 objectives, and they quickly became convinced that the task was likely to be very difficult until the airborne forces, their headquarters and their supporting air transport formations deployed to the continent. On 1 September Brereton wrote to Eisenhower arguing that 'from the bases now occupied in the United Kingdom, the Allied Airborne Army can only operate as far as the line Amsterdam – Utrecht – Eindhoven – Liège'.[23] In his view, bases would be required east and northeast of Paris before an airborne assault could be mounted across the Rhine.

Weather in the United Kingdom is often different from weather on the Continent at the same period. With bases on the Continent, weather over the target area and bases is more likely to be similar, thus decreasing the chances of having to call off operations for weather reasons.

Brereton was also worried about the geographical separation of many key Allied command, control and communication nodes. Based in France,

The Headquarters, First Allied Airborne Army, would be physically in closer contact with Supreme Headquarters AEF, Army Group Headquarters and Communication Zone; and with Advance Headquarters, AEAF.[24]

It might be contended that Brereton's letter merely represented a further attempt by American elements in First Allied Airborne Army to frustrate plans for employing the airborne forces in support of 21st Army Group, but the chronology of events does not support such an interpretation. On 1 September the Allies were still expecting that the original Linnet plan would be executed in the British sector, well inside the line that Brereton identified. Hence he can only have been looking ahead to the operations that might potentially follow on from Linnet, although it is highly probable that he was thinking about future American airlift requirements too. By August 1944 US glider plans assumed so-called 'double-tow' arrangements, whereby one Dakota was used to pull two gliders; this practice substantially reduced the Dakota's operational radius. Of course, the aircraft's effective range could be extended if it was used to tug only a single glider, but this halved the potential deployment rate of glider-borne elements.

The surviving files do not contain any response from Eisenhower, nor was action taken in the short term to address the issues Brereton raised. Realistically, very little could have been achieved in early September, given that preparations began immediately afterwards for a Rhine crossing. The letter nevertheless sheds an interesting light on some of the problems that were later encountered during Market Garden. The difficulties involved in mounting an airborne crossing of the Rhine from England were foreseen by First Allied Airborne Army, and the clearest possible warning was placed before SHAEF.

Brereton was informed of the prospective Arnhem–Wesel operation on the evening of 3 September, after which (at 10.30 p.m.) his Chief of Staff formally directed Browning to initiate detailed planning.[25] For this purpose, Browning duly convened a conference at his Moor Park headquarters the following morning. Then, in answer to Montgomery's summons, he flew out to France. Having seen Montgomery, he met de Guingand and Dempsey at Second Army headquarters and they renewed their deliberations the following morning, after which Browning returned to England. According to Dempsey's diary, the decision to target Arnhem rather than Wesel had been taken by the time he met Browning on the 4th.[26]

Why was Arnhem chosen as the objective? One common argument is that the Allied air forces favoured Arnhem and Nijmegen because fewer anti-aircraft defences were deployed in the area, and it is certainly true that Wesel (located inside the German frontier on the western edge of the Ruhr) lay near one of the most formidable anti-aircraft artillery belts in the world. Moreover, Arnhem and Nijmegen are somewhat closer to the UK than Wesel. Yet the belief that air force opposition was the decisive factor in the rejection of Wesel is based entirely on an account given verbally by Montgomery to the journalist and historian Chester Wilmot after the war.[27] It is notable that the version of events Montgomery recorded in his memoirs did not suggest that the air forces had anything to do with the decision to choose the more northerly axis.[28] No air force objections to a crossing at Wesel are recorded in the (admittedly few) surviving files, whereas air concerns over flak in the Arnhem and Nijmegen areas are very well documented, and at least one account maintains that they were raised at Browning's Moor Park conference.[29]

Arnhem would thus appear to have been preferred for other reasons. It is sometimes suggested that the town was the more logical objective because it lay beyond the most northerly stretch of the fortifications that guarded Germany's western frontier – the Siegfried Line. Yet this advantage was offset by the fact that the Rhine divides into the Lower Rhine and the Waal north of Wesel. In other words, the capture of Arnhem required two Rhine crossings, whereas the capture of Wesel would have involved only one; the route to Arnhem was also intersected by a major canal that linked the Waal to the Maas. Furthermore, the Siegfried Line provided only very limited protection to Wesel and would probably not have seriously delayed Allied ground forces.[30] It is notable that by 10 September Dempsey was advocating a Rhine crossing at Wesel rather than Arnhem.[31] But the Wesel option would have required the preliminary crossing of the Maas to be staged in the Venlo area, necessitating a Second Army advance almost along the line of their boundary with the Americans. In the view of 21st Army Group's former head of intelligence, it was this factor more than any other that caused Montgomery to favour Arnhem. Targeting Wesel would have been impossible to reconcile with the 'narrow thrust' strategy for it would have necessitated careful co-ordination with American operations. By contrast, a crossing at Arnhem required Second Army to strike off very sharply to the north and away from Bradley's forces, and any follow-up offensive would likewise have been separated from them.[32] It is possible that such reasoning was influenced by the role American troops played in the cancellation of Operation Linnet.

*Map 7: Second (British) and First (US) Army dispositions,
mid-September 1944*

On the very day that this decision was taken Antwerp unexpectedly fell into
Allied hands. Had Montgomery's forces then swung northwest they could
have trapped the 100,000 German troops of Fifteenth Army in Belgium,
winning a victory greater even than Falaise. Equally, if British forces had
evicted the Germans from the Scheldt Estuary and opened Antwerp to shipping, the Allies' logistical position would have been massively improved. Such
considerations were foremost in Eisenhower's thinking when he directed
Montgomery to clear the estuary on the 5th. Yet the diversion of Second Army
to operations around the Scheldt would also have brought Montgomery's
advance to an abrupt halt, leaving Germany to the Americans and ending any
prospect of British forces capturing the Ruhr in 1944. Communication problems are said to have prevented him from receiving Eisenhower's directive in
full until the 7th, by which time Comet's launch was thought to be imminent;

he also, by his own admission, underestimated the difficulties involved in evicting the Germans from the Scheldt Estuary, believing that the task could be left to the already overstretched Canadians. But it is unlikely that an earlier signal from Eisenhower or a different analysis of the Scheldt operation would have persuaded Montgomery to re-examine his priorities. The truth is that, by 4 September, he was already determined to press on northeast of Antwerp with the objective of crossing the Rhine. Again, in the view of his former intelligence chief, he hoped that by establishing a bridgehead at Arnhem he would 'tilt the centre of gravity and give the British priority of supplies before the US armies'. Eisenhower would have no option but to reinforce the breakthrough.[33]

Montgomery did propose using the American airborne divisions in the Scheldt Estuary area in an assault on Walcheren Island, but Brereton raised a number of objections to this scheme. He maintained that plans were still under consideration to use the American divisions in the Aachen-Köln area ahead of US ground forces, that Walcheren's flak defences were too heavy, that the island made a dangerously small parachute drop zone and that its terrain was unsuitable for glider landings.[34] All of this was probably true, but it is also very likely that Brereton, his predominantly American staff and the US airborne divisional commanders were hoping to see their forces committed to a higher profile action, preferably in support of Bradley's advance on Germany. In any event, whereas Montgomery's scheme took for granted a rapid overland advance to Walcheren, which would have been essential to relieve the airborne, First Canadian Army in fact required the whole of October to clear the south and east of the estuary. If an airborne assault had been launched against the island in September the consequences would have been catastrophic.

* * *

In seeking to identify the key instigator of Market Garden, historians remain divided over the roles respectively played by Montgomery and Browning. Browning has always been seen as an obvious and very easy target. We have already noted how, from an early stage in the development of Britain's airborne forces, he blatantly used them to further his own career. In October 1941 he was given the task of forming 1st Airborne Division, but within months he was arguing for the creation of a higher airborne headquarters.[35] As there would have been little justification for the organization he had in mind unless further airborne divisions were established, it is very probable that he was already both anticipating and actively encouraging this development, and it is not surprising to read in the official War Office history that he was at this time 'looking ahead and insisting on the strategic, long-range possibilities of employing large formations of airborne forces'.[36] When the decision was finally taken to form

Lieutenant General F.A.M. 'Boy' Browning

6th Airborne Division in April 1943 and a higher headquarters came into being, Browning was, predictably enough, appointed to command it as Major General Airborne Forces (MGAF).[37] It is interesting to note that the Americans, with their significantly larger airborne arm, did not identify a need to establish an equivalent command level in the European theatre until August 1944. Yet, as MGAF, Browning was dismayed to find that he exercised only limited and advisory powers relative to the airborne divisional commanders, who were also major generals. 'A headquarters was required which had the ability and authority to command more than one division in operations and to prepare them during training', he wrote after just four months in post, recommending the elevation of his existing organization under a Lieutenant General Airborne Forces. At the end of 1943 he duly became (as Lieutenant General) Commander Airborne Troops within Montgomery's 21st Army Group, with responsibility for the two airborne divisions and other elements, such as the Poles and the SAS.[38]

Browning strongly believed that only one of the two British airborne divisions should be employed in the assault phase of any future operation, with the other being retained as a reserve.[39] He formed this opinion as early as August 1943, and it provided the basis for all British airborne planning during the build-up to Neptune. While 6th Airborne Division would be deployed on D-Day, '1st Airborne Division [were] to stand ready for employment as a

Division at any time after D+6'.[40] Whatever the rights and wrongs of this ruling, the result was that 1st Airborne Division were held in a state of inactivity throughout the summer of 1944.

As Commander Airborne Troops, Browning developed close relations with Montgomery and thus placed himself in a strong position to promote his ideas about how the airborne should be employed.[41] He was at least partly responsible for the flawed concept of using a single division to secure the eastern flank of the Normandy landing area, and for the hugely problematic 'Wild Oats' scheme for dropping 1st Airborne Division south of Caen.[42] Both plans reflected his inability to grasp the basic limitations of airborne forces, which stemmed directly from the fact that he had no operational command experience. Brigadier General James Gavin, who led 82nd Airborne Division in Market Garden, at one stage recorded in his diary that Browning 'unquestionably lacks the standing, influence and judgement that comes from a proper troop experience … [and] his staff was superficial … Why the British units fumble along … becomes more and more apparent. Their tops lack the knowhow, never do they get down into the dirt and learn the hard way.'[43]

By late August 1944 there had still been no opportunity for Browning to demonstrate that operational imperatives fully justified the creation of two British airborne divisions, or indeed the higher command post that he had occupied for more than eight months. He was disappointed not to have been given overall command of the Allied airborne forces, frustrated by the succession of cancelled operations and desperate to lead I Airborne Corps into battle.[44] Eisenhower's decision to assign First Allied Airborne Army to 21st Army Group then signalled the imminent launch of a new large-scale airborne venture and finally offered Browning an opportunity to fulfil this aspiration. His personal commitment to deploying the airborne in support of Montgomery's advance may be gauged from his threat to resign when Brereton proposed mounting Linnet 2 in the American sector at the beginning of September.

In short, then, there were many good reasons for Browning to have strongly promoted Comet and its subsequent expansion into Market Garden, and he was very well placed to do so. Yet despite the efforts of Montgomery's apologists to blame Browning for the Allied defeat, the documents clearly show that the Comet plan originated at 21st Army Group headquarters and that the scheme was already in being when Montgomery instructed his staff to call Browning over from England to discuss it. Browning's role was limited to providing guidance on how airborne troops could best fulfil the role that Montgomery envisaged for them. It is to Montgomery's credit that he did at least recognize the importance of obtaining advice from the airborne community, but ideally this should have taken the form of an objective and critical assessment of the Comet concept and of its chances of success. Browning could hardly have been expected to provide such an appraisal; on the contrary, by September 1944 his own very personal agenda ensured that he was only ever likely to offer his whole-hearted support to the Rhine crossing proposals. He may well have seen in them 'the airborne's last chance of getting into action' in the European theatre.[45]

Montgomery's reliance on Browning reflected a broader problem in the way he chose to exercise command. By the second half of 1944 he had largely isolated himself from the remainder of the Allied command chain. His intent was largely communicated by intermediaries – doubtless with varying degrees of accuracy. He kept contact with SHAEF to the barest minimum, rarely spoke directly to senior American officers and also chose to reside at his tactical head-quarters rather than at the headquarters of 21st Army Group – as if a tactical HQ would be an appropriate location for a field marshal and army group commander.[46] Furthermore, although in the past he had often stressed the importance of close co-operation between the Army and the Allied air forces, by September he was maintaining hardly any direct contact with them. As a result, there was no top-level air input at the inception of Comet. Montgomery's approach appears extraordinary given the role of the RAF and the USAAF in determining the outcome of earlier airborne operations and was completely at odds with the joint War Office and Air Ministry ruling issued after Operation Husky, which had sought to increase the influence of the air forces within the airborne planning process.

Montgomery and the Allied Expeditionary Air Force commander,
Air Chief Marshal Sir Trafford Leigh-Mallory

In theory, Montgomery should have devised his plans in direct consultation with four senior officers. One of these was clearly the responsible Army commander, Dempsey. But it is important to remember that Montgomery was (in modern parlance) a land component commander and not a joint commander; he was not empowered to command the Allied air forces. The Comet concept should therefore have been developed through liaison with at least one airman – Air Marshal Sir Arthur Coningham, Air Officer Commanding Second Tactical Air Force (Second TAF – the deployed RAF component responsible for supporting 21st Army Group) – and ideally also with Air Chief Marshal Sir Trafford Leigh-Mallory who, as commander of the AEAF, was responsible for co-ordinating supporting air operations from

Coningham, of Second TAF, and Brereton, commanding general
of First Allied Airborne Army

Britain. Leigh-Mallory and other air force officers had participated in planning the Neptune airborne operations from their very beginning.[47] Additionally, proposals for employing the airborne forces should have involved direct contact between Montgomery and Brereton. Yet in practice, Comet was devised by Montgomery, Dempsey and Browning, after which Brereton and Leigh-Mallory were simply presented with the concept and instructed to commence detailed preparations; Coningham was not consulted at all.[48]

Montgomery deliberately employed this approach to overcome any potentially inconvenient objections to his proposals, such as those that had halted Operation Wild Oats; his intention was to confront the air forces with a fait accompli. This was very much in keeping with a political strategy he discussed with the CIGS in July. 'The only real answer,' he wrote, 'is to proceed very carefully and to lead "the air" down the garden path.'[49] The consequences were only too predictable. Montgomery's tactics ensured that the basic Comet plan was not influenced by air considerations. No thought was given to the potential problems that Brereton had described to Eisenhower only a few days before. Air issues likely to affect the outcome of the entire operation would therefore only be identified later on.

* * *

Operation Comet was conceived as a pursuit operation in the aftermath of Second Army's spectacular advance across northern France – a headlong dash that brought Dempsey's forces from the Seine to Antwerp in just one week. It appeared that the Germans were incapable of offering much further resistance and that, given sufficient logistical support, the pace of the British advance could be maintained. Early in September there seemed to be a genuine prospect of entering Germany within days if only bridges over the Maas and the Rhine could be captured intact.

In Montgomery's view, such a task was eminently suited to airborne forces. And yet, as this chapter has shown, the decision to use the airborne was not in any way based on a careful, reasoned or objective analysis of what they had achieved in the past, or of what they might plausibly be expected to accomplish in the future. Instead, the Allies found themselves contemplating another large-scale airborne venture primarily to find a use for First Allied Airborne Army, and this operation became one element within the much broader debate on how to carry the war from Normandy to Berlin. Eisenhower's desire to deploy the airborne gave Montgomery an opportunity to incorporate them into his 'narrow thrust' at a time when Bradley was showing little interest in airborne operations and was seeking to switch transport aircraft to routine supply work. Yet Montgomery had virtually no knowledge or understanding of airborne warfare. If, to overcome this handicap, he had opted to consult First Allied Airborne Army and the responsible Allied air commanders, his plans would nevertheless have been shaped by a very substantial body of operational expertise and experience, but instead he preferred to rely solely on Browning. Browning, for his part, was desperate to exercise operational command of the airborne forces and to secure employment for I Airborne Corps, if not for the entire airborne army and, like most other senior British Army officers, he was determined that 21st Army Group should win the race into Germany. The historically neglected plan 'Linnet' was the first operation to emerge from this process; Comet – the initial Rhine crossing concept – was the second.

Notes

1. Lamb, *Montgomery in Europe*, pp. 177, 188, 207, 209.
2. Warren, *Airborne Operations*, p. 81.
3. AIR 37/776, Eisenhower to Marshall, 8 July 1944.
4. Otway, *Airborne Forces*, p. 204. The Commanding General and the Chief of Staff were American, and Americans were placed in charge of personnel, intelligence, operations, planning and communications – in other words, five of the six main divisions within the headquarters.
5. AP 3231, *Airborne Forces*, p. 146.
6. Extract from Joint War Office/Air Ministry Report on the Employment of Airborne Forces, Part B, Recommendations for Future Employment of Airborne Forces, Appendix D to Appendix V/19, Wing Commander W.D. Macpherson to SASO, 27 November 1943, Notes on the Planning and Preparation of the Allied Expeditionary Air Force for the Invasion of North West France in June 1944, appendices.
7. Ibid., pp. 146–147.
8. Warren, *Airborne Missions in the Mediterranean*, p. 81.
9. Warren, *Airborne Operations*, p. 86.
10. Ibid.
11. Lamb, *Montgomery in Europe*, p. 190.
12. WO 219/2186, paper entitled 'Operation Linnet', issued by SHAEF G-3 Division, 2 September 1944.
13. Warren, *Airborne Operations*, p. 27.
14. WO 219/2186, memorandum for the record by Major General H.R. Bull, 2 September 1944.
15. Omar N. Bradley, *A Soldier's Story* (New York, Henry Holt and Company, 1951), pp. 401–03.
16. Lamb, *Montgomery in Europe*, pp. 194–195.
17. Warren, *Airborne Operations*, p. 87

18. Nigel Hamilton, *Monty: The Battles of Field Marshal Bernard Montgomery* (Hodder & Stoughton, London, 1994), p. 420.

19. Warren, *Airborne Operations*, p. 87

20. WO 219/2186, paper entitled 'Operation Linnet', issued by SHAEF G-3 Division, 2 September 1944.

21. CAB 44/253, War Office narrative entitled 'Liberation Campaign North West Europe', p. 65. 'Bradley ... does not require airborne drop on Liege line. We both consider that all available aircraft should go on to transport work.'

22. Ibid.

23. WO 219/2186, Brereton to Eisenhower, 1 September 1944.

24. WO 219/2121, memorandum by SHAEF planning staff, 4 September 1944. This memorandum set out the basic arguments Brereton submitted to Eisenhower on 1 September.

25. WO 219/3068, Brigadier General Parks to GOC British Airborne Corps, 4 September 1944 ('confirming telephone message 032230').

26. WO 285/9, Dempsey diary, 4 and 5 September 1944.

27. Wilmot, *The Struggle for Europe*, p. 543, note 1.

28. Field Marshal the Viscount Montgomery of Alamein, *Memoirs* (Collins, London, 1958), pp. 274–275.

29. Lamb, *Montgomery in Europe*, p. 206; Lamb cited WO 219/4998, minutes of a meeting at Airborne Corps HQ, 4 September 1944. However, WO 219/4998 does not contain minutes of any such meeting. It is unclear whether the citation is incorrect or whether the document has been removed from the file since *Montgomery in Europe* was published in 1983.

30. For an Allied assessment of the Siegfried Line from early September 1944, see WO 171/341, Appendix A to XXX Corps intelligence summary 499, 11 September 1944. 'North of Aachen the Siegfried Line is at its weakest, consisting only of a thin line of forts following the frontier, and becoming very widely separated in the north. Photographic reconnaissance in the Goch area [just west of Wesel] discloses only four forts in a strip of 8 miles.'

31. WO 285/9, Dempsey diary, 9 September 1944.

32. Lamb, *Montgomery in Europe*, p. 214.

33. Ibid., pp. 209–212, 262.

34. WO 205/197, Brereton to Montgomery, 9 September 1944.

35. AP 3231, *Airborne Forces*, p. 101.

36. Otway, *Airborne Forces*, p. 59.

37. AP 3231, *Airborne Forces*, p. 101.

38. Otway, *Airborne Forces*, pp. 137–139.

39. Royal Air Force Airborne Assault Operations, 1940–45, Vol. 1, minutes of a meeting held at Norfolk House on 10 August 1943 to discuss future policy relating to the employment of airborne forces.

40. Minutes of the Airborne Air Planning Committee, 18 May 1944, Appendix V/41, Notes on the Planning and Preparation of the Allied Expeditionary Air Force for the Invasion of North West France in June 1944, appendices.

41. Buckingham, *Arnhem*, p. 74.

42. Browning's presence at Montgomery's headquarters during the planning of Wild Oats is recorded in Hamilton, *Monty*, p. 277.

43. http://en.wikipedia.org/wiki/Frederick_Browning, accessed 29 June 2010.

44. Buckingham, *Arnhem*, pp. 76–77.

45. Ryan, *A Bridge Too Far*, p. 87, quoting Major Brian Urquhart, of Browning's intelligence staff.

46. Hamilton, *Monty*, pp. 401–403.

47. Leigh-Mallory was already working closely with the airborne forces within a month of Husky. See Royal Air Force Airborne Assault Operations, 1940–45, Vol 1, minutes of a meeting held at Norfolk House on 10 August 1943 to discuss future policy relating to the employment of airborne forces.

48. US Army Military History Institute Papers, Supreme Command, Forrest Pogue Interviews, interview with Air Chief Marshal Sir Arthur Coningham, 14 February 1947.

49. Vincent Orange, *Coningham: A Biography of Air Marshal Sir Arthur Coningham* (Centre for Air Force History, Washington DC, 1992), p. 204.

2.2. From Comet to Market Garden

OPERATION COMET WAS initially scheduled for 6 or 7 September. The plan drawn up by Montgomery, Dempsey and Browning envisaged that 1 Parachute Brigade would capture the road and rail bridges across the Lower Rhine at Arnhem, while 4 Parachute Brigade, 1 Air Landing Brigade and the Polish Parachute Brigade were tasked to take bridges across the Waal at Nijmegen and the Maas at Grave. They would also have had to secure at least one bridge over the Maas-Waal Canal, between Grave and Nijmegen. In conjunction with the airborne assault, XXX Corps would begin a northward advance from the Antwerp-Brussels-Luvain area. This was originally to begin on 7 September, but XXX Corps were ordered to 'adjust their advance from this area so that the surprise of the airborne landings will not be prejudiced'.[1] The plan envisaged that they would quickly link up with the airborne troops and cross the various waterways, their ultimate objective being a bridgehead on the north bank of the Lower Rhine at Arnhem.

Following Browning's return to England the details of the airborne lift were finalized. The Arnhem, Nijmegen and Grave bridges were each to be seized by *coup-de-main* parties, each party being conveyed by six gliders. The *coup-de-main* troops would land close to the bridges and hold them until relieved by the various brigades converging from the main DZ/LZ areas. The *coup-de-main* operations were scheduled for 05.45 – before daybreak. Otherwise, the 1st Airborne Division and Polish Parachute Brigade requirement for more than 600 glider sorties necessitated two airlifts, one reaching its objectives at 08.00-09.00, the other at 17.30-18.30.[2] With the exception of the 12 Stirlings assigned to the pathfinders, RAF aircraft were to be employed solely for glider towing; the parachute brigades would be carried by Williams' 9th TCC.

Had the Germans been unable to offer any organized resistance between the Albert Canal and Arnhem, Comet might possibly have succeeded. In any other circumstances it would have been a desperately risky venture. To begin with, the rationale for selecting Arnhem as the objective was dubious in the extreme. Located on rising ground on the north bank of the Lower Rhine, it would have made an excellent defensive position for any force seeking to block an advance from the south across typical Dutch low-lying polderland – a point firmly established by the Dutch Army between the wars.[3] The bridge area would have been very vulnerable to artillery fire from the high ground north of the town, and any Allied troops that made the crossing would then have found themselves confronted by a difficult urban battle. The task that Comet assigned to 1 Parachute Brigade – the capture of the Arnhem bridges – did not alone guarantee a breakout north of the town.

Equally, Arnhem could not be captured unless Nijmegen was secured first, and this also promised to be a formidable undertaking. With one brigade plus divisional troops committed to Arnhem, 1st Airborne would be left with three brigades to secure the bridge at Grave, a bridge over the Maas-Waal Canal and a bridge over the Waal in Nijmegen itself. In addition, it was necessary for part of the airborne force to capture and hold an area of high ground southeast of Nijmegen at Groesbeek, only a few miles from the German frontier. German possession of the Groesbeek Heights might have left XXX Corps' eastern flank dangerously exposed to counter-attack. Hence the Comet plan suffered from the same basic shortcoming that had characterized a number of earlier airborne operations, in that resources were stretched across too many different tasks in an excessively large geographical area. To put the challenge into context, a perimeter line drawn around the four main Nijmegen objectives would have extended to a distance of approximately 25 miles.[4] Nevertheless, Montgomery's plan required 100 per cent mission success – something as yet unknown in large-scale airborne operations. Failure to capture a single objective would jeopardize the entire XXX Corps offensive; failure to secure the Nijmegen bridges would leave part of 1st Airborne Division cut off at Arnhem.

A number of other substantial risks were involved in Comet. The double airlift was hugely problematic: the component brigades of 1st Airborne would have been unable to deploy at full strength until the second lift arrived, and would in the meantime have had to divert some troops from the first lift to the defence of DZ/LZ areas. The Germans would, on the other hand, have begun mobilizing in response to the three *coups-de-mains*, which would also have revealed the precise Allied objectives. The benefit of any shock or surprise effect from the initial landings would soon have been lost, and 1st Airborne would rapidly have found themselves outnumbered and outgunned. In such circumstances, they stood little chance of success without prompt relief by XXX Corps. And yet Browning – their principal spokesman – simply did not grasp the vulnerability of their position. Indeed, by his own admission, he at one stage told Montgomery 'that he was prepared to hold that area till D+4 day with airborne forces only'.[5] On the basis of past airborne history, this was an extraordinary undertaking, and one that could only have been given by an officer lacking direct operational experience. For, in truth, no airborne force deployed in the European theatre since September 1939 had held an objective for much longer than 48 hours without relief or reinforcement from either ground forces or air-landed troops.

However, it would have been highly optimistic to expect 1st Airborne to be relieved more rapidly. The ultimate goal – Arnhem – lay some 70 miles inside enemy-occupied territory, and even the distance to Nijmegen was nearly 60 miles. To attempt an airborne assault against such deep objectives was at odds with established Allied airborne practice and with the main lessons identified from earlier operations, which had, of course, laid great emphasis on the critical importance of a rapid link-up with ground forces. The risks might have been somewhat reduced if XXX Corps' route to Nijmegen had been relatively free of obstacles, but this was not the case. Indeed, confronting XXX Corps was a succession of substantial water barriers, including the Meuse-Escaut Canal, the Wilhelmina Canal and the Zuid Willemsvaart Canal. Additionally, in Eindhoven and Nijmegen there were two large conurbations where even limited defensive action might have proved enormously difficult to overcome. And then there was the road along which XXX Corps had to advance. It was barely more than a country lane, raised on an embankment in some areas, bordered by soft ground or thick woodland in others and wide enough for only one tank. It should not have required an exceptional act of foresight to realize that it would be vulnerable to blocking action and susceptible to congestion. By contrast, Arnhem was very well linked into the German and Dutch railway networks and the Germans were thus well placed to move reinforcements to the area quickly.[6]

Finally there were the three preliminary *coups-de-mains*. It might be supposed that these deliberately mimicked the brilliantly executed Orne River and Caen Canal operations of 6 June, but in fact they were planned to address yet another basic flaw in the decision to mount Comet against Arnhem and Nijmegen – the lack of suitable DZs and LZs near the main bridge objectives. To understand this issue it is necessary to recall that Comet originated at 21st Army Group headquarters on 2 September and was not considered in detail by First Allied Airborne Army until the 4th. It was then quickly decided that the main airlifts should be executed in daylight.

There were two basic grounds for staging daylight lifts. Moon conditions were one consideration, but the key factor was almost certainly the failure of earlier night operations – particularly the American landings in western Normandy. Located nearly 100 miles inland, Arnhem would have been a very challenging night target under any circumstances, and German anti-aircraft fire en route would probably have complicated the navigational task still further. The more experienced crews of 38 Group RAF might have staged a reasonably accurate night-time airlift to Arnhem or Nijmegen; their role in supporting clandestine elements such as the SAS involved regular night infiltration and supply drops, which were usually executed very accurately.[7] But nothing in the performance of 9th TCC or 46 Group in Normandy suggests that they would have delivered 1st Airborne Division accurately to the Comet objectives in darkness.[8] By contrast, the navigational benefits of daytime lifts had been clearly demonstrated by Operation Mallard (the British lift on the evening of 6 June) and by the second airlift in Dragoon. By September 1944 it was clear that day lifts had the potential to achieve levels of accuracy and concentration completely unprecedented in the otherwise troubled history of Allied airborne warfare.[9]

Yet in a deep assault such as Comet daytime airlifts would have been impossible unless enemy air defences were either avoided or suppressed to an extent previously unknown to Allied airborne planners, and to some, at least, the risks appeared excessive. The prospect of staging day lifts to objectives so far inside German-occupied territory led the commanding officer of 38 Group, Air Vice-Marshal Leslie Hollinghurst, to argue that Comet was impracticable and that the casualties (aircraft lost or damaged) inflicted by enemy fighters and anti-aircraft fire might be as high as 40 per cent. He met Browning and Leigh-Mallory on the evening of 5 September to voice these opinions. But Hollinghurst was told that 'the military aim, if attained, outweighs the casualties incurred by the air and ground troops in the air operation'. Leigh-Mallory in any case believed Hollinghurst's estimate of likely casualties to be too high.[10]

Still, even if they took issue with Hollinghurst on this point, Browning and Leigh-Mallory evidently agreed that very serious risks were involved in targeting at least two key objectives – the Arnhem and Nijmegen bridges – which lay immediately adjacent to large towns with significant flak defences. The Allies had never previously dropped airborne troops next to a substantial urban area in darkness, let alone in broad daylight. The presence of defended, built-up areas directly north of the Lower Rhine at Arnhem and south of the Waal at Nijmegen limited the range of DZ/LZ options that Allied planners could consider, and confronted the air forces with the formidable prospect of over-flying both the towns and other nearby anti-aircraft artillery concentrations. To complicate matters further, much of the terrain in the Arnhem area was found to be unsuitable for glider landings.

These were issues which should have been addressed in consultation with the Allied air forces when the primary objectives for Comet were being selected. Instead, the decision to target Arnhem and Nijmegen was taken without any consideration of where landing areas might be located, and the problem had then to be tackled retrospectively. The *coup-de-main* scheme was the result. Hollinghurst apparently believed that at least some of his 38 Group glider tug crews would be able to navigate successfully to the Arnhem-Nijmegen area in darkness and that limited numbers of glider-

*An RAF reconnaissance photograph of the Arnhem road bridge
in September 1944*

borne troops might thus theoretically be landed safely next to the bridges.
The first main airlift would then follow after daybreak, employing DZ/LZ
areas outside the two towns. Browning accepted the plan and signalled
Dempsey on the evening of 5 September 'that he considered it essential to
land *coup-de-main* glider parties on each bridge on the night of 7/8 Sep and
then bring in the first main lift early daylight 8 Sep, otherwise surprise would
be impossible'.[11]

This does not mean that the *coups-de-mains* would have worked. The navigational challenge alone was of an entirely different order to that facing the
tug and glider crews involved in the assault on the Orne bridges, which lay just
a few miles from the Normandy coast. And, whereas the personnel who
participated in the D-Day operations had undertaken innumerable practice
landings, neither the aircrew nor the air landing troops committed to Comet
would have conducted any rehearsals at all, as no time was available. It was
also extremely ambitious to expect that forces of around 150 lightly equipped
infantry might be able to capture and then hold objectives as large as the

Arnhem or Nijmegen road bridges for several hours if confronted by more than the most limited opposition.

In summary, then, Comet was an extremely high-risk venture that counted on a near-total absence of enemy forces in eastern Holland, and which ignored a succession of lessons identified in the aftermath of earlier airborne operations. It was ultimately halted for several reasons. First, while Montgomery had originally intended the airborne assault to take place on 6 or 7 September, weather predictions and the time required for essential preparations pushed the date back to the 8th. By then the German presence in Second Army's sector was increasing, both on the immediate battlefront in the areas of the Meuse-Escaut and Albert Canals and elsewhere, as we shall see. This caused Montgomery to postpone the operation again. Simultaneously, he was becoming increasingly concerned about his logistical position. On the 7th the head of administration at 21st Army Group had inconveniently warned that it would be impossible to advance beyond Arnhem before the Channel ports were open and without a substantial increase in airlifted supplies.[12] 'My maintenance is stretched to the limit', Montgomery signalled Eisenhower on the 7th.

> First instalment of 18 locomotives only just released to me and balance still seems uncertain. Require an air lift of 1,000 tons a day at Douai or Brussels and in last two days have had only 750 tons total. My transport is based on operating 150 miles from my ports and at present I am over 300 miles from Bayeux ... I cannot go on for long like this. It is clear therefore that based as I am at present on Bayeux I cannot capture the Ruhr.

He finished by asking Eisenhower to visit him to discuss the situation.[13]

* * *

The circumstances of Montgomery's decision to transform Comet into Market Garden are recorded in the documents in outline but not in detail, and therefore they remain the subject of some conjecture. On 9 September he signalled the CIGS:

> Second Army are meeting with very determined resistance on the Albert Canal line and rapid progress here cannot now be expected. The Airborne drop in the Arnhem area on the Rhine has now been postponed for the present.[14]

It is in fact almost certain that by the time Montgomery sent this message the possibility of mounting a larger airborne operation was already being investigated. A meeting between Browning and Dempsey the following morning is documented, and it is also well established that Browning met Montgomery, possibly at the same time or earlier. It is therefore highly probable that he flew out from England on the 9th; if not, he would certainly have received the order to visit Montgomery that day.[15] Moreover, writing in his diary on the evening of the 9th, Dempsey was still pondering the wisdom of the Arnhem operation, which hardly indicates that the postponement was expected to last for very long. Yet Dempsey by this time harboured the very gravest doubts about crossing the Rhine at Arnhem. 'It is clear', he confided to his diary that evening,

'that the enemy is bringing up all the reinforcements he can lay his hands on for the defence of the Albert Canal and that he appreciates the importance of the area Arnhem-Nijmegen. It looks as though he is going to do all he can to hold it.'

Dempsey much preferred the idea of establishing a left flank along the Albert Canal, and recorded that he wanted to 'strike due east, towards Cologne, in conjunction with First [US] Army'. This again raised the possibility of bridging the Rhine at Wesel.[16]

The very next morning, at 09.00, he met Montgomery at the 21st Army Group tactical headquarters and the fateful step was taken. Dempsey afterwards wrote in his diary:

In view of increasing [German] strength in the Arnhem-Nijmegen area the employment of one airborne division in this area will not be sufficient. *I got from C-in-C his agreement to the use of three airborne divisions.*[17]

Dempsey's account is interesting because it is often suggested that Comet was enlarged into Market Garden primarily to cope with stiffening German resistance around the Albert Canal, ahead of XXX Corps.[18] Clearly this was not the case; on the contrary, the main enemy threat was located around the airborne objectives – hence the importance of expanding the airborne force.

Assuming Dempsey's version of events is accurate – and there is no reason to believe that it is not – Market Garden emerges as one of two options placed before Montgomery on the morning of 10 September. Both were proposed for the same reason, namely concern over the 'increasing [German] strength in the Arnhem-Nijmegen area'. If Dempsey could not persuade Montgomery to adopt a more easterly axis of advance, he could alternatively back the enlarged airborne operation as an insurance against strengthening German defences around the two towns. Montgomery later claimed in his memoirs to have favoured the more northerly route because of the need to 'rope off' V2 rocket launch areas around Rotterdam and Amsterdam, after the first V2 attacks on London on 8 September.[19] He apparently left Dempsey with the impression that this was his chief concern.[20] Yet this is far from convincing given that he had in fact selected Arnhem as the objective for Comet a week earlier. For Montgomery, Arnhem remained the preferred goal primarily because it accorded with his desire to advance well north of the nearest American ground formations. 'Monty knew if he made the Rhine crossing at Wesel he would have had to share it with the Americans.'[21]

For Browning there would have been obvious practical advantages in maintaining the focus on Arnhem because of the large amount of planning work already undertaken for Comet. But despite this, he was in no way responsible for the decision to retain Arnhem as the operational objective. On the contrary, the former Brigadier General Staff at 21st Army Group, David Belchem, recorded that Browning, like Dempsey, would have preferred to redirect the offensive against Wesel.[22] Historians often puzzle over the meaning of Browning's famous comment that Arnhem represented 'a bridge too far', assuming he was proposing a halt at Nijmegen. This would have been pointless if the Allied objective was to cross the Rhine.[23] Yet his phrase makes perfect sense in the context of a choice between Arnhem and Wesel, given that a Rhine crossing at Arnhem involved one additional bridge.

Again, the absence of air force input is striking. Market Garden involved the lift of 35,000 troops from a multiplicity of British airfields into a narrow corridor of airspace, much of which was over enemy-occupied territory. Quite apart from the airlift required, an enormous air effort would be needed to suppress German anti-aircraft defences and prevent any interference by the Luftwaffe. More broadly, air power had of course played a crucial role both in the Allied victory in Normandy and in the subsequent advance through northern France. There was no reason to expect that its contribution would be less decisive in Holland. And yet, at its inception, not a single air force officer was consulted over Market Garden. The expertise of a troop carrier commander such as Williams would have been particularly valuable at this stage, but it was not sought. Second TAF remained on the periphery of the operation; Coningham played no part whatsoever in the events of 10 September 1944.[24]

After conferring with Dempsey, Montgomery met Eisenhower at Brussels airport – a direct consequence of his earlier request for an audience with the Supreme Commander. Gaining approval to use the whole of First Allied Airborne Army appears to have been little more than a formality. Broader strategic issues proved far more contentious. The only record prepared immediately after the meeting (by the Deputy Supreme Commander, Tedder) confirms that Montgomery's concept of advancing to Berlin was dismissed out of hand, but he remained desperate to secure logistical priority for his northern thrust. He was particularly anxious to ensure that First Army (fighting on Second

Army's right flank) received priority over Patton's formations further south, and apparently hoped that First Army might be placed under his direction, if not his formal command. 'Argument on such a basis [is] obviously futile', Tedder wrote.

> Eisenhower made it clear that he could not accept such an interpretation. We must fight with both hands at present and a moment for the left hook had not come yet and could not come until Northern Army Group maintenance was based securely on the Channel ports.[25]

Historians still sometimes contend that the innumerable risks inherent in Market Garden were justified on the basis that the operation, if successful, might have ended the war by Christmas 1944.[26] Yet Tedder's account shows that Eisenhower had no such expectation; in his view, Antwerp or the Channel ports were needed to sustain a major 21st Army Group offensive into the German heartland. The Supreme Commander was, of course, very anxious to find a use for First Allied Airborne Army, but he authorized the operation primarily because it accorded with his view that both US and British forces should advance on a broad front. It would at the same time remove any residual threat of a counter-attack on Antwerp from the north while Allied troops were clearing the Scheldt Estuary. So Market Garden was to be, in his own words, 'merely an incident and extension of our eastward rush to the line we needed for temporary security. On our northern flank that line was the Lower Rhine itself.'[27] Eisenhower naturally appreciated the potential value of a Rhine bridgehead, and he was prepared to defer opening Antwerp for a limited period if one could be captured quickly; Market Garden offered him this prospect. But he saw no justification for backing Montgomery's offensive at Patton's expense. As Tedder put it, 'robbing the American Peter who is fed from Cherbourg will certainly not get the British Paul to Berlin'.[28] Rather, Eisenhower hoped that his relatively limited aspirations for Market Garden might be achievable without any substantial redistribution of supplies.

Why did Eisenhower ignore Brereton's recent warning that an airborne operation extending as far east as the Rhine would be very difficult to mount from England? Possibly the Supreme Commander assumed that there had been prior consultation between Montgomery and First Allied Airborne Army, but in actual fact Brereton had no knowledge of the plan at this stage. Indeed, Montgomery quite deliberately went over his head to avoid any further objections. 'Airborne Army HQ had refused my demand for airborne troops to capture Walcheren,' he informed the CIGS, 'and they are now going to be ordered by Ike to do what I ask.'[29]

The exceptionally challenging nature of the enterprise Eisenhower had sanctioned became clear to First Allied Airborne Army as soon as Browning returned to England that afternoon. His first action was to inform Brereton of the decision to launch Market Garden between 14 and 16 September. This left only three days to plan an operation of monumental complexity – a hopelessly inadequate period of notice. History regularly portrays Brereton's planners as (at best) inexperienced and (at worst) incompetent; yet on 10 September they were confronted by a task that would have stretched even the most seasoned military staff. The timetable was dictated partly by the intelligence on strengthening German resistance and partly by the pressing need to free up First Allied Airborne Army's air transport resources.

Upon Browning's return, Brereton convened a conference of his senior troop carrier and airborne commanders to determine the main features of the operation. Yet the time constraints were inevitably to have a marked impact on First Allied Airborne Army's preparations. Whereas, before Neptune, Allied commanders had sufficient notice to subject particular proposals to detailed scrutiny, questioning, discussion and consequently sometimes revision, no such deliberations could occur before Market Garden. Plans had simply to be drawn up and implemented, as constant last-minute changes would have caused chaos.[30] Equally, there was no opportunity to organize the training programmes, rehearsals or exercises, which earlier operations had shown to be so vital and which, in other circumstances, might have drawn attention to potential problems.[31] To make matters worse, key participants in Market Garden could not always be consulted in the very limited time available. The location of First Allied Airborne Army's headquarters in England when 21st Army Group and Second TAF were based in Belgium made joint planning between these formations particularly difficult. Brereton had, of course, strongly advocated the deployment of his headquarters and troop carrier formations to northern France partly to address this specific problem.

Operation Market Garden was essentially an enlarged version of Comet, which also drew heavily on Linnet; the earlier airborne plans were recycled to save time.[32] Yet the new scheme represented at most a marginal improvement on Comet. Although it envisaged the deployment of many more airborne troops in total, the Allies did not possess nearly enough transport aircraft to bring them all into Holland in a single lift. Several consecutive airlifts would therefore still be needed and once again tactical surprise would be lost after the first lift, allowing German forces around Arnhem and Nijmegen to begin mobilizing long before the second lift arrived. In such circumstances, it would be very difficult to exploit much of the additional combat power that the new plan theoretically provided.

1st Airborne Division and the Polish Parachute Brigade were now exclusively assigned to Arnhem, but with broader divisional objectives encompassing the entire town. The American airborne divisions would in the meantime create a 'corridor' for XXX Corps' advance. The Nijmegen area,

The railway and road bridges over the Waal at Nijmegen

with its multiplicity of dispersed goals, was at first given to 101st Airborne, while tasking further south was allotted to Gavin's 82nd Airborne. But almost immediately this allocation was reversed because 82nd Airborne were stationed further to the north in England; it was desirable that the two divisions should not cross in mid-air.[33] When Gavin's senior executives first became acquainted with the Nijmegen plan, his Chief of Staff, Colonel Robert Wienecke, is said to have protested, 'We'll need two divisions to do all that.'[34] Gavin nevertheless accepted the task he had been given, whereas 101st Airborne flatly rejected their assignment further south.

Montgomery, Dempsey and Browning had between them allotted to the most southerly of the three airborne divisions the job of plugging the gap between XXX Corps and the objectives around Nijmegen. Yet this would have required their deployment along a 40-mile stretch of the corridor via landings both to the north and south of Eindhoven on no fewer than seven separate drop zones. The Germans had been strengthening their presence south of Eindhoven: a Second Army intelligence summary dated 9 September remarked that 'fresh units keep appearing on the scene, none of them of divisional size but all of them adding weight to the infantry defences'.[35] XXX Corps were also confronted by some potentially troublesome minor water crossings south of the city. Hence there were good reasons for staging an airborne assault in this area. The problem was that the dispositions thereby required of 101st Airborne (stretching from within artillery range of XXX Corps in the south to the town of Grave in the north) would have been impossibly dispersed; the airborne troops would have

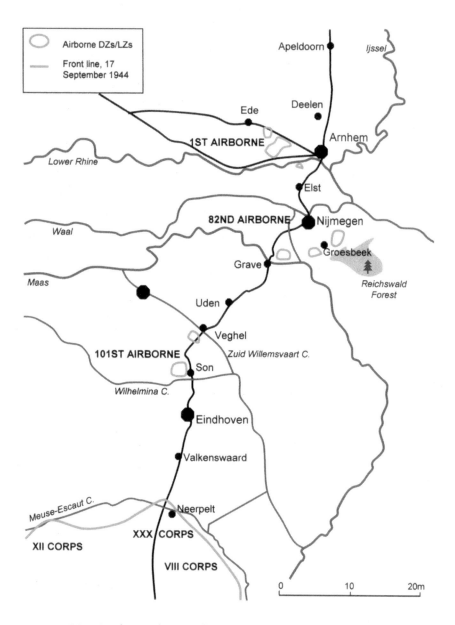

Map 8: The Market Garden area, showing main waterways and DZ/LZ areas

been far too thinly spread across innumerable objectives – a point immediately raised by their commanding officer, Major General Maxwell Taylor. Brereton strongly supported Taylor's protests and was also understandably concerned about the 'difficulty of dropping accurately on so many small pinpoint dropping zones' – an approach that directly contravened Allied airborne tactical doctrine.[36] He therefore took up the issue with Montgomery.

Montgomery was opposed to any revision of the plan, but he reluctantly agreed to let Taylor and Dempsey negotiate a compromise and they duly met in Belgium on 12 September. No record of the meeting survives but it is clear that Dempsey accepted the thrust of Taylor's arguments, and the result was a substantial reduction of 101st Airborne's tasking. The divisional objectives would now be confined to a 16-mile stretch of road from Eindhoven to Grave; they would include bridges over the Wilhelmina Canal and the Zuid Willemsvaart Canal and it was envisaged that there would be a link-up with XXX Corps at Eindhoven by the end of Market Garden's first day, or early on the second day.[37] Taylor's forces would consequently be far less scattered, although their responsibilities would still be extensive. Unfortunately, of course, the revised scheme left German units south of Eindhoven free to concentrate against XXX Corps' advance. There would no longer be any threat of vertical envelopment.[38]

Another assumption made by Montgomery, Dempsey and Browning on 10 September was that the airlift employed in Market Garden would be similar to that planned for Linnet.[39] This had envisaged the deployment of all three airborne divisions in two waves, with an initial lift soon after daybreak and another in the evening; only the Poles and a small glider lift were scheduled to arrive the next day. For the Americans the realization of this timetable was dependent on the 'double-towing' of all assault gliders.[40] There were, however, two important differences between the operations. First, the Market Garden objectives were significantly further from Britain than those of Linnet; second, hours of daylight had declined since late August, when Linnet was originally scheduled. To any air force officer with planning experience the implications would immediately have been obvious: if the lift had to be executed in daylight it was not safe to expect that a schedule designed to target the western Franco-Belgian border area in late August would automatically be appropriate for eastern Holland in mid-September. Equally, such issues were never likely to occur to army officers lacking such experience.

Only the most limited scrutiny of Browning's outline plan was required before the 9th TCC staff concluded that there was no prospect of using the Linnet airlift timetable. In Market Garden only one full-scale lift could be completed in the daylight hours of any given day.[41] Moreover, as the Market Garden objectives lay too far from the UK for the 'double-towing' of gliders to be practicable, nearly half of the American gliders had to be moved from the second to the third lift.

Hence, as well as accepting the basic risk of using multiple lifts, the Allies would also have to contend with a slower airborne reinforcement rate than originally envisaged. And the revised schedule required three consecutive days of favourable weather rather than just two; in the event of adverse weather conditions over this period the airborne build-up might be set back even further. This does not mean, of course, that an airlift employing the Linnet schedule would have been invulnerable to weather disruption – particularly to the morning fog which featured in Allied forecasts in mid-September.[42]

The known difficulties regarding DZ/LZ location at Arnhem and Nijmegen appear to have exerted no influence at all during the expansion of Comet into Market Garden. But whereas in Comet a solution of sorts had at least been found in the form of the three *coups-de-mains*, in Market Garden no equivalent operations could be conducted. This was not, as Harclerode maintains, 'because of an RAF veto on the use of terrain south of the river'.[43] It must be remembered that the Comet *coups-de-mains* had been scheduled as night-time assaults, preceding the first main lift. Browning's original hope for Market Garden was that the first airlift would take place early in the evening.[44] However, as this would have required the preliminary *coups-de-mains* to be executed in daylight – a proposition he knew to be unacceptable to the RAF – it is very probable that he had abandoned the whole idea before his return to England on 10 September. In the event, the alternative daytime lift plan selected by First Allied Airborne Army was also impossible to reconcile with the *coups-de-mains*. Timed shortly before the first main lift, the three operations would again have had to take place in broad daylight; on the other hand, if the night-time plan had been retained, the handful of troops involved would have faced German counter-attacks for the entire day pending relief from the main landing zones. As before, the *coups-de-mains* would also have signalled to the Germans that larger airborne assaults on the bridges were imminent.[45]

So the *coups-de-mains* were cancelled. Their chances of success had always been slight. Furthermore, in the context of Market Garden (as opposed to Comet), so many bridges had to be captured by the airborne that the organization of discreet, small-scale assaults on every objective would have been impracticable, introducing numerous additional complications into an already over-complex airlift and causing the further dispersal of units into small and vulnerable penny packets. Yet the *coups-de-mains* had originally been proposed to address a specific and acknowledged weakness in the Arnhem-Nijmegen plan. Indeed, Browning's signal to Second Army on 5 September had strongly implied that the operation could not be staged without the *coups-de-mains*.[46] Presumably, he now withheld similar arguments because of their potential to throw the entire enterprise into jeopardy. At Arnhem, 1st Airborne Division turned their Reconnaissance Squadron into an alternative *coup-de-main* force, which was tasked with driving into the town ahead of 1 Parachute Brigade, but, at Nijmegen, Gavin made no equivalent arrangements for the Waal bridges.

So much for the airborne plan; what of the preparations for XXX Corps' offensive? Since the fall of Antwerp there had been a limited further advance to the north, which culminated on the evening of 10 September in the establishment of a bridgehead across the Meuse-Escaut Canal at Neerpelt. But this still meant that the most forward elements of XXX Corps would be 64 miles from Arnhem when Market Garden began. Moreover, their northward advance, veering off at a tangent from the American forces southeast of Second Army, would leave their right flank dangerously exposed. By 10 September it was clear to Montgomery that this area would have to be covered by other elements of Second Army, namely VIII Corps – at that time halted on the River Seine by the shortage of supplies. So having agreed at his meeting with Eisenhower that day that Market Garden would be launched within a week, Montgomery signalled the Supreme Commander the very next morning that it would not be possible to begin the advance until the 23rd, when VIII Corps would be in a position to provide support. The news was received with utter dismay at SHAEF, where it had been recognized that even the original plan would yet again prevent the air transport fleet from being transferred to supply work. 'This was the fourth time that air lift had been diverted for an operation which so far had not materialized.' Eisenhower responded by immediately dispatching his Chief of Staff, Bedell Smith, to 21st Army Group with a promise of extra supplies and transport, and an assurance that elements of First Army would operate on the British right.[47]

Bedell Smith's promises were not fulfilled. With the Allies' general logistical situation deteriorating daily, Montgomery received a far smaller increase in supplies than he had sought, and First Army became too heavily engaged in fighting around Aachen to play any part in Market Garden. Montgomery was left to choose between reducing XXX Corps' supplies in order to move up VIII Corps, or, alternatively, launching the operation as planned but before VIII Corps were able to bring their full combat power to bear. He opted for the latter course of action – a desperate gamble that could only invite German counter-attacks from the east against XXX Corps' narrow axis of advance.[48] In such circumstances, the forward impetus of the offensive would be slowed as troops were diverted from their primary objectives by the undesirable but essential task of keeping the airborne corridor open.

British historians have often blamed the Americans for SHAEF's failure to provide the support promised on 11 September. Bradley is said to have connived with Patton, whose forces were deliberately committed so extensively beyond the Moselle that no redirection of the American main effort further to the north (and nearer to the British) was possible.[49] While there is undoubtedly some truth in these allegations, they fail to acknowledge Montgomery's very personal responsibility for the northerly orientation of Market Garden, and they overlook the secretive and duplicitous manner in which he dealt with Bradley during the preceding days. For barely one week before the operation was conceived Montgomery had of course met Bradley and had agreed with his recommendation 'that all available aircraft should go on to transport work so that we can maintain momentum of the advance'.[50] By this Bradley had meant the *Allied* advance on a broad front. It is therefore not difficult to imagine his indignation at learning on 13 September – *three days* after Montgomery's meeting with Eisenhower – that almost the entirety of the Allied air transport force had been assigned to an airborne assault in the British sector. Bradley had been comprehensively hoodwinked. He wrote later:

> I had not been brought into the plan. In fact Montgomery had devised it and sold it to Ike several days before I even learned of it from our liaison officer to 21st [Army] Group. Monty's secrecy in planning confused me, for although the operation was to be confined to his sector, the move would nevertheless cripple the joint offensive we had agreed upon a few days before.[51]

If Montgomery was determined to ensure that he did not win the enthusiastic co-operation of his American opposite number, this was exactly the right way to go about it.

Even as tens of thousands of Allied troops began their final preparations for Market Garden the operation was falling apart. In addition to the elementary flaws that it inherited from Comet, Market Garden was also mounted at excessively short notice and on the basis of completely (and in many respects deliberately) inadequate consultation between 21st Army Group and other elements within the Allied command chain, including First Allied Airborne Army, the Allied air forces and the American armies to the southeast. Most of the difficulties with which Montgomery was confronted in mid-September 1944 can be traced to this fundamental and entirely self-inflicted cause. There was, however, one further issue, which profoundly influenced the Market Garden plan – namely Allied assessments of German strength in the proposed area of operations. To this subject we must now turn.

Notes

1. WO 205/692, HQ Airborne Troops Instruction No. 1, 6 September 1944.
2. AIR 37/979, 38 Group Operation Order 524, 'Comet', 6 September 1944. The airlift schedule was apparently subject to revision; these times were pencilled in against the original times, which were crossed out.
3. Sir John Hackett, 'Operation Market Garden', in M.R.D. Foot (ed.), *Holland at War Against Hitler: Anglo-Dutch Relations, 1940–1945* (Frank Cass, London, 1990), p. 164.

4. Warren, *Airborne Operations*, p. 130.

5. CAB 106/1133, official historian's notes of an interview with Lieutenant General Sir Frederick Browning, 7 October 1954.

6. AIR 37/1217, Operation Market, 1st Airborne Division Planning Intelligence Summary No. 2, 14 September 1944.

7. AP 3231, *Airborne Forces*, pp. 138–139.

8. AIR 37/13, An Account of the Organization, Training and Operations (and Lessons Learned) of 46 (Transport Support) Group Royal Air Force during the Invasion of Hitler's Europe, p. 68. Predictably enough, 46 Group later claimed that they could have operated at night, and that the real problem lay in the fact that American air transport crews were not trained for night operations.

9. AIR 37/1214, Allied Airborne Operations in Holland, September–October 1944.

10. AIR 37/775, Hollinghurst to Leigh-Mallory, 6 September 1944.

11. CAB 44/253, p. 69.

12. WO 285/9, Dempsey diary, 7 September 1944.

13. Tedder papers, Duplicates 1944, July–September, Montgomery to Eisenhower, 7 September 1944 (held at AHB).

14. Hamilton, *Monty*, p. 437.

15. WO 285/9, Dempsey diary, 10 September 1944; Montgomery, *Memoirs*, pp. 274–275.

16. WO 285/9, Dempsey diary, 9 September 1944.

17. WO 285/9, Dempsey diary, 10 September 1944 (author's italics).

18. See for example Buckingham, *Arnhem*, p. 69.

19. Montgomery, *Memoirs*, pp. 274–275.

20. Wilmot, *The Struggle for Europe*, p. 543, note 1.

21. Lamb, *Montgomery in Europe*, p. 224, quoting Brigadier Williams, Montgomery's former head of intelligence.

22. Stephen Hart, *Colossal Cracks: Montgomery's 21st Army Group in Northwest Europe, 1944–45* (Stackpole, Pennsylvania, 2007), p. 129.

23. Buckingham, *Arnhem*, p. 75.

24. Dempsey did meet the AOC of 83 Group Second TAF that afternoon, but contact at this level was primarily concerned with the air support requirements of Second Army and not with the broader issue of Second TAF's role in Market Garden as a whole. See WO 285/9, Dempsey diary, 10 September 1944.

25. Tedder papers, Duplicates 1944, July–September, Tedder to Portal, 10 September 1944; see also Hamilton, *Monty*, p. 448.

26. Middlebrook, *Arnhem*, pp. 441–442.

27. Dwight D. Eisenhower, *Crusade in Europe* (Heinemann, London, 1948), p. 336.

28. Tedder papers, Duplicates 1944, July–September, Tedder to Portal, 10 September 1944.

29. Hamilton, *Monty*, p. 451.

30. Harvey, *Arnhem*, p. 37.
31. Warren, *Airborne Operations*, p. 99.
32. Ibid., p. 89; Report by First Allied Airborne Army, Operations in Holland, September–November 1944, 22 December 1944.
33. WO 219/4998, minutes of a meeting called by Commanding General, First Allied Airborne Army, 10 September 1944.
34. Ryan, *A Bridge Too Far*, p. 89.
35. CAB 44/253, p. 7.
36. WO 219/4997, memorandum by Brereton, 11 September 1944; extract from Joint War Office/Air Ministry Report on the Employment of Airborne Forces, Part A, Lessons of Airborne Operations in Sicily, Appendix D to Appendix V/19, Wing Commander W.D. Macpherson to SASO, 27 November 1943, Notes on the Planning and Preparation of the Allied Expeditionary Air Force for the Invasion of North West France in June 1944, appendices.
37. Warren, *Airborne Operations*, p. 89.
38. This sequence of events is completely misrepresented in Buckingham's study of Market Garden. Buckingham asserts that the plan for 101st Airborne originated with Brereton, and was 'carried over from the British planning for Comet'. In fact, Brereton had nothing at all to do with their proposed tasking, nor had the British plans for Comet envisaged any airborne landings in the areas assigned to 101st Airborne. See Buckingham, *Arnhem*, p. 84.
39. WO 219/4998, Operation Sixteen Outline Plan, 10 September 1944.
40. AIR 37/509, No. 11 Group Operation Instruction No. 39/1944, 2 September 1944; memorandum entitled 'Air Support, Operation Linnet', Appendix B, 30 August 1944.
41. WO 219/4998, Lieutenant Colonel T. Bartley to Chief of Staff, 1st Allied Airborne Army, 10 September 1944.
42. CAB 44/254, p. 8. Operations Linnet and Comet were both postponed by adverse weather before their ultimate cancellation.
43. Harclerode, *Arnhem*, p. 161.
44. WO 219/4998, Operation Sixteen Outline Plan, 10 September 1944.
45. CAB 106/1133, Browning to Harris, Cabinet Office Historical Section, 12 October 1954.
46. CAB 44/253, p. 69.
47. Hamilton, *Monty*, pp. 450–451.
48. Lamb, *Montgomery in Europe*, pp. 221–222.
49. Ibid; Harclerode, *Arnhem*, pp. 28–29.
50. CAB 44/253, p. 65.
51. Omar Bradley, *A Soldier's Story*, pp. 416–418.

2.3. The Market Garden Intelligence Legend

ACCURATE AND TIMELY intelligence is an important factor in any military undertaking, but it has a particularly critical role to play in airborne warfare because of the exceptional risks involved. Airborne troops are typically conveyed in large and slow transport aircraft that are very vulnerable to enemy air defences. Moreover, the airborne invariably lack heavy weapons and much in the way of motorized transport and logistical support; against more numerous conventional ground troops possessing armour and artillery, mechanized units and ample supplies, airborne forces inevitably operate at a considerable disadvantage. Airborne operations must therefore be planned with the most precise and up-to-date information available on enemy dispositions in the battle area. In surveying airborne operations prior to Market Garden, we have already seen how failures in intelligence collection, interpretation or dissemination could substantially reduce the prospects of mission success.

The role of intelligence in Operation Market Garden has generated a lengthy historiography since the end of the Second World War and continues to provoke controversy. The emotive nature of the subject stems in large part from the tendency of many historians to rely for their source material on anecdotal evidence, while paying insufficient attention to the surviving official records. This approach has allowed innumerable inaccuracies and misunderstandings to shape popular perceptions of the intelligence story. The result has been the emergence over time of a Market Garden intelligence legend: it is maintained that Montgomery ignored intelligence, while Browning deliberately suppressed it, and that 1st Airborne Division was denied intelligence to an extent that fundamentally influenced their fate at Arnhem. At the same time, the threat posed by German air defences is often said to have been exaggerated. Not one of these assertions is sustained by the War Office and Air Ministry files held by the UK National Archives, and yet the divergence between the majority of published histories and the official record has yet to be properly corrected.

The aim of this chapter is to consider the documented availability and application of intelligence on German ground dispositions in the Market Garden area in September 1944 (Allied intelligence on German air defences can more appropriately be covered later). Once again, it will be shown that Montgomery played a pivotal role in the story; indeed, his personal influence can be identified at a number of different levels of the British command chain.

Central to the Market Garden intelligence legend is the role of two SS panzer divisions, 9th and 10th SS Panzer, which, as II SS Panzer Corps, came under the command of General Wilhelm Bittrich. Their precise part in the destruction of 1st Airborne Division at Arnhem has been widely misunderstood and misrepresented. The British Airborne did not land right on top of two crack SS panzer divisions, nor were they at first prevented from achieving their objectives at Arnhem by large formations of German tanks. For by mid-September 1944 – after operating against the Allies in Normandy and during the subsequent retreat across northern France – 9th and 10th SS Panzer were severely depleted. It has been estimated that their combined strength was between 6,000 and 7,000 personnel, whereas, at full establishment, a single SS panzer division would have numbered 18,000. Very little of their armour survived the retreat, and some of their few remaining self-propelled guns were then deployed into forward positions as part of the more general German effort to establish a defensive line along the Albert Canal in front of XXX Corps, 70 miles south of Arnhem.[1]

On 17 September, the remnants of the two divisions were otherwise positioned north and northeast of Arnhem, 9th SS Panzer to the west of the River Ijssel, 10th SS Panzer to the east. As 10th SS Panzer were then sent south to hold the bridges at Nijmegen, only the 9th could be committed to the Arnhem battle, initially with just a handful of tanks. Indeed, the first tank units to become engaged in the fighting at Arnhem in any strength (but not until 19 September) were not affiliated to II SS Panzer Corps at all, but came from the Wehrmacht Assault Gun Brigade 280, largely equipped with Sturmgeschutz III self-propelled guns. However, Assault Gun Brigade 280 had not been located near Arnhem on 17 September but had instead been diverted there from Aachen in response to the airborne landings. More German tanks were subsequently encountered by 1st Airborne Division, but all had been dispatched to Arnhem from Germany or from other parts of the front.[2] In summary, then, the Allied intelligence failure in Market Garden was not of the magnitude sometimes suggested: on 17 September 1944 large numbers of German tanks were not deployed in the immediate vicinity of Arnhem.

Indeed, it could even be argued that the key Allied failure did not relate to II SS Panzer Corps at all. Rather, it concerned the Germans' capacity to deploy as infantry at very short notice an extraordinary array of auxiliary personnel, many of whom had little or no appropriate training or experience. They included miscellaneous elements retreating from France, Belgium and southern Holland, Dutch SS, Luftwaffe and naval personnel, convalescents, home defence and garrison troops. According to a later study,

> On the basis of information received about the enemy, the Germans antici-pated airborne operations. Furthermore, the commanders in the nearby home defence zones (Wehrkreis VI and Luftgau VI) as well as in Holland had made arrangements well in advance, in order to be able in such cases to quickly organize motorized auxiliary forces (so-called 'alert units') with home defence troops and occupation forces, which would be available immediately.[3]

These preparations allowed the Germans to create ad hoc formations such as Kampfgruppe von Tettau and 406 Division and mobilize them against 1st Airborne and 82nd Airborne (respectively) within 24 hours of the initial land-ings.[4] Not surprisingly, many of the units involved suffered very heavy casualties, but they made a vital contribution to the German victory. The Allies captured orders concerning their deployment in defence of crossings over the Rhine, but they were not circulated until 15 September and the British intel-ligence staff offered no meaningful assessment of the numbers or potential fighting capability of the units concerned.[5] There were merely periodic, fleeting references to low-quality occupation troops who would be incapable of offering serious resistance.

Over recent years, the important part played by these forces has become clearer. This is not to underestimate the role of II SS Panzer Corps in the failure of Market Garden, but it does mean that history can be more precise about the nature of the threat that they posed. Bittrich's troops were for the most part well led, well trained and very experienced. By contrast, 1st Airborne Division numbered many inexperienced personnel, having been substantially reconstituted since returning from Italy, and were led by an officer with no previous experience of airborne warfare. The two German divisions had lost nearly all their tanks; nevertheless, they still possessed armoured cars and half-tracks, other motorized transport and some heavy weapons, together with ample resources of excellent small arms and plenty of ammunition. They were also, of course, sustained by overland supply lines, which their airborne adver-saries inevitably lacked. Furthermore, before the Allied landings in Normandy, II SS Panzer Corps had been intensively schooled in counter-airborne warfare.[6] Hence, although only one half of a severely degraded SS Corps confronted the British airborne, this formation could still boast a significant combat capability.

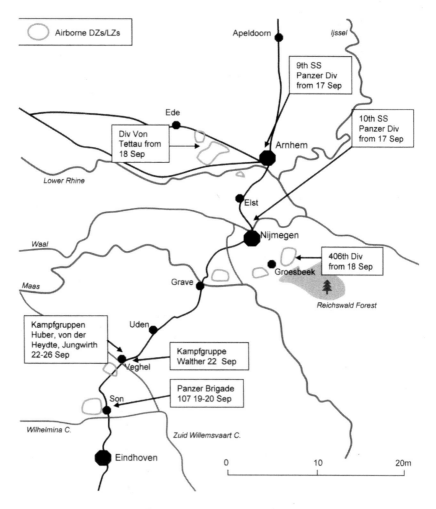

Map 9: Principal German responses to the Allied offensive

However, as events turned out, the precise circumstances of the Arnhem battle would be particularly favourable to the Germans. For, by 17 September, they were aware of a potential Allied threat to Arnhem[7] and, like other German forces in this region, the II SS Panzer Corps battalions north of the town had been formed into alert units. 'On paper the Hohenstaufen [9th SS Panzer] could muster 19 quick reaction or equivalent company strength groups, spread over 12 locations, numbering an approximate total of 2,500 men.' Their average distance from Arnhem was 10 to 15 km – a 2-hour march for heavily laden troops, or a half-hour vehicle ride.[8] On the afternoon of 17 September, elements of 1st Airborne Division (1 Parachute Brigade) had to cover a distance of around 10km from their landing areas to the Arnhem road bridge, but their progress was slowed by determined resistance from a single SS training battalion, which had by chance been deployed along their route. The delay was sufficient to allow 9th SS Panzer to send blocking forces into the west of the town before many British troops could reach the road bridge.[9] From then on, the Germans possessed a further advantage in that they were fighting in urban or wooded environments that inevitably favoured defence.

Beyond this, the presence of SS troops in significant numbers so close to Arnhem meant that the Germans could potentially consider a range of tactical responses to the airborne landings extending far beyond the measures that they actually chose to employ. It also meant that any airborne insertion based on more than one lift was very likely to fail, and rendered completely impracticable one important part of 1st Airborne Division's battle plan, which envisaged the deployment of 4 Parachute Brigade around the northern edge of the town after the 18 September lift. The brigade never stood the slightest chance of establishing this perimeter line against strong enemy forces that had been mobilizing since the previous afternoon. Equally, the immediate availability of II SS Panzer Corps gave the Germans ample scope to confront Allied airborne and ground forces at Nijmegen in order to delay or prevent the relief of Arnhem. As events turned out, 10th SS Panzer beat 82nd Airborne to the Nijmegen bridges and then halted the American paratroops as they approached their objectives. This single critical airborne mission failure of 17–18 September fundamentally influenced the outcome of Market Garden as a whole.[10]

Given that II SS Panzer Corps posed a major threat to both 1st Airborne at Arnhem and 82nd Airborne at Nijmegen, prior knowledge of their dispositions would certainly have been of great value to the Allies. What intelligence was actually available? After narrowly escaping from the Falaise Pocket, II SS Panzer Corps withdrew across France only slightly ahead of the Allied ground forces, straddling routes along which Dempsey's Second Army and Hodges' First Army were advancing. They were regularly mentioned in intelligence reports at the end of August and in early September. On 30 August, 101st Airborne Division – then preparing for Operation Linnet – were warned of the presence of 10th SS Panzer in northern France.[11] The next day Second Army captured German maps which revealed 'as part of the enemy's intentions a concentration area for 9th and 10th SS Panzer Divisions just east of Amiens'. So rapid was the Allied advance that this plan could not, in the event, be implemented.[12]

On 2 September, Second Army identified 10th SS Panzer around the town of Albert, and their intelligence summary also mentioned a report that around 40 tanks belonging to 9th SS Panzer had left Amiens on 30 August and were moving to St Quentin.[13] On the same day, elements of 9th SS Panzer were in action against First Army forces around Cambrai.[14] On the 3rd their whereabouts were said to be 'somewhat of a mystery', but Second Army speculated that they were probably moving back towards Germany on their right flank. Even then, there was said to be evidence of 9th and 10th SS Panzer east of Arras.[15] On 4 September, the day Montgomery selected Arnhem as the objective for Operation Comet, neither division featured in Second Army's intelligence summary, probably because by this time they were located around Maastricht, well inside First Army's area of responsibility.[16]

Yet their whereabouts did not remain unknown for very long. On the afternoon of 4 September they were ordered together with two other panzer divisions to withdraw to the area Venlo–Arnhem 's Hertogenbosch to 'rest and refit'.[17] This message – encrypted using the Enigma cipher machine – was intercepted by the Allies and decrypted at Bletchley Park within 24 hours. Moreover, a further signal decrypted on the 6th clearly placed II SS Panzer Corps' headquarters and 9th SS Panzer Division in the more northerly part of this area.[18] In the event, both 9th and 10th SS Panzer began arriving at Arnhem on 7 September.[19] Over the following days, decrypts would also reveal that the Germans were expecting a British offensive on the general Eindhoven–Arnhem axis.[20]

Circulation of the so-called 'Ultra' intelligence produced at Bletchley Park was of course very tightly controlled. At the Army Group and Army level, Montgomery and Dempsey had access to Ultra, but it was not made directly available to corps or divisional commanders.[21] Nevertheless, particularly important Ultra could sometimes be 'sanitized', or attributed to conventional intelligence sources such as aerial reconnaissance or prisoner of war (POW) interrogations to allow for wider distribution, and this was precisely what happened to the Ultra on II SS Panzer Corps. It was already influencing Second Army's intelligence summaries (which were sent to both XXX Corps and I Airborne Corps) by the 6th, when it was attributed to German POWs.[22]

Bearing in mind the planning in progress for Operation Comet, II SS Panzer Corps' move to Holland would have made unwelcome news but it would hardly have been very surprising, given that Allied intelligence had successfully tracked most stages of their flight from Normandy. Moreover, so great was the level of attrition that Bittrich's forces had sustained that Second Army's intelligence staff were disinclined to accept that they posed a serious threat. 'There can either be rest and refit or defence of the West Wall and Holland. There cannot be both.'[23] The intelligence officers at XXX Corps took a very similar view. Following reports (attributed to the Dutch resistance) that 9th and 10th SS Panzer had been moved into Holland, their 8 September intelligence summary pointed out that 10th SS Panzer had been 'so badly mauled around Mons a few days ago as to be virtually written off'.[24]

But it would have been very optimistic to think that the rest and refit of II SS Panzer Corps around Arnhem completely precluded their involvement in its defence against a relatively small force of lightly-armed airborne troops, and Dempsey was not prepared to make any such assumption. On the contrary, his conclusion was that the Germans were determined to defend the Arnhem–Nijmegen area. As we have seen, it was on this basis that he proposed to Montgomery on 10 September either avoiding Arnhem altogether or else expanding Operation Comet. In short, Allied intelligence made both Montgomery and Dempsey aware of the presence of II SS Panzer Corps at Arnhem; Montgomery's decision to convert Comet into Market Garden was in part a direct response to this intelligence.

It is apparent, however, that such information as Montgomery subsequently supplied to SHAEF about his basic rationale for revising the plan did not state explicitly that the enhanced German defences around Arnhem included armoured formations. Hence, intelligence on the presence of II SS Panzer Corps near the town was received by Eisenhower's staff with both surprise and alarm over the following days. But having secured SHAEF's support for Market Garden, Montgomery altered his assessment of the risks involved in the operation. Apart from his obvious desire that the offensive should proceed as planned, he presumably persuaded himself that any threat from the Germans would be offset by the very much larger number of airborne troops being employed, despite warnings to the contrary from his head of intelligence.[25] So when Bedell Smith suggested to Montgomery that Market Garden might be revised or halted, his objections were dismissed out of hand.[26]

* * *

If Montgomery and Dempsey were made aware of II SS Panzer Corps' dispositions, how much intelligence was available at lower levels of the command chain? This has proved to be the most contentious part of the Market Garden intelligence legend. It has been widely maintained that Browning failed to warn his subordinates that German armour was in the prospective battle area – a claim largely founded on the recollections of Major Brian Urquhart, former head of intelligence at I Airborne Corps' headquarters (no relation to the commander of 1st Airborne Division). One recent history dramatically accuses Browning of 'withholding intelligence reports from the men at the sharp end … Browning deliberately suppressed intelligence showing the presence of SS troops and armour at Arnhem.' In the process, he is said to have misled 1st Airborne Division into basing their battle plan on the assumption that they were facing the equivalent of a low-category brigade, possibly bolstered by a few mobile battalions and flak troops.[27] To assess the validity of such accusations it is first of all necessary to consider Urquhart's story in some detail.

Urquhart recalled that during the planning of Market Garden he became increasingly concerned as accumulating evidence suggested that the Germans were strengthening their defences in Holland. He later told Cornelius Ryan that he noticed a reference to II SS Panzer Corps in a Second Army intelligence summary and subsequently concluded that German armour had been deployed around Arnhem.[28] However, he was unable to persuade any senior officers at I Airborne Corps headquarters to take the warnings seriously. In his memoirs he wrote that,

> There seemed to be a general assumption that the war was virtually over and that one last dashing stroke would finish it. The possibility of German opposition was scarcely considered worthy of discussion. The 'Market Garden' operation was constantly referred to as 'the party'.[29]

When Urquhart raised with Browning and his chief of staff the specific issue of II SS Panzer Corps' reported presence, 'they seemed little concerned and became quite annoyed when I insisted on the danger'.[30] Urquhart was allegedly told not to worry, that the reports were probably wrong and that the German troops were refitting and not up to much fighting in any case. His account continues:

> To convince Browning of the danger, I decided to try to get actual pictures of the German armour near the 1st Airborne Division's dropping zone, and asked for oblique photographs to be taken of the area at a low altitude by the acknowledged experts in this art, an RAF Spitfire squadron stationed at Benson in Oxfordshire ... The pictures when they arrived confirmed my worst fears. There were German tanks and armoured vehicles parked under the trees within easy range of the 1st Airborne Division's main dropping zone. I rushed to General Browning with this new evidence, only to be treated once again as a nervous child suffering from a nightmare.

Soon afterwards he was relieved of his duties on medical grounds.[31]

Many historians have accepted this disturbing account at face value, assuming simultaneously that the tanks must have belonged to II SS Panzer Corps. Yet it raises several questions that have proved extremely difficult to answer. The order of events is questionable, in certain respects, particularly the claim that the first reports mentioning the presence of the two SS panzer divisions at Arnhem appeared after Market Garden was approved. In fact, as we have seen, they were circulated during the planning for Operation Comet, several days earlier. Indeed, Comet's enlargement into Market to deal with the enemy threat is completely overlooked in Urquhart's account.

No less significant, however, is the fundamental mismatch between the capabilities of the RAF Benson squadrons – the only squadrons that operated in support of the airborne forces – and the task that Urquhart described. Of the various units at Benson, 541 Squadron had specific responsibility for Holland. To capture oblique imagery at low level, their Spitfires were equipped with wing-mounted forward-facing synchronized 8-inch lens cameras. As they only produced photographs of a limited area, the target location had to be established and briefed to the pilot in advance, and the aircraft had to be flown directly towards the target when the photographs were taken. Consequently, this technique was reserved for fixed points of interest. Indeed, of the few low-level missions flown by 541 Squadron in the summer of 1944, not one was launched to photograph mobile tactical targets, such as mechanized ground formations.[32]

In short, to stand any realistic chance of obtaining low-level obliques showing elements of II SS Panzer Corps, 541 Squadron would have had to possess other information identifying the exact location of the enemy formation at some kind of fixed facility, such as a barracks. Yet Urquhart's account clearly placed the tanks in a more tactical setting, 'parked under trees'. Moreover, even if he had obtained detailed intelligence of where the armour was positioned at a particular time, subsequent relocation was not merely possible but highly probable while the reconnaissance sortie was being requested, approved and mounted.

This raises the question of whether the mission, as described, would have been officially sanctioned, for it would have involved considerable risks without much likelihood of operational gain. Low-level missions were nicknamed 'dicing' quite literally because they involved dicing with death. In this regard, it is important to remember that all requests for air reconnaissance tasks involving the Benson squadrons had to be approved by a body named the Joint Photographic Reconnaissance Committee (JPRC), a subcommittee of the Joint Intelligence Committee, through which it was responsible to the Chiefs of Staff.

It is unthinkable that the JPRC would have acceded to a request for a low-level air reconnaissance mission to search some general area around Arnhem for German armour, when the proposed task would have been carried out by a squadron that had no established low-level capability against mobile tactical targets and was only equipped to take low obliques of fixed points of interest. The probability of mission success would have been negligible, especially in the densely forested terrain north of Arnhem, which offered the Germans abundant scope for concealment. In actual fact, when 541 Squadron was required to photograph smaller, tactical targets, like V-2 launchers, without specific knowledge of their whereabouts, their approach was typically to operate at high altitude using cameras with 36-inch lenses to take vertical imagery of areas, rather than pinpoints. Photographs of particular interest would then be magnified many times over to provide tactical detail.

Urquhart's account is therefore somewhat perplexing. Further problems arise if we seek to document the events he described. While he and at least one other former 1st Airborne Division officer could recall the photographs in sufficient detail to identify the tanks as Panzer IIIs and IVs, several extensive searches in the British archives failed to locate any air imagery of German armour near Arnhem before Market Garden. Moreover, although the Benson missions were systematically recorded in squadron and group-level diaries, not one record matches the sortie Urquhart described. Low-level missions targeting the Arnhem and Nijmegen bridges on 6 September were scrupulously noted down, but all other recorded reconnaissance sorties over the airborne objectives were flown at higher altitude and captured vertical imagery.

The mystery was only solved after Dutch holdings of Allied air reconnaissance photographs were released online. The Allies gave a significant amount of imagery to Holland after the war to assist with a range of post-war economic and legal tasks. Duplicates were not retained in the UK. The digitization of these photographs provided the means to achieve rapid enlargement, allowing them to be examined in far greater detail than had previously been readily available to researchers. The imagery included the only surviving photographs from a high-level 541 Squadron mission, 106G/2816, flown from Benson on 12 September 1944 by Flight Lieutenant Brian Fuge. It was evidently mounted for the airborne forces, for its geographical parameters were confined to the Arnhem and Nijmegen area.

Fuge began his first run near Deelen airfield over a forested area known as the Deelerwoud. Almost immediately after activating his camera, he photographed multiple German tanks and armoured vehicles near the intersection of two woodland tracks; halted near supply dumps, they were apparently moving south. Some were partly obscured by tree cover, while others were in the open. The larger tanks included Panzer IVs of early design, with short-barrelled 75mm guns; there were also smaller tanks, including Panzer IIIs, which were again early models equipped with 37mm guns.

The preponderance of antiquated equipment in the photograph eliminates any possibility that it belonged to II SS Panzer Corps. Indeed, there was only one unit in this area of Holland that possessed a considerable number of older tanks. This was the Hermann Goering Parachute Panzer Training and Replacement Regiment, which was responsible for supplying replacements to its parent division, the Herman Goering Parachute Panzer Division, then fighting in the east. Based at Utrecht, it is recorded that the regiment had previously used Apeldoorn and other locations north of Arnhem for training purposes – a fact well known to Allied intelligence. Early in September, it was

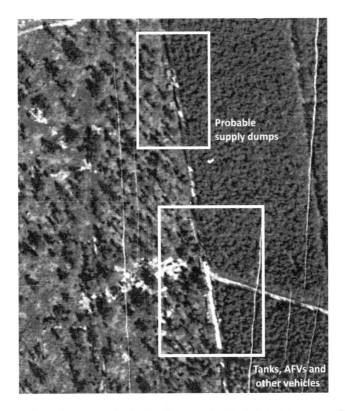

German tanks and armoured vehicles photographed by Flight Lieutenant Brian Fuge north of Arnhem on 12 September 1944.

allocated to the 1st Parachute Army, formed under Generaloberst Student with the aim of constructing a defensive line on the Albert Canal to block the British advance from Antwerp.

The regiment's Second Battalion (responsible for panzer, self-propelled gun and panzer grenadier training) was then sent south. It suffered heavy losses fighting at Hechtel between the 7th and the 10th but managed to extricate at least some tanks. On the 11th, all remaining Hermann Goering units were ordered to move from their bases to Eindhoven. The remnants of the Second Battalion were positioned north of the city. It is known that they were equipped with early model Panzer IIIs and IVs as these tanks were encountered near Son by 101st Airborne Division on the first day of Market Garden. Three were destroyed by Allied fighter-bombers; the remainder fled.

A possible scenario is that at least part of the Second Battalion was held back from the fighting at Hechtel – perhaps the less battle-worthy of their six companies – and was training north of Arnhem when orders for the move came through. It may well be that, in preparation, these elements refuelled and restocked from the dumps near Deelen, where they were photographed by Flight Lieutenant Fuge. The photographs subsequently produced for Brian Urquhart were probably maximum-scale enlargements of a single high-level frame.

How significant was the imagery? Although the tanks could have represented a potential threat to 1st Airborne Division, the issue was not straightforward. The appearance of modern tanks such as Panthers or Tigers in the photographs would certainly have provided grounds for serious concern, but the prevalence of older model Panzer IIIs and IVs could well have suggested that they belonged to a second-line unit of questionable combat capability. A reasonable conclusion might have been that the photographs reinforced the broader picture of German militarization in the Market Garden area but did not necessarily point to a specific threat from a first-line panzer formation at Arnhem.

The popular obsession with Brian Urquhart's story has caused historians to neglect other intelligence sources that might have been available to 1st Airborne Division before Market Garden. The enduring mythology is that 1st Airborne were sent into Arnhem without any prior knowledge of the presence nearby of II SS Panzer Corps. Hence their plans were designed only to cope with limited opposition. How accurate is this picture?

Within 1st Airborne Division the task of capturing the Arnhem road bridge (and the rail bridge) on 17 September 1944 was assigned to 1 Parachute Brigade, commanded by Brigadier Gerald Lathbury. After the war Lathbury was contacted by the official Cabinet Office historian and asked when and how he had first learnt that II SS Panzer Corps were in the Arnhem area. In his reply he referred to the planning for Operation Comet, in the week before Market Garden was initiated. 'During the initial briefing by the Corps Commander [Browning] the suspected presence of II [SS] Panzer Corps refitting in the area was mentioned.' The basis for this statement would again almost certainly have been the 5–7 September Enigma decrypts, suitably sanitized. Lathbury went on to say that no further reference to this formation had been contained in later briefings. 'I certainly never considered it in my plan.'[33] Nevertheless, it is at the very least certain that Browning *did* warn 1st Airborne Division of a potential threat. Moreover, contrary to Lathbury's account, there *was* further mention of II SS Panzer Corps in later intelligence reports. Among these, the most notable was 1st Airborne Division Planning Intelligence Summary 2 of 7 September 1944, which stated:

It is reported that one of the broken Panzer divisions has been sent back to the area north of Arnhem to rest and reüt; this might produce some 50 tanks … There seems little doubt that our operational area will contain a fair quota of Germans, and the previous estimate of one division may prove to be not far from the mark.[34]

Again, the words 'rest and refit' directly reproduced the terminology of the Enigma decrypts.

The divisional commander, Major General Urquhart, was initially far more reluctant than Lathbury to admit that he had received any prior intelligence on II SS Panzer Corps.[35] It is notable, however, that the post-operation report he prepared immediately after Market Garden was completely silent on this issue, which hardly suggests that he believed at the time that he had been seriously misled about the strength of German resistance at Arnhem. Moreover, when Urquhart published his memoirs in 1958, he did not at any stage claim to have been entirely ignorant of the presence of 9th and 10th SS Panzer. On the contrary, 'Dutch resistance reports had been noted to the effect that "battered panzer remnants have been sent to Holland to refit" and Eindhoven and Nijmegen were mentioned as the reception areas.'[36] Urquhart was quoting directly here from a corps-level report issued on 7 September.[37] Urquhart otherwise implied that I Airborne Corps controlled the distribution of intelligence and massively understated the threat: 'Browning himself told me that we were not likely to encounter anything more than a German brigade group supported by a few tanks.'[38] This was the estimate of German strength in the Arnhem area that Urquhart chose to employ at his orders group on 12 September.[39] Yet it is impossible to reconcile his account with Lathbury's frank admission that Browning *did* brief 1st Airborne about II SS Panzer Corps, nor does it accord with the calculation of enemy strength contained in the 7 September divisional intelligence summary.

In general, First Allied Airborne Army as a whole were poorly placed to make objective assessments of the ground situation in Holland in the week before Market Garden. To reiterate, although assigned the task of *executing* the airborne assault, Brereton and his staff (Browning excepted) played no part in devising the conceptual plan, and only Browning directly witnessed the deliberations which resulted in the enlargement of Comet into a multi-division operation on 10 September. We do not know whether he described this decision-making process accurately or in detail upon his return to England. Nevertheless, there is enough evidence in the surviving files to demonstrate that Browning issued a discouraging picture of German defensive preparations in the Market Garden area to Allied airborne commanders. The outline airborne plan that he drew up with Montgomery and Dempsey and which formed the basis of his initial brief to First Allied Airborne Army stated that 'there is every sign of the enemy strengthening the river line through Arnhem and Nijmegen'.[40]

First Allied Airborne Army received a limited amount of 'Ultra'.[41] Additionally, a member of their intelligence staff, Wing Commander Asher Lee, had previously worked in Air Ministry intelligence handling Ultra and had succeeded in retaining access to material that would not otherwise have reached the airborne. Yet it is not clear that such information as was obtained via this route added anything to the reports received on 5 and 7 September; indeed, after 7 September, II SS Panzer Corps did not reappear in the Enigma decrypts. In any case, denied the opportunity to influence the broader operation plan, Brereton was not in a position to exploit strategic intelligence, and he would also have known that Montgomery had access to Ultra and had nevertheless decided that Market Garden should proceed. Hence, on alerting Brereton to reports that German armoured formations were in the Arnhem area, Lee was ordered to refer the matter directly to 21st Army Group. He duly visited the Army Group headquarters but was unable to gain access to any officers of senior rank, and his warnings apparently fell on deaf ears.[42]

Otherwise, First Allied Airborne Army depended very heavily on 21st Army Group and Second Army for their supply of intelligence. The picture constructed within the airborne divisions on the basis of this information immediately after 10 September is reflected in a 1 Parachute Brigade summary that appeared on the 13th, and which pointed out that 'the whole Market area' was being 'feverishly prepared for defence' – a statement entirely in accord with Dempsey's diary notes of the 9th and 10th. There was said to be little information about German forces located around Arnhem at that time, but before the Normandy landings the area north of the town had been used for training armoured and motorized units and was thought to have contained some 15,000 troops, including 4,900 in Arnhem itself and a similar number at the nearby town of Ede. Some 2,000 Luftwaffe personnel were also thought to have been located at Deelen airfield, only a few miles to the north.

Since June there was likely to have been a reduction in training activity around Arnhem, and some troops had been moved from northern Holland into Germany. But others, the report noted, 'have come down to the Arnhem-Nijmegen area, if not further'. Of the formations previously identified in northern Holland, some had moved forward to the Albert Canal line, and some had gone southeast to face the Americans. But there were still thought to be troops 'staying in Nijmegen or possibly Arnhem'.

> Meanwhile, a reported concentration of 10,000 troops SW of Zwolle [40 miles north of Arnhem] on 1 September may represent a battle-scarred Pz Div or two reforming, or alternatively the result of emptying the Arnhem and Ede barracks to make room for üghting troops....[43]

This could hardly be described as a confident or encouraging assessment, and it was manifestly not a basis for supposing that 1st Airborne Division would encounter nothing more than 'a German brigade group supported by a few tanks'. It suggested that Arnhem had been important to the German military for some time, that up to 15,000 German troops had been stationed in the area only a few months earlier and that as recently as 1 September a 10,000-strong formation had been located not far to the north. It also specifically warned of the possibility that German units from northern Holland or other 'fighting troops' might have been moved to Arnhem. The reference to the 'battle-scarred Pz Div or two reforming' is further incontrovertible evidence that intelligence on the presence of II SS Panzer Corps *had* been passed down to the airborne divisions, 1st Airborne included.

It was presumably to update this appreciation that First Allied Airborne Army's assistant head of intelligence, Lieutenant Colonel Anthony Tasker, flew to France on 11 September. There, he visited 21st Army Group, Second Army, and XXX Corps. At this point, Dempsey's diary record should again be recalled, with its two explicit references to 'increasing [German] strength in the Arnhem-Nijmegen area'. We might expect in Tasker's reports to find details of the German reinforcements that so concerned Second Army's commanding officer. But in fact, Tasker received an entirely different picture: the threat had miraculously receded and the only German reinforcements to have appeared in the Low Countries 'had been put in to thicken up the line' they were attempting to form on the Albert Canal. Tasker found 'no direct evidence that the area Arnhem–Nijmegen is manned by much more than the considerable flak defences already known to exist'.[44]

Tasker's findings were conveyed too late to influence 1st Airborne Division intelligence on 12–13 September. But almost as soon as the 1 Parachute Brigade summary appeared on paper, 1st Airborne's divisional intelligence officer began presenting a more upbeat assessment. On the basis of Tasker's reports, he wrote, 'a more optimistic estimate can be made of enemy forces actually in the Divisional area'.

> The main factor, on which all sources agree, is that every able-bodied man in uniform who can be armed is in the battle – the Germans are desperately short of men and it is improbable that any formations capable of üghting will be found in an L[ine] of C[ommunication] area, however important it may be. The barracks and billeting areas in Ede and Arnhem are not likely, then, to contain üghting troops unless they are in transit from NW to SE or regrouping in the area, and there are precious few troops left in Northern Holland now to move. Identiücations in the Albert Canal area satisfactorily prove that practically all the enemy troops which could have been in Northern Holland are now actually engaged.[45]

The emphasis here on troops being moved from the north into Arnhem is striking and there can be little doubt that this section at least was written with the specific aim of dismissing the threat identified by 1 Parachute Brigade the previous day. Perhaps Tasker had shown the brigade (or an equivalent divisional) summary to his sources at 21st Army Group or Second Army headquarters. Whatever the truth is, one of its most problematic threat warnings was effectively eliminated within 24 hours – a bitterly ironic development given the role of the SS training battalion in the disaster that befell 1st Airborne Division on the afternoon of 17 September. In a similar vein it was also stated that,

> The garrison of the airüeld … will have been combed to provide üghting troops and will probably be considerably less than the estimate of 2,000 given in our previous summary.[46]

This very much more positive picture was reinforced by Tasker on the 15th, when he repeated that the only Germans arriving in Holland were being deployed straight to the front line. 'Large forces of airborne troops having the audacity to drop in daylight may well scare the enemy into a state of complete disorganization.'[47]

This series of documents again illustrates how intelligence was used between 10 and 17 September, initially to make a case for enlarging Comet into Market Garden, then conversely to prevent any objections being raised to the plan on the basis of anticipated German opposition. Yet the optimism emanating from 21st Army Group and Second Army was still to some extent tempered by more cautious judgements. The divisional report issued on 14 September did acknowledge that Arnhem was of strategic importance to the Germans, and the author believed that they would fight to hold both Arnhem and Nijmegen. He also drew attention to the fact that Arnhem was an important railway junction to which reinforcements could quickly be conveyed from other areas.

> One thing is certain – German reactions to a successful airborne landing in the Arnhem area will be immediate and to his [sic] maximum capacity. It is here that he is most favourably placed to produce troops from the East, North or West and any major reactions (which will include tanks) to the airborne armies' intrusion must be borne by 1st Airborne Division.[48]

And then there were the reports of German armour.

> Rather fragmentary Dutch reports conürm that there are twenty thousand German troops east of the Ijssel in the Hengelo-Bocholt-Cleve area where tanks have previously been reported. The same sources also state that defences are being prepared along the line of the [River] Ijssel.[49]

As with so many statistics provided by relatively untrained resistance or other civilian elements, the figure of 20,000 was probably exaggerated. But the precise numbers are less important than the reference to 'previous reports' of German armour, which again reflects the fact that 1st Airborne Division had already received warnings of a potential threat.

At the same time it is appropriate to ask whether such generalized intelligence appreciations might not have been strengthened and more sharply focused. This latter section of the 14 September summary bears a marked similarity to another warning transmitted the very same day by the Dutch resistance to MI6 in London – a warning that may also have been the catalyst for Beddell Smith's visit to Montgomery two days later. It should be noted here that the 1st Airborne Division report was essentially third-hand information – an edited précis by the divisional intelligence officer of material supplied to Tasker on the continent. The Dutch resistance report on the other hand contained 'raw' intelligence:

> SS Div Hohenstau— [9th SS Panzer Division] along Ijssel. Units from this division noticed from Arnhem to Zutphen and along road Zutphen-Apeldoorn. HQ perhaps at Eefde. Field fortiücations are being built along Ijssel.[50]

Given that the information came in both cases from Dutch sources, that it was in both cases issued on 14 September and that it focused in both cases on the River Ijssel, there can be little doubt that the two reports shared a common origin. But whereas the Dutch resistance signal clearly pointed to a threat *west* of the Ijssel and specifically linked the German formations concerned to Arnhem, the British summary subtly shifted the suspected German presence to the east bank of the river and completely ignored its proximity to Market Garden's primary objective. Enemy forces deployed 'east of the Ijssel' could still have been less than 20 miles from Arnhem. As already stated, 10th SS Panzer Division *had* taken up position on the east bank of the river, while 9th SS Panzer were on the west bank; a straight line drawn from Hengelo to Cleve would have passed only slightly to the east of the area occupied by 10th SS Panzer Division. A SHAEF summary suggested on 16 September that Bittrich's divisions had been withdrawn to the Arnhem area and were being refitted from a depot at Cleve and it is clear that similar intelligence had been received several days earlier, for the Market Garden Field Order (issued on the 13th) was accompanied by a map which showed near Cleve a location that 'may be pool for refitting Pz Divs'.[51]

What intelligence was available to 1st Airborne Division before 17 September 1944? Even the rather watered down summaries prepared from the information supplied to Tasker warned that substantial German formations, possibly including tanks, were located perhaps 20 to 30 miles from Arnhem. They also pointed out that the Germans would be well placed to bring reinforcements to Arnhem quickly once the fighting began, and they indicated that the town was of such strategic significance to the Germans that they were likely to fight hard to retain it. At the same time, the available intelligence suggested that there were unlikely to be many enemy combat troops *in* Arnhem when the airborne landings began. All of this was broadly correct. Moreover, while on 17 September 9th SS Panzer Division were closer to Arnhem than any of 1st Airborne's later reports indicated, this does not necessarily mean that Major General Urquhart and his senior staff were completely unaware of their presence. Indeed, Browning had informed them that II SS Panzer Corps might be in the Arnhem area and it is clear that 1st Airborne received other intelligence, including at least six air reconnaissance photographs, suggesting that German armour was in the vicinity. It may be that Browning did not repeat his warning, but equally there is no record that he withdrew it.

It was on this basis that Lathbury devised a battle plan for 1 Parachute Brigade 'based on comparatively minor enemy opposition of poor quality'.[52] Although the plan succeeded in so far as one parachute battalion reached the Arnhem road bridge, it was otherwise a lamentable failure. Yet this does not necessarily mean that a better plan might have been developed if either Lathbury or Urquhart had received clearer intelligence on the presence of II SS Panzer Corps. The truth is that 1st Airborne stood very little chance of executing any plan successfully if the Germans were able to react in strength around Arnhem or Nijmegen within hours of the initial airlift. The challenge of effectively exploiting the available intelligence on the two panzer divisions should not have been left to brigade, division or even corps commanders. It should have been factored into the higher-level deliberations about whether to target Arnhem or another Rhine crossing point. Objectively considered, the fact that Arnhem would involve not only the capture of the Waal bridges but also an early confrontation with Bittrich's troops should have tilted the balance decisively. But sadly the essential element of objectivity was decidedly lacking.

Hence the Market Garden intelligence legend, with its emphasis on the alleged neglect or suppression of operationally vital information, does not stand up to careful scrutiny. The true picture is more complex. Beginning at the top of the command chain, Montgomery initially exploited the information at his disposal quite logically: when it became clear that the Germans were reinforcing the Arnhem–Nijmegen area, he sought and obtained Eisenhower's backing for the enlargement of Operation Comet into Market Garden. Afterwards, however, he sought to ensure that the augmented enemy presence in Holland did not become a basis for halting the operation. In his defence it must be kept in mind that Market Garden involved three Allied airborne divisions whereas Comet had involved only one. This represented a far larger increase in the number of airborne troops in the proposed area of operations than in the number of German troops being reported by Allied intelligence. On the other hand, though, it would not be possible for the airborne to deploy at full strength until the three airlifts had been completed.

Montgomery's change of stance was presumably communicated to subordinate command levels, and a similar shift was certainly in evidence in numerous intelligence assessments prepared after Market Garden had been authorized. Browning returned from his meeting with Montgomery and Dempsey on 10 September and reported that the Germans were strengthening their defences around the airborne objectives; yet when Tasker afterwards visited 21st Army Group and Second Army to obtain more detailed information about enemy dispositions he could find few grounds for concern. The warnings contained in earlier reports did not disappear, but they could certainly have been reiterated in more direct and explicit terms and related more specifically to Market Garden's ultimate goal – Arnhem. It is difficult to avoid the impression that at least some of the later British reports 'massaged' the intelligence to a certain extent, so that it delivered a message broadly acceptable at the higher command levels.

This interpretation is supported by a further intelligence appreciation prepared by Second Army when, on 18 September, they received the MI6 report on 9th SS Panzer Division and their deployment along the River Ijssel. It is highly likely that, by this time, Second Army had already obtained broadly the same information directly from the Dutch; Tasker had been given intelligence on the Ijssel defences by British Army sources on the Continent, and Second Army had on 13 September recorded that 9th and 10th SS Panzer had 'been seen in small packets', although their exact geographical position was not mentioned.[53] Nevertheless, the 18th was the first occasion on which they referred specifically to 9th SS Panzer's location near the river. Yet while they now acknowledged the division's presence, they chose not to reproduce the MI6 report in its entirety:

> From Arnhem there is no deünite news ... But further north, digging is reported on the banks of the rivers Waal and Ijssel, in the latter case at Olst and Wijhe. Civilian sources report that 9th SS Panzer Division is located along the Ijssel River, but it cannot be the whole division, for part of it is known to be in the Escaut Canal area northeast of Neerpelt.* A reasonable guess to account for its

* By this time, the forward elements of 9th SS Panzer Division had been encountered by XXX Corps during their advance from Neerpelt.

identiücation in both places is that the elements on the Ijssel River were sent there to recover from the effects of the long retreat, leaving behind them such troops as were still capable of continuing the struggle without a refresher.[54]

This assessment was partially accurate but it is impossible not to be struck by the near-reflex tendency of Second Army's intelligence staff to play down the threat by emphasizing that the elements of 9th SS Panzer spotted along the Ijssel did not represent the entire division, and by implying that they were less than battle-worthy. Furthermore, although the report sent to MI6 had related the threat directly to Arnhem, the Second Army summary once again failed to do so. Indeed, the sections of the MI6 report that specifically placed units from 9th SS Panzer 'from Arnhem to Zutphen and along road Zutphen-Apeldoorn' were omitted. Yet this intelligence suggested that elements of the division might be positioned within 15 miles of Market Garden's primary objective.

However, it would be wrong to suppose that British commanders from Montgomery down to Urquhart or even Lathbury completely discounted any threat from II SS Panzer Corps near Arnhem after 10 September. Rather, their mistake was that they underestimated the residual fighting capability of the two very battered panzer divisions and, most of all, the speed of their reaction after the first airborne landings. As Montgomery himself wrote,

> The 2nd SS Panzer Corps was reütting in the Arnhem area ... We knew it was there. But we were wrong in supposing that it could not üght effectively; its battle state was far beyond our expectation.[55]

At the same time, he no less fatally overestimated the fighting prowess of 1st Airborne Division and the speed of XXX Corps's advance up the airborne corridor. His assumption was that 1st Airborne would establish strong defensive positions around the Arnhem bridges and that two heavily depleted panzer divisions were unlikely to overwhelm them before they were relieved. He was wrong on both counts.

Notes

1. Kershaw, *It Never Snows in September*, pp. 16, 28, 38.
2. Ibid., p. 78.
3. *Airborne Operations: A German Appraisal*, Ofüce of the Chief of Military History, Department of the Army (US Army Foreign Military Studies Series, 1950), pp. 54–55.
4. Kershaw, *It Never Snows in September*, pp. 108–112, 119–120.

5. WO 171/376, Appendix A, Captured Order for Defence of the Rhine Crossings, 15 September 1944.

6. Kershaw, *It Never Snows in September*, pp. 38–43; Buckingham, *Arnhem*, pp. 52, 101–102.

7. F.H. Hinsley, E.E. Thomas, C.A.G. Simkins and C.F.G. Ransom, *British Intelligence in the Second World War: Its In8uence on Strategy and Operations*, Vol. 3, Part 2 (Her Majesty's Stationary Ofüce, London, 1988), p. 386.

8. Kershaw, *It Never Snows in September*, p. 41.

9. Ibid., p. 102.

10. Ibid., pp. 304–306.

11. WO 219/605, Annex 1a to Field Order 3 for Operation Linnet, G2 estimate of enemy situation, 30 August 1944.

12. WO 285/3, Second Army Intelligence Summary, 1 September 1944.

13. WO 285/3, Second Army Intelligence Summary, 2 September 1944.

14. Kershaw, *It Never Snows in September*, pp. 11–13.

15. WO 285/3, Second Army Intelligence Summary, 3 September 1944.

16. Kershaw, *It Never Snows in September*, p. 38.

17. DEFE 3/221, XL 9188, 5 September 1944.

18. DEFE 3/221, XL 9245, 6 September 1944.

19. Kershaw, *It Never Snows in September*, p. 38.

20. Hinsley, *British Intelligence in the Second World War*, Vol. 3, Part 2, p. 386.

21. Ibid., p. 384. For details of Ultra circulation during the campaign to liberate Northwest Europe, see pp. 780–786 and 975–978.

22. WO 285/3, Second Army Intelligence Summary, 6 September 1944.

23. Ibid.

24. WO 171/341, intelligence summary 494, 7 September 1944, and intelligence summary 496, 8 September 1944.

25. Lamb, *Montgomery in Europe*, pp. 224–225.

26. C.B. Macdonald, *The Siegfried Line Campaign* (Ofüce of the Chief of Military History, Washington, 1965), p. 122.

27. Buckingham, *Arnhem*, pp. 76–77, 95.

28. Ryan, *A Bridge Too Far*, pp. 85–87.

29. Brian Urquhart, *A Life in Peace and War* (Harper & Row, New York, 1987), p. 71.

30. Ibid., p. 72.

31. Ibid., p. 73.

32. This analysis can be consulted in more detail in Sebastian Ritchie, *Arnhem: The Air Reconnaissance Story* (Ministry of Defence, 2015), pp. 9-26.

33. CAB 106/1133, Lathbury to Harris, 5 April 1954.

34. WO 171/393, 1st Airborne Division War Diary, Planning Intelligence Summary 2 of 7 September 1944.

35. CAB 106/1133, Urquhart to Harris, 22 November 1952.

36. Urquhart, *Arnhem*, pp. 19–21.

37. WO 171/341, XXX Corps intelligence summary 494, 7 September 1944. 'Dutch resistance sources report that battered Panzer formations have been sent up to Holland to reüt, and mention Eindhoven and Nijmegen as the reception areas.' Correspondence in this üle indicates that the report was sent by XXX Corps to I Airborne Corps, who presumably then passed it to 1st Airborne Division; see GSI XXX Corps to HQ Airborne Troops, 091345.
38. Urquhart, *Arnhem*, pp. 19–21.
39. CAB 106/1133, pp. 64–65.
40. WO 219/4998, Operation Sixteen Outline Plan, 10 September 1944.
41. For example, the distribution code 'GU' on the two Ultra decrypts of 5 and 6 September shows that they were sent to First Allied Airborne Army; see DEFE 3/221, XL 9188 of 5 September 1944 and XL 9245 of 6 September 1944.
42. Lamb, *Montgomery in Europe*, p. 225; Harclerode, *Arnhem*, pp. 44–45.
43. WO 219/5137, 1 Parachute Brigade Intelligence Summary No. 1, by Capt W.A. Taylor, 13 September 1944.
44. AIR 37/1217, Information from Northern Group of Armies, Second Army and XXX Corps, as at 11.00 hrs, 12 September 1944, by Lieutenant Colonel A. Tasker, G-2, FAAA, 12 September 1944.
45. AIR 37/1217, Operation Market, 1st Airborne Division Planning Intelligence Summary No. 2, dated 14 September 1944, prepared by G2 (I), 1st Airborne Division, 14 September 1944.
46. Ibid.
47. WO 219/4998, Enemy Situation on Second Army Front, report by Lieutenant Colonel A. Tasker, 15 September 1944.
48. AIR 37/1217, Operation Market, 1st Airborne Division Planning Intelligence Summary No. 2, dated 14 September 1944, prepared by G2 (I), 1st Airborne Division, 14 September 1944.
49. Ibid.
50. CAB 106/1133, Netherlands Military Attaché to Harris, Cabinet Ofüce Historical Section, 30 March 1953.
51. WO 219/1924, SHAEF intelligence summary 26 of 16 September 1944; AIR 37/1217, Headquarters Troop Carrier Forces, US Army Air Forces, Field Order No. 4 for Operation Market, 13 September 1944. Curiously, there was no elaboration on this subject in the accompanying intelligence brief.
52. CAB 106/1133, Lathbury to Harris, Cabinet Ofüce Historical Section, 5 April 1954.
53. WO 285/4, Second Army Intelligence Summary, 13 September 1944.
54. WO 285/4, Second Army Intelligence Summary, 18 September 1944.
55. Montgomery, *Memoirs*, p. 297.

Part 2: Conclusion

ONTGOMERY HAS TOO often been presented as a near-peripheral figure in the events of September 1944. Some British authors still have great difficulty accepting that he is a legitimate target for criticism and instinctively point the finger of blame elsewhere. Yet the foregoing chapters clearly demonstrate that virtually every aspect of the Market Garden operation plan was critically influenced by decisions taken at the top of 21st Army Group. Montgomery (ably assisted by Dempsey and Browning) effectively established a very restrictive conceptual framework for his operation, which in turn profoundly affected detailed planning. His notion that after the Normandy landings frequent airborne operations could be mounted at very short notice also contributed significantly to some of the identified 'planning failures' for which First Allied Airborne Army has so often been held responsible, as did his self-imposed isolation, which additionally created the conditions in which Browning became influential despite his lack of operational experience.

Lacking any direct contact with Brereton or his staff, Montgomery had no knowledge of the range, weather, command, control and communication problems that would potentially accompany an airborne Rhine crossing mounted from England. No plan requiring multiple airlifts made sense given the growing strength of German defences around Arnhem and Nijmegen, but, astoundingly, Montgomery and Browning managed to design Market Garden around a lift timetable that would literally have been impossible for First Allied Airborne Army to implement. Browning also brought back from 21st Army Group a hopelessly flawed plan for the deployment of the most southerly of the three airborne divisions. In other respects, the Market Garden concept merely reproduced glaring weaknesses in the Comet plan. The ultimate operational objectives were nearly as deep; the key axis of advance remained the single narrow road with its innumerable obstacles; the lack of suitable DZ/LZ areas near the Arnhem bridge objectives – an issue identified as early as 5 September – became more problematic; the number of tasks confronting the airborne troops around Nijmegen remained wholly excessive. None of these deficiencies were the responsibility of First Allied Airborne Army, yet all were to play their part in Market Garden's failure.

Beyond this, the process whereby British commanders sought to play down any threat posed by German forces near the airborne objectives also began with Montgomery. His response to the deteriorating intelligence picture involved enlarging Comet into Market Garden on the assumption that the greater number of airborne troops deployed around Arnhem and Nijmegen would be sufficient to deal with II SS Panzer Corps. Consequently, he dismissed subsequent warnings about German armour in the Arnhem area, and the staffs of 21st Army Group, Second Army and XXX Corps followed his lead, rejecting or watering down unpalatable reports and assessments. Even 1st Airborne Division elected not to give serious consideration to the various reports that they received on the refitting panzer divisions near Arnhem.

Had airborne warfare proved more effective in the past – had the airlifts been more accurate, had the level of mission success been higher or had casualty rates been lower – there might have been stronger grounds for accepting the enormous risks involved in Market Garden. But the Allied experience of airborne operations had in fact been fraught with difficulty, as we have seen. Hence in the planning process there was, if anything, a necessity for risk reduction or, at the very least, risk management. Yet instead, risks were allowed to accumulate throughout Montgomery's plan in an entirely uncontrolled way. This would have been a hazardous approach under any circumstances, but it was courting disaster in an operation such as Market Garden, in which a failure to secure any one objective implied the failure of the operation as a whole.

PART THREE

The Allied Air Forces and Market Garden

Introduction

THE HISTORIOGRAPHY OF Operation Market Garden is punctuated by numerous disagreements over details – over the roles of particular personalities such as Montgomery, Browning and Urquhart, over the actions of formations like XXX Corps or 82nd Airborne Division, or over the relative importance of key occurrences in the Arnhem battle or in XXX Corps' advance north. But while debate continues about events on the ground, there is broad agreement in much of the published literature that the Allied air forces played a decisive part in the operation's failure. This consensus has been reached on the basis of three main lines of argument: first, the RAF insisted on landing 1st Airborne Division too far from their objectives at Arnhem; second, the airlift was spread out over an excessively long period; third, inadequate air support was provided to the ground and airborne troops.

Surprisingly, despite their supposedly crucial contribution to the Allied defeat, these issues have hardly ever been subjected to detailed scrutiny or analysis. Most historians appear content with the notion that Market Garden was primarily ruined in the air, rather than on the ground. The aim of the following chapters is to rectify this imbalance by carefully examining the allegations so consistently levelled at the air forces. Chapters 3.1 and 3.2 offer the first ever detailed study of the circumstances that governed the selection of the Arnhem DZ/LZ areas; among other things they assess the role of intelligence in DZ/LZ selection and the largely neglected relationship between planning for Operation Comet and for Market Garden. They also address the associated issues of 1st Airborne Division's battle plan for 17 September 1944 and the German response. Chapter 3.3 examines the no less controversial subject of the Market Garden airlift plan, exposing the standard critique of First Allied Airborne Army's lift schedule to a sceptical investigation that is long overdue. It also considers the manner in which the available lift capacity was employed on the first two days of the operation. Chapters 3.4 and 3.5 cover the subject of air support, surveying the background to the problems encountered during Market Garden, Allied air dispositions in theatre and air command and control, before providing a blow-by-blow analysis of the air battle based on British, American and German records.

3.1. The Arnhem Landing Areas: Operation Comet

IN THE MYTHOLOGY of Market Garden, the selection of DZs and LZs for 1st Airborne Division occurred shortly after Browning presented his outline operation plan to First Allied Airborne Army on 10 September 1944. Desk-bound RAF planners allegedly forced Urquhart to accept a landing area west of the town, near Wolfheze, that was too far from his bridge objectives. The distance from this area to the bridges is held to be primarily responsible for the operation's failure. The most potent weapon in the airborne arsenal – tactical surprise – was needlessly thrown away; 1 Parachute Brigade were confronted by a long march into central Arnhem, and the Germans were given ample opportunity to deploy blocking forces before the airborne troops neared their ultimate objectives. Consequently, only about 740 troops (chiefly from Lieutenant Colonel John Frost's 2 PARA) reached the road bridge, and they had been overwhelmed by the time XXX Corps began their northward advance from Nijmegen. The implication is that the bridge would have been held until XXX Corps' arrival at Arnhem if only a larger airborne force had landed nearby.[1]

This line of argument dates back to Urquhart's original after-action report but has since been repeated in the vast majority of published histories of Market Garden. Buckingham's study of the Arnhem battle is typical:

> It should be remembered that a scratch force of less than 700 men, built around two companies of Lieutenant Colonel John Frost's 2nd Parachute Battalion, succeeded in holding out around the north end of the Arnhem road bridge for three and a half days. Consider what a single, or indeed two full brigades might have achieved had they been delivered almost directly to the same location at the outset of Market.[2]

Historians regularly cite the memorandum drawn up by the War Office and the Air Ministry after Operation Husky in 1943, which is simplistically said to have ruled that airborne operations be considered air operations until the airborne troops hit the ground. On this basis, it is maintained that the RAF exercised 'untrammelled control over the air side of airborne operations'.

The result was an airborne planning machine totally controlled by the RAF, in which the planners formulated their schemes totally divorced from any operational considerations but their own, and with no requirement to act upon, or even acknowledge, those of the airborne soldiers tasked to carry them out.'[3]

In particular, the RAF supposedly possessed the power to overrule airborne commanders over the location of DZs or LZs – a facility that the commanding officer of 38 Group, Air Vice-Marshal Hollinghurst, exercised in Market Garden, despite strident protests from 1st Airborne. The RAF's determination to locate the landing area at Wolfheze is said to have been motivated by a self-interested desire to protect their aircraft from Arnhem's anti-aircraft defences. Yet the threat of flak was grossly exaggerated. The Allied air forces should have delivered 1st Airborne Division into the area immediately south of the road and rail bridges. Such arguments are invariably employed in an attempt to show that primary responsibility for 1st Airborne's failure rests with the RAF.[4] However, they are constructed on a basis that is not merely superficial and misleading, but in many respects factually inaccurate.

Throughout the Second World War, drop zone selection proved to be one of the most problematic aspects of airborne warfare. It will be recalled that in the early years the German airborne tended to stage landings directly onto enemy airfields, or in their immediate vicinity. But while this approach at first worked very well, the targeting of airfields in western Holland and Crete ended in disaster. When the Allies sought to mimic German tactics in North Africa they were spared heavy casualties only by the absence of significant resistance on the ground. Another appalling selection decision involved 2 PARA's mission in Tunisia in November 1942, when a DZ was chosen some 15 miles from the ultimate objective at Oudna. In Sicily poor drop zone selection played a part in creating a near-impossible night navigation task for American troop carrier crews, and the British Air Landing Brigade were directed to put their gliders down in terrain covered by potentially lethal obstacles. In Normandy, in both the American and British sectors, DZs were chosen that were either close to or within flooded areas.

In Operation Varsity – the Rhine crossing in March 1945 – glider LZs were selected by 6th Airborne Division which were in certain respects too close to their objectives. They were found by the glider pilots to be shrouded in smoke, generated partly by the ongoing battle and partly by the British Army's smoke-screen over the Rhine, and the landings also ran into strong opposition in the form of German flak and small arms fire.[5] Chaos ensued: 6th Airborne's glider lift went so badly wrong that the airborne troops lost 46 per cent of their jeeps, 44 per cent of their trailers, 50 per cent of their light tanks, 50 per cent of their 25-pounder artillery pieces, 56 per cent of their 17-pounder anti-tank guns, 56 per cent of their weapon carriers, and much else besides. Moreover, during the first critical hours of Varsity, between 20 and 30 per cent of the equipment ultimately recovered was unavailable for battle.[6] It should be noted here that not one of the zones employed in these operations was chosen by airmen, except to the extent that the German airborne arm was part of the Luftwaffe. Rather, the catalogue of selection errors was very largely the responsibility of the airborne forces themselves.

Allied airborne doctrine did not address the issue of DZ/LZ selection in any detail. The joint War Office and Air Ministry memorandum on the employment of airborne forces merely stated that 'the dropping zone should be an easily recognisable area rather than a pin point chosen for tactical reasons'. Otherwise, the only ruling of some relevance was that,

> Airborne troops should not be landed in an area where active operations are in progress, nor should they be routed over a heavily defended area (enemy or friendly), unless the vital importance of their objectives justifies the acceptance of heavy losses.[7]

American doctrine declared almost in one breath that 'the route for troop carrier aircraft should be selected so as to avoid anti-aircraft fire' but that 'the objective should be sufficiently close to the landing area to ensure surprise'.[8] But what procedure should be employed if these two criteria proved difficult to reconcile? On this point no guidance was forthcoming.

It is perhaps surprising, given the difficulties described, that the selection of airborne landing areas appears not to have generated much argument. Equally, while issues such as air navigation and DZ marking featured prominently and repeatedly in airborne after-action reports, little attention was paid to the question of where DZs should be located or to such issues as their topographical suitability. The first recorded objections raised to a proposed LZ came from the Glider Pilot Regiment and the RAF prior to Operation Husky, but these were ignored by the airborne forces.[9] In the aftermath of Husky, the joint War Office and Air Ministry memorandum may well have sought to increase air force influence within the airborne planning process, but its impact was in fact very limited. There were, for example, legitimate concerns within the RAF about the likely difficulties involved in navigating to DZ V in eastern Normandy, but, as a drop in the vicinity of DZ V was deemed operationally essential by 6th Airborne Division, the risks were apparently accepted without dispute.[10] In April 1944 staff at Allied Expeditionary Air Force Headquarters criticized the location of the Neptune landing areas on several grounds. It was argued that some airborne troops would be landing so close to enemy forces that they were likely to come under attack before they had formed up, that troop carriers would have to be routed over defended areas to reach their assigned DZs and that some of the DZs chosen might well be obscured by fires, lights and smoke produced by naval or air bombardments. There was some basis for all of these objections and they were supported by several Allied doctrine papers, but none exerted the slightest impact on the airborne plans.[11]

Otherwise, the only serious controversy of some relevance was concerned more with routing than with specific DZ/LZ selection. Yet it is worth considering because historians have sometimes contended that the RAF's behaviour on this particular occasion was characterized by exactly the same self-interest as supposedly emerged during the planning of Market Garden.[12]

The extensive revision of American airborne plans for western Normandy on 27 May 1944 – barely a week before D-Day – was described earlier in this study (see page 60). The two airborne divisions, previously destined for quite separate and distinct locations, were now to be dropped in adjacent landing areas. Confronted at the last moment by this new scheme, the Allied Air Commander-in-Chief, Air Chief Marshal Leigh-Mallory, warned of the threat posed by German air defences and produced an estimate of probable casualties among the USAAF troop carriers and glider tugs amounting to 50 per cent.[13] This figure would ultimately prove to be a massive overestimate in relation to the number of aircraft destroyed, although 'casualties' in terms of aircraft destroyed or damaged in the parachute and glider missions did amount to 30 per cent.[14]

Most Allied commanders anticipated far higher casualties on D-Day than were actually incurred. Moreover, although Leigh-Mallory placed his concerns before Eisenhower, it is clear from the surviving records that his position in the Allied Command chain did not give him sufficient authority to block the American airborne operations, and he afterwards fully acknowledged his mistake.[15] His anxiety is nevertheless easy to understand. He had that day been presented with new intelligence suggesting a substantial increase in German defences in western Normandy, which implied some similar strengthening of their air defences. The new airborne plan originally envisaged routing the two US divisions via a single approach to the DZs. An enormous stream of aircraft would thus have been required to fly east over 20 miles of enemy-occupied territory and it should be recalled that, at this time, Allied air and land commanders assumed that the airborne operations would be launched in clear weather or not at all. The troop carriers would be flying in close formation, straight and level, at low speed and at low altitude. Clearly the 82nd Airborne formations at the rear of the stream would in these circumstances have been exceptionally vulnerable.

In the event casualties were limited partly by action upon which Leigh-Mallory himself insisted: the troop carriers were routed to their DZs in two parallel streams, thus reducing 82nd Airborne Division's potential exposure to flak.[16] Otherwise, the cloud cover across western Normandy provided valuable but completely unexpected protection. Nevertheless, the basic issue that Leigh-Mallory identified was far from insignificant: anti-aircraft fire throughout 9th TCC's extended overland approach played a major part in the wide dispersion of the American parachute drops.[17] Leigh-Mallory's stance was thus in no way self-interested (he was, after all, an RAF officer, whereas the dispute related to USAAF aircraft). On the basis of the most up-to-date intelligence available he identified a genuine problem, which exerted a profound influence on the execution of the American airborne missions on 6 June.[18]

Beyond this one episode and the altercation between Leigh-Mallory and Montgomery over Operation Wild Oats later in June,* the planning of airborne operations in the Second World War did not give rise to serious inter-service friction. Yet history now implies that the selfish pursuit of narrow single-service interests by the Allied air forces was to blame for what is deemed the most fundamental flaw in the Market Garden plan – the location of the Arnhem landing areas. How fair is this judgement?

Arnhem was first selected as the objective for Montgomery's proposed Rhine crossing on 4 September. That morning, Browning held a meeting with the principal airborne and air commanders involved, and afterwards travelled to France to meet Montgomery and Dempsey. He returned to England on the 5th, but telegraphed Dempsey that evening to advise him that it had not been possible to identify any suitable DZs or LZs near the bridges at Arnhem and Nijmegen. For this reason, *coup-de-main* operations were being planned to capture them; the main airborne formations would land outside the two towns.[19] On the following day, written orders for Operation Comet were issued, which included sketch maps showing the same principal landing areas as were ultimately used in Market Garden.[20] It is therefore clear that the Arnhem DZs and LZs were identified between the morning of 4 September and the evening of 5 September and were not the subject of lengthy deliberations. Beyond this, sadly, no official records relating to their identification have ever been found. Nevertheless, the fact that this issue arose several days before Comet was transformed into Market Garden is clearly an important part of the story. By 10 September Arnhem was already well known to be a highly problematic objective where landing area selection was concerned; it

* See Chapter 1.3

is quite possible that this factor helped persuade Browning that a switch to Wesel should be considered.*

During the deliberations on Comet it appears that Hollinghurst raised objections to staging daylight landings close to the bridges; his reasoning was presumably supported by the Air Officer Commanding 46 Group. In the case of Nijmegen, Hollinghurst's stance has never generated any controversy. Broadly the same landing zones proposed for Comet were subsequently employed in Market Garden by 9th TCC and 82nd Airborne. But where both operations were concerned, the airborne troops had so many objectives beyond central Nijmegen that it would have been almost impossible for them not to have dropped near one or another. It was simply accepted that the Waal bridges would have to be dealt with later.[21]

In the case of Arnhem, the circumstances were rather different. The landing zones selected for Comet were located in an area, which at its nearest point was around five miles west of the road bridge; at its furthest point it was seven miles. The equivalent distances from the rail bridge were three and five miles. According to the report prepared by Major General Urquhart after Market Garden, the established practice in choosing landing areas was that they should be no more than five miles from the objective. Hence, at the very most, the landing areas extended two miles beyond this limit and it is therefore hardly accurate to describe them as 'distant'. Ideally, nonetheless, an area closer to the road bridges would have been preferable.

Hollinghurst has recently been portrayed as some kind of pen-pushing functionary who had no knowledge of the realities of airborne warfare,[22] yet nothing could be further from the truth. He was actually one of the most experienced members of the British airborne community – far more experienced than Urquhart, who knew nothing of air power and had never executed an airborne operation plan before Market Garden. Moreover, before September 1944, Hollinghurst's work with the airborne forces had not been characterized by inter-service bickering but rather by the closest possible collaboration. The Glider Pilot Regiment commander, Colonel Chatterton, recorded that it was to Hollinghurst that he 'owed the virtual existence and success of the regiment, and he made it a reality'.[23] General Sir Richard Gale, former commander of 6th Airborne Division in Normandy, held similar views:

I next met him [Hollinghurst] when, as commander of the 6th Airborne Division, I had to work in very close co-operation with him when he was AOC of the now famous 38 Group. 'Holly's' keenness and his original and

* See Chapter 2.2.

inspired methods of training of his pilots meant that one of the greatest airborne operations went off with the success that is now well known.[24]

The two officers began their collaboration some ten months before the Normandy landings, initially to address the problems encountered during Operation Husky.[25] Later, in April 1944, they established a combined planning room near 38 Group headquarters at Netheravon, where all the key details of the Normandy operation were developed. And on the night of 5/6 June Hollinghurst would not have been found sitting safely pushing pens behind his desk, for he was in fact airborne in one of the pathfinder aircraft over Normandy.[26]

It is clear that Hollinghurst did not enjoy with Urquhart anything like the close relationship that he had with Gale. The reasons for this have never been properly established, but it can hardly have helped that 38 Group's headquarters was located in the West Country whereas 1st Airborne Division set up base in Lincolnshire. Equally, while the long build-up to Normandy created scope for months of mission-specific joint planning, in September 1944 there was minimal time to orchestrate a similar approach. This was one of the many handicaps imposed on First Allied Airborne Army by the decision to stage a Rhine crossing at exceptionally short notice. Nevertheless, Hollinghurst's earlier record demonstrates that he was in no way averse to intimate collaboration with the airborne forces.

To understand Hollinghurst's position as Comet was evolving into Market Garden it is first necessary to bear in mind two fundamental points. First, transport aircraft and glider combinations are slow, unwieldy and very vulnerable; they are particularly vulnerable in airborne operations, which have to be executed at low altitude. Moreover, the Dakotas – the backbone of the Allied air transport fleet in 1944 – were equipped neither with armour nor with self-sealing fuel tanks. Transport aircraft may of course derive some security from escort fighters or aircraft assigned to the suppression of enemy air defences, but both aircrew and passengers also depend for their protection on the responsible air commander, who must ensure that his forces are appropriately employed. Inevitably this means that the exercise of air command partly involves determining precisely when air forces may not be committed. It may be that a proposed course of action does not conform to extant rules of engagement, or stretches or even exceeds the technical parameters of the aircraft; or it may be that the operation exposes air platforms to exceptional risks in relation to such operational benefits as are expected to accrue. Whatever the exact circumstances, the air commander periodically has the difficult and unpopular task of holding up the red card – a fact as true today as it was during the Second World War.

Air Vice-Marshal Leslie Hollinghurst, the Air Officer Commanding 38 Group

Second, the enduring lessons derived by the Allied air forces from airborne operations in Sicily and Normandy had largely been concerned with the inaccuracy of the various airlifts. Sicily had been a disaster; for the USAAF Normandy was generally perceived to have been a failure and for the RAF it had been, at best, only a partial success. As we have seen, Brereton was appointed to command First Allied Airborne Army with a specific brief from Eisenhower to improve the standard of troop carrier navigation. It was thus inevitable that this issue should have loomed particularly large in the minds of Allied air planners in September 1944. The decision to stage operations such as Linnet, Comet and Market Garden in daylight went a long way towards eliminating one of the main problems that had previously confronted the Allied air forces. But by opting for daylight operations the Allies were consciously taking far greater risks with enemy air defences than they had accepted in the past. This was especially the case with Comet and Market Garden, given that their objectives lay so far inside enemy-occupied territory and so close to the German frontier. Apart from the casualties involved, it could be expected that anti-aircraft fire would yet again break up the airborne formations and drive them off course.

Had the Allies acquired more experience in mounting daylight airborne operations in support of earlier campaigns, it is possible that different decisions would have been taken. But since the North African fiasco daylight landings had been limited to the evening missions on 6 June in Normandy and the second lift in Dragoon, and neither of these ventures provided a sound basis for predicting the outcome of a daylight assault around Arnhem and Nijmegen. They did not involve deep objectives, nor were they confronted by comparable enemy air defences. Equally, no previous airborne objective had been located at or even near a substantial enemy-held conurbation. Hence there was literally no scope for determining how effective such counter-measures as evasive routing or flak suppression might be, and it was by no means certain that Allied escort fighters would succeed in preventing interference by the Luftwaffe. There was only the available intelligence on German air defences, the knowledge that transport aircraft made very easy targets and the experience of how even limited flak in Sicily and Normandy had scattered the troop carrier formations, resulting in widely dispersed and inaccurate drops.

With tactical surprise, a massive counter-flak effort, equally substantial fighter escort cover and a route plan that carefully avoided known flak concentrations, it would ultimately transpire that the first airlift could take place relatively safely. But in early September 1944 there was no prior experience that might have enabled the air force planners to foresee this happy outcome. Moreover, it is documented that, because Arnhem lay so far inland, they did not expect to attain outright tactical surprise. The Comet air warning order stated,

> Tactical surprise is extremely unlikely and the enemy will undoubtedly have knowledge of the approach of Troop Carrier formations either by radar alert or visual reconnaissance.[27]

This was not an unreasonable assumption. It will be recalled that the Germans were confronted by a very similar problem in 1940 when planning their operations around The Hague. Furthermore, even if an initial airlift achieved surprise and emerged relatively unscathed, the Germans could subsequently be expected to mobilize their air defences against any follow-up lifts or air re-supply missions. Arnhem's distance from RAF and USAAF fighter bases and its proximity to Germany would increase the dangers still further.

In summary, although Hollinghurst evidently held strong views on the location of the Arnhem and Nijmegen DZ/LZ areas, his concerns extended far beyond tactical planning issues. He was opposed to the entire concept of mounting a deep airborne operation against a defended objective in daylight – a point he spelled out to Leigh-Mallory verbally on 5 September and in writing on the 6th.[28] The vast majority of modern-day airborne planners would accept the validity of Hollinghurst's objections. On the other hand, he was willing to attempt limited *coup-de-main* operations near to the main bridge objectives if they could be executed under cover of darkness. He was not prepared to consider such tactics in daylight; equally, it is very unlikely that he would have agreed to mount the Pegasus Bridge *coup-de-main* in daylight.

What, then, were the more direct influences on DZ and LZ selection at Arnhem? The procedure by which Allied airborne operations were planned has been described as a reverse process. Following the identification of the operational objective, the first planning issue was normally deemed to be the selection of the landing zones; this had to take place immediately. Once the landing area had been determined, a flight plan could be drawn up; the flight plan in turn largely dictated the allotment of airborne troops to airfields in England.[29] Where Comet and Market Garden are concerned, however, it

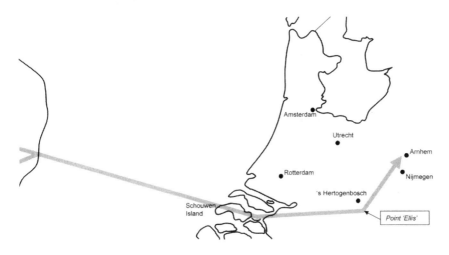

Map 10: The northern Operation Comet airlift route, later used for 1st Airborne Division in Market Garden

appears that the flight plan exerted at least some impact on the choice of DZs and LZs; in other words, the 'reverse process' was itself reversed. This can be deduced from the fact that the northern air route devised for Comet and ultimately assigned to 1st Airborne Division in Market Garden did not follow a direct easterly path from England to the Arnhem area, but instead tracked southeast to the Dutch islands before turning east to route across the mainland. This course was maintained up to an initial point labelled 'Ellis' about three miles south of 's Hertogenbosch. From Point Ellis the route veered sharply northeast to Arnhem (see Map 10).

The routing was entirely dictated by the need to avoid known concentrations of German anti-aircraft guns as well as main roads along which mobile flak might be encountered.[30] Flak clearly represented the primary threat to the effectiveness and security of the Comet and Market Garden airlifts, and evasive

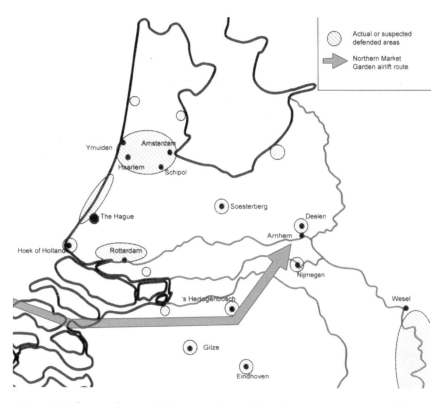

Map 11: The northern airlift route planned for Operation Comet and later used for 1st Airborne Division in Market Garden, showing actual or suspected German flak deployments (based on an RAF flak map dated 3 June 1944, Air Historical Branch)

routing was thus one of the fundamental principles on which both operation plans were based. Here, it is necessary to bear in mind Holland's geographical position between Britain and Germany. The vast majority of Allied bomber formations bound for Germany flew over Holland and for this reason a substantial network of air defences had long been located there. The RAF flak maps show that in northern Holland the strongest of these defences were sited around Rotterdam, The Hague and Amsterdam. It was therefore essential for the airborne formations to track south of Rotterdam and to maintain a course south of other potential threat areas such as Dordrecht, 's Hertogenbosch, and the various roads that ran parallel to the Waal and the Lower Rhine (see Map 11).

It was this routing that necessitated the abrupt northward turn up to Arnhem from Point Ellis; but the sharp change of course was also required to

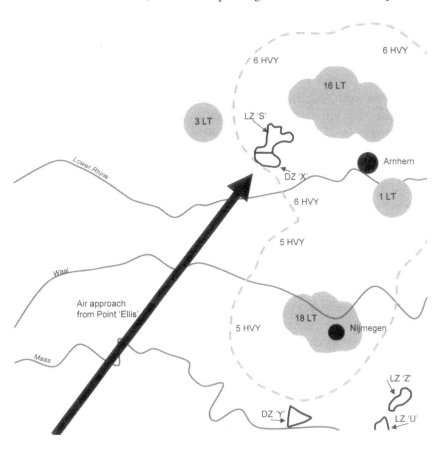

Map 12: A flak map prepared for Operation Comet, also showing the proposed DZ/LZ locations and the air approach route from Point Ellis to the Arnhem landing area

avoid flying directly over Nijmegen or the area between Arnhem and Nijmegen, where aircraft would potentially have been vulnerable to anti-aircraft fire from both towns. In other words, aircraft bound for Arnhem might have found themselves under fire throughout much of their final approach from Point Ellis. From the air forces' perspective this consideration could only have lent weight to arguments for using landing areas west of Arnhem. A course to the west would keep the airlift clear of German air defences at Nijmegen and would also avoid light flak at Arnhem, although the proposed DZs and LZs were still believed to lie within range of heavy flak concentrations. This routing would also have enabled aircraft to execute a simple north-westerly turn away from the main threat areas after the drop had been made, whereas any alternative course would have involved an egress directly over Arnhem or Nijmegen, or the danger of a possible incursion into German airspace.[31]

Given the more general Allied concerns about anti-aircraft fire during the air transit across Holland – the legitimacy of which cannot be contested – it is hardly surprising that enemy flak dispositions at Arnhem and Nijmegen also influenced the selection of specific DZs and LZs. Indeed, it would have been both inconsistent and illogical to expend so much effort on evasive routing if flak threats near the airborne objectives were then to be ignored. Allied intelligence reports stated that there was a flak battalion at Arnhem and a flak map obtained by 1st Airborne Division on 6 September noted 'heavy concentrations at Deelen airfield, Arnhem and Nijmegen – respectively 30 light and 24 heavy guns, 36 light and 36 heavy guns, 24 light and 12 heavy guns'. These numbers were expected to increase.[32] No record of the precise location of German anti-aircraft guns at Arnhem has survived from the period when Comet was planned, but the limited mapping available points to substantial deployments slightly to the north of the town.[33] On the 3rd a number of Luftwaffe airfields in Holland, including Deelen, were targeted in a large day raid by Bomber Command. The attacks had nothing at all to do with flak suppression or with Operation Comet; the airfields were targeted because they were being used by tactical support aircraft that had been withdrawn from northern France.[34] The raid clearly resulted in some temporary reorganization of Deelen's flak batteries, which was picked up in Allied air reconnaissance imagery after a few days. From this source it was initially concluded that Deelen's anti-aircraft defences had been removed, but this assessment was subsequently revised. A flak estimate produced by First Allied Airborne Army on 12 September recorded: 'Flak is apparently still present in rather large quantity, there being seventeen (17) heavy guns and fifty-five (55) light guns shown as [sic] occupied positions on the latest photo cover.'[35]

It thus made eminent sense to ensure that the airlift routed well clear of Deelen; consequently no serious consideration was given to potential landing areas north of Arnhem.[36] But as DZs or LZs in this vicinity would have been very vulnerable to counter-attack by 9th SS Panzer Division, it can hardly be argued that they would have been more suitable than the areas near Wolfheze that were actually chosen. The country south of the Lower Rhine was clearly studied far more carefully, and the Arnhem and Nijmegen anti-aircraft defences unquestionably played some part in persuading the air planners that this area should be avoided. If locations south of the bridges had been chosen, the transport aircraft would subsequently have had to fly straight across the main German flak concentrations just north of Arnhem (at 300 feet and at speeds of between 100 and 150 mph).

But it is by no means certain that this was the decisive consideration. In fact, Hollinghurst recorded that 'the overriding reason for disregarding the southern bank of the Rhine' was the terrain, which was typical Dutch polder, criss-crossed by dykes and drainage ditches and prone to flooding in some places.[37] Allied appreciations of the topography of this area are usually said to have been based on aerial photographs and the reports of Dutch liaison officers. Recently, however, the existence of this intelligence has been called into question on the basis that none of the relevant documents has ever been located.[38]

This is a perfect illustration of the poor scholarship that has blighted the historiography of Market Garden over the years. If the records concerned had been buried in some obscure corner of the UK National Archives, the proposition that there was actually no genuine topographical intelligence might be more defensible. But in fact, the nature of the terrain south of the Arnhem bridges is very well described in 1st Airborne Division's War Diary – perhaps the most obvious of all Market Garden reference sources. Annex A to 1st Airborne Division's Planning Intelligence Summary of 5 September 1944 stated that 'the areas between the Waal and the [Lower] Rhine and south of the Waal are mainly flat, dyked clay polderland, intersected by innumerable drainage ditches'. According to their Planning Intelligence Summary of 7 September, the smallest of these ditches were 5–6 feet wide, while the largest were 12 feet wide. 'The wider ditches may be vaulted with a 12-foot pole, which is the practice in the Royal Dutch Army.'[39] A post-war official account refers in even more detail to the terrain features south of Arnhem, suggesting that the author at the time had access to material that has since been lost or destroyed. According to this study,

> The land here is divided by ditches into areas of around 50 to 100 metres in width and 100–200 metres long. The ditches are 2–3 metres wide and 1½ deep with usually ½ metre of water in them.[40]

It is difficult to believe that such a detailed description could simply have been invented.

In any case, elaborate intelligence assessments are not required to demonstrate that this area was unsuitable for airborne operations. All the detailed period maps of Arnhem (such as, for example, the maps included with the various Market Garden after-action reports) vividly illustrate the problem with the terrain (see Map 13). No responsible Allied commander could conceivably have authorized a substantial assault glider landing into such extensively subdivided country. To have done so would have involved a high risk of serious damage to the gliders and their cargoes, injury or worse to their passengers and acute difficulties unloading and transporting vital equipment.[41] According

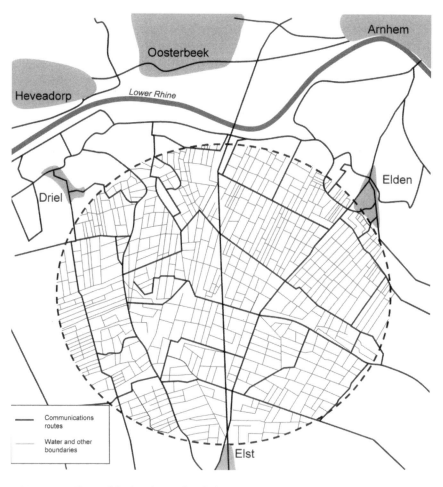

Map 13: The polderland south of the Lower Rhine at Arnhem (based on Report by First Allied Airborne Army, Operations in Holland, September to November 1944, 22 December 1944, mapping at Appendix 2)

to Hollinghurst this was fully appreciated by what he termed 'the glider people', who 'felt they could not land closer in' than the Wolfheze area.[42]

It is sometimes maintained that paratroops could and should have been dropped in this area independently of the gliders. Yet there is no record that any such course of action was suggested by or on behalf of 1st Airborne Division at the time. There were clearly concerns that the terrain features, which effectively ruled out a large-scale glider landing, would also pose serious problems for the parachute brigades. Past experience – particularly in Normandy – had illustrated the dangers of ignoring topographical intelligence and none of the British planners could have failed to note that the country south of the Lower Rhine replicated very closely the conditions of the western Dives valley, with its mass of streams and irrigation ditches and its propensity for periodic inundation. As Hollinghurst put it, 'We had some experience on D-Day in 'V' Zone of the dangers of releasing heavily laden paratroops over such country.'[43]

The first paratroops to drop would of course have been the pathfinders. The decision to stage Comet and Market Garden in daylight in no way reduced the importance that the British airborne community attached to their role and there was always a possibility of the airlifts encountering marginal visibility conditions – especially the early morning or late afternoon lifts scheduled for Comet. The pathfinders' failure in Normandy had misled aircraft bound for DZ K and was partly responsible for scattering the formations sent to DZ V far and wide, and the lesson drawn from the experience was that more rather than fewer pathfinders were required in future. 'Greater accuracy might have been achieved if there had been more insurance in the shape of more pathfinder teams for each dropping zone.'[44] Consequently, the Arnhem landings were ultimately assigned twice as many pathfinder aircraft as were allocated to 6th Airborne Division in Normandy.[45] In Normandy the pathfinders failed to illuminate DZ V primarily because of the nature of the surrounding terrain, which resulted in the loss or breakage of equipment and prevented half the force from reaching and marking the drop zone before the main airlift reached the French coast. The officers who planned later airborne operations can hardly be blamed for seeking to learn lessons from this debacle.

However, there was another very obvious argument against landing the paratroops and gliders at separate locations. As one Neptune planning document put it,

Paratroops may be dropped in zones unsuitable for glider landings ... On the other hand paratroops, once landed, lack striking power. If, therefore, a balanced military force is to be dropped it will be necessary for the paratroop force to be dropped in the area in which the glider-borne force is landed.[46]

The paratroops were in fact dependent on a glider-borne divisional infrastructure and also employed gliders for the carriage of their vehicles, equipment and supplies. Ultimately, for example, some 43 gliders were assigned to 1 Parachute Brigade at Arnhem.[47] The five anti-tank guns employed in the defence of the road bridge were all conveyed to Arnhem by glider; without them the bridge would have been recaptured far more rapidly. Hence, to put paratroops down some miles away from the gliders and on the other side of the Lower Rhine would have substantially weakened their combat capability, particularly if events then prevented a link-up. The fragmentation of the British airborne, which ultimately played such a large part in their destruction, would have commenced even before they hit the ground.

After Comet had metamorphosed into Market Garden plans were drawn up for the Polish Parachute Brigade to drop onto an area just south of the Arnhem road bridge on the third day of the operation (19 September), while their gliders employed either the main LZ at Wolfheze on the 18th or separate fields on the other side of the village on the 19th. Ostensibly this might appear to support the case for a 1st Airborne Division parachute drop to the south of the Lower Rhine. Yet it is important to bear in mind the context in which the Polish mission was devised. The intention was originally that 1st Airborne Division would relinquish their hold on the Wolfheze landing area after the second airlift on 18 September and withdraw to a perimeter line just outside Oosterbeek; hence an alternative drop zone had to be found for the Poles. Sosabowski's troops were tasked with taking up positions on the eastern edge of Arnhem, so they would obviously have favoured a more easterly DZ, even if the terrain was far from suitable. As long as 1st Airborne succeeded in establishing firm control of Arnhem by the time the Polish paratroops arrived, they would have no great difficulty linking up with their glider-borne elements. Equally, it could be expected that 1st Airborne Division would by then have put all German anti-aircraft units in Arnhem out of commission. Indeed, they were assigned this specific objective by the Market Garden operation instructions, which stated,

> You will do all in your power to destroy the flak in the area of your DZs, LZs and Arnhem to ensure the passage of your subsequent lifts.[48]

Urquhart would later confirm this point to one of the official historians:

> You were right in assuming that the DZ for the third [i.e. Polish] lift just south of the Arnhem road bridge was chosen because it was assumed that by then the flak in the town would have been overcome.[49]

The flak defences in Nijmegen would also have been overwhelmed by Allied ground forces by this time.

In summary, the Polish plan was designed to deal with a very different scenario from that which was expected to confront 1st Airborne Division when they staged their initial landings at Arnhem. For a number of reasons it was not a plan that would have appealed to the British airborne, and its inherent disadvantages were all too graphically illustrated (as events turned out) by the fact that the Polish paratroops never made contact with their glider-borne headquarters and support infrastructure or with any of their heavy equipment.

*   *   *

It is impossible to judge whether the flak threat at Arnhem would have been accepted by Allied planners if the terrain south of the road bridge had been more suitable. But the prospect of heavy and extended anti-aircraft fire, combined with yet another chaotic glider landing and further terrain-related problems, was evidently decisive. There had simply been too many failed airlifts in the past for these risks to be accepted. So the search moved north of the river. The country east of Arnhem was no more attractive than the south, while landings to the north were ruled out for the reasons already noted. To the west, Arnhem was bordered by extensive suburb and woodland completely unsuitable for parachute drops or glider landings. The first substantial stretch of open ground was the area actually chosen at Wolfheze.

Notes

1. Buckingham, *Arnhem 1944*, p. 231.
2. Ibid., p. 91.
3. Ibid., p. 9.
4. Ibid., pp. 83–91.
5. Warren, *Airborne Operations*, p. 178.
6. Otway, *Airborne Forces*, pp. 304–305, 318.
7. Extract from Joint War Office/Air Ministry Report on the Employment of Airborne Forces, Part A, Lessons of Airborne Operations in Sicily, Appendix D to Appendix V/19, Wing Commander W.D. Macpherson to SASO, 27 November 1943, Notes on the Planning and Preparation of the Allied Expeditionary Air Force for the Invasion of North West France in June 1944, appendices.
8. Extract from US War Department Training Circular 113, Appendix V/8/1, Notes on the Planning and Preparation of the Allied Expeditionary Air Force for the Invasion of North West France in June 1944, appendices.
9. Tugwell, *Airborne to Battle*, p. 157; Warren, *Airborne Missions in the Mediterranean*, p. 23.

10. Report by 38 and 46 Group RAF on the British Airborne Effort in Operation Neptune, HQ 38 Group, October 1944.
11. Memorandum on the Employment of Airborne Forces in Operation Overlord, April 1944, Appendix V/8, Notes on the Planning and Preparation of the Allied Expeditionary Air Force for the Invasion of North West France in June 1944, appendices.
12. Buckingham, *Arnhem*, p. 69.
13. Notes of a conference held at SHAEF, 27 May 1944, Appendix V/45, Notes on the Planning and Preparation of the Allied Expeditionary Air Force for the Invasion of North West France in June 1944, appendices.
14. Calculated from Warren, *Airborne Operations*, p. 224. A total of 1,324 missions were flown and 399 aircraft troop carriers or glider tugs were damaged or destroyed.
15. Leigh-Mallory to Eisenhower, 7 June 1944, Appendix V/60, Notes on the Planning and Preparation of the Allied Expeditionary Air Force for the Invasion of North West France in June 1944, appendices. Leigh-Mallory's acknowledgement was written before the inaccuracy of the American landings was fully appreciated.
16. Notes of a conference held at SHAEF, 27 May 1944, Appendix V/45, Notes on the Planning and Preparation of the Allied Expeditionary Air Force for the Invasion of North West France in June 1944, appendices.
17. Warren, *Airborne Operations*, p. 79.
18. Notes on the Planning and Preparation of the Allied Expeditionary Air Force for the Invasion of North West France in June 1944, by PS to C-in-C, AEAF, p. 297. On 28 May Leigh-Mallory told Montgomery that 'since the American pilots were mostly untried in active service conditions, the formations would be likely to break up when they came under fire, and the troops would be dropped over a very wide area. He thought that only a very small proportion would be able to provide effective opposition to the enemy – certainly not more than 50%, possibly less.'
19. CAB 44/253, p. 69.
20. AIR 37/979, 38 Group Operation Order 524, 'Comet', 6 September 1944.
21. Ryan, *A Bridge Too Far*, pp. 89–90.
22. Buckingham, *Arnhem*, pp. 84–85, 232.
23. Chatterton, *Wings of Pegasus*, p. 241.
24. *The Times*, 12 June 1971.
25. Royal Air Force Airborne Assault Operations, 1940–45, Vol. 1, minutes of a meeting held at Norfolk House on 10 August 1943 to discuss future policy relating to the employment of airborne forces.
26. AP 3231, *Airborne Forces*, pp. 118, 125.
27. WO 205/850, Advanced Headquarters 9th Troop Carrier Command, Warning Order for Airborne Operation, 6 September 1944.

28. AIR 37/775, Hollinghurst to Leigh-Mallory, 6 September 1944.

29. Report by 38 and 46 Group RAF on the British Airborne Effort in Operation Neptune, HQ 38 Group, October 1944.

30. AIR 25/589, Appendix D to 38 Group Operational Order 524, 6 September 1944.

31. This point is best illustrated by AIR 37/1214, Appendix D, Headquarters Troop Carrier Command Intelligence Trace No. 4 for Operation Market; the equivalent map for Operation Comet is contained in WO 205/850.

32. WO 171/393, 1st Airborne Division Planning Intelligence Summary 1, 6 September 1944.

33. See flak map in WO 205/850, Advanced Headquarters 9 Troop Carrier Command, Warning Order for Airborne Operation, 6 September 1944.

34. WP (44) 539, Memorandum by the Secretary of State for Air, 21 September 1944, summarizing Bomber Command operations for the four weeks ending 10th September (held at AHB).

35. This assertion appears in Harclerode, *Arnhem*, pp. 64–65, and was based on imagery gathered by a 541 Squadron Spitfire on 6 September; for the correction, see WO 219/4997, HQ First Allied Airborne Army, Flak Estimate, Operation Market, prepared by Major T.J. Lowe, 12 September 1944.

36. Otway, *Airborne Forces*, p. 293.

37. AIR 37/1214, Allied Airborne Operations in Holland, September–October 1944; Hollinghurst papers, AC 73/23/49, comments on AHB monograph on the history of the airborne forces, p. 2.

38. Buckingham, *Arnhem*, p. 85.

39. WO 171/393 1st Airborne Division War Diary, September 1944.

40. Air Historical Branch, *The Liberation of North West Europe Vol. 4, The Breakout and the Advance to the Lower Rhine, 12 June to 30 September 1944*, p. 169, note 1.

41. Hollinghurst papers, AC 73/23/49, comments on AHB monograph on the history of the airborne forces, p. 2.

42. Ibid., p. 3.

43. Ibid., p. 2.

44. Otway, *Airborne Forces*, pp. 199–200.

45. AP 3231, *Airborne Forces*, pp. 124, 155.

46. Memorandum on the Use of Aircraft to Accelerate the Concentration of Land Forces in 'Operation Overlord' and for their subsequent supply, Appendix V/17, Notes on the Planning and Preparation of the Allied Expeditionary Air Force for the Invasion of North West France in June 1944, appendices.

47. Urquhart, *Arnhem*, p. 217.

48. Urquhart, *Arnhem*, p. 209.

49. CAB 106/1133, Urquhart's comments on Chapter VII, section III.

3.2. The Arnhem Landing Areas: Market Garden

THE RATIONALE THAT underpinned the initial selection of the Wolfheze landing area for Comet was reinforced in every respect during the planning of Market Garden. To begin with, 1st Airborne Division's mission at Arnhem became primarily a glider operation rather than a parachute drop – another issue that has been ignored by the vast majority of historians. On 17 September, 321 assault glider sorties were scheduled for Arnhem compared to 155 parachute sorties; on the following day a further 296 glider sorties were flown but only 126 parachute sorties.[1] It is absurd to contend that so many gliders could possibly have been brought down safely in the country south of the Arnhem bridges. The diagrams prepared afterwards depicting the precise location of every single glider on the main Wolfheze LZs present a picture of extraordinary complexity and confusion (see Map 14). Yet the landings were ultimately successful because the LZs were sufficiently large, firm and open. By contrast, an attempt to put down 300 or more heavily laden assault gliders into the polder south of the Lower Rhine would have been akin to a swarm of insects seeking to fly through a very large spider's web. Moreover, after the landings, 1st Airborne would have found their subsequent unloading, assembly and movement impeded by literally hundreds of minor water obstacles.

Secondly, Allied intelligence indicated that German flak dispositions were being strengthened throughout the Market Garden area. As early as 7 September XXX Corps recorded that heavy and light flak at both Arnhem and Nijmegen was increasing considerably. 'Guns getting into position (with vehicles and pits under construction) can be seen on several photos and there is railway flak at Arnhem.'[2] The 1st Airborne Division intelligence report of the 14th noted a substantial increase in flak deployments since early September: at Arnhem there were by this time estimated to be 73 light flak positions occupied and a further 31 unoccupied, while there were also 17 heavy emplacements occupied and 6 unoccupied. New flak positions had appeared in the immediate vicinity of the Arnhem bridges. At Deelen, some 57 light positions were occupied and 13 unoccupied; there were 17 heavy positions

A Stirling tug taking off for Arnhem with a Horsa glider in tow

1st Airborne Division gliders at Wolfheze

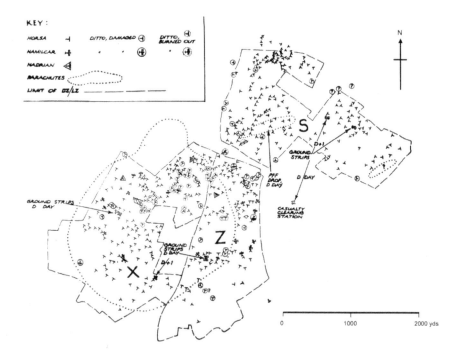

*Map 14: Plot of 1st Airborne Division glider landings at Arnhem on
17 and 18 September 1944*

occupied and 12 unoccupied.[3] These developments would have been
worrying enough under any circumstances, but the build-up of German flak
around Arnhem and Nijmegen gave cause for particular concern because it
was suspected of being far from coincidental. It is important to bear in mind
that, by the time this report was written, elements of Second Army had been
positioned in northern Belgium awaiting an Allied airborne assault on
Arnhem for ten days, and that, for much of this period, they had been
engaged in a series of actions against German forces in the area. Maintaining
operational security in this environment proved extremely difficult. As the
report stated,

> From the German point of view the chief nigger in the wood-pile is the
> FAAA [First Allied Airborne Army]. And so while the hastily formed new
> divisions go south to protect the Reich from the invading American armies,
> all available flak is concentrated in Arnhem, Nijmegen and the ideal landing
> sites in the area of Deelen airfield to discourage the launching of the much
> heralded airborne armada in so vital an area....

It is odd, if one thinks of it, this heavy build-up of flak to protect bridges which are at least as important to us as to the enemy. They cannot suppose that we would bomb them to prevent the escape of 25,000 disorganized troops. The guns are curiously sited and the concentration unduly heavy if their main purpose is to protect the supply line or escape route of what 21st Army Group consider is a low priority battle area. Perhaps as usual the Germans have misappreciated our intention and they really do think we wish to destroy the bridges which we photograph but do not bomb, or perhaps they perceive as we have that the bridges are a suitable airborne target. Even if they do not realize this, the security for the operation has been so appalling that some breeze must have reached them. There cannot be many troops in XXX Corps in contact with the enemy who have not been warned of an impending airborne operation. Some thirty thousand fully briefed personnel, including aircrews, have been unleashed. Telephone security goes from bad to worse and avoidable breaches of security which, prior to D-Day, would have incurred a severe penalty, now pass unchecked.[4]

Similar but less overtly stated concerns almost certainly lay behind a letter Hollinghurst addressed to Williams on 11 September, in which he drew attention to air photographs showing 'that the heavy flak around the three towns in which we are interested has approximately doubled during the last two days.'[5] On 14 and 15 September there was a heated exchange between Hollinghurst and Browning over a serious breach of security involving the leakage of one potential Market Garden launch date to airborne troops at a 38 Group airfield,[6] and Hollinghurst would later recall the concerns he had shared with Browning over operational security:

> There was always the risk that if security was blown, the Germans might have deployed mobile flak on the route, when with such 'sitting birds' as glider trains, casualties would have been much higher than they were. We were, of course, working under the Americans, and their security measures were hardly the same as ours. I certainly, and also I think Browning and AOC 46 Group, thought that there was a strong possibility something might leak out.[7]

It is only in this context that the Allied air forces' anxiety about German anti-aircraft artillery can be appreciated properly. Officers such as Hollinghurst and Williams were not merely concerned about routine enemy anti-aircraft provisions. By mid-September they had to consider the possibility that the airborne formations would be confronted by flak batteries forewarned of their approach and deployed with a specific counter-airborne role in mind. The inaccurate terminology employed by 21st Army Group to explain German strategy in Holland, typified by such terms as 'low priority battle area', made other potential explanations for the augmented flak defences appear implausible.

Some of the rights and wrongs of the Allied intelligence picture were considered earlier in this book. Breaches of security there certainly were, but, while the Germans were expecting an Allied ground offensive in Holland, they appear not to have identified Arnhem as a potential *airborne* objective. However, Luftwaffe records do confirm that flak was being strengthened in the Market Garden area as a direct result of the decision early in September to establish a new forward defensive line between Antwerp and Maastricht. Both the formation and sustainability of this line depended upon the integrity of the communication routes behind it. Presumably because these were felt to be vulnerable to air interdiction, orders were issued to strengthen anti-aircraft defences at key points. On 5 September, Luftgau Belgium-Northern France Field Headquarters received orders 'to put A.A. [anti-aircraft] artillery into the German western position to provide defence against air attack for troops fighting there, and also to cover defiles, bridges, etc. on supply routes'. The headquarters was specifically instructed to protect the area 'between Antwerp and Maastricht'.[8] The lines of communication serving the more westerly sector of this region ran directly through Arnhem and Nijmegen, and could have been severed if their vital bridges over the Lower Rhine and the Waal had been destroyed. This doubtless explains why they were singled out for the additional flak cover noted by Allied intelligence.

In his memoirs Urquhart would strongly imply that the threat of flak was exaggerated, and this view has been expressed in far more explicit terms by other former 1st Airborne Division personnel. Many historians have accepted their arguments uncritically.[9] Yet their recollections hardly provide a reliable basis for gauging the true extent of Arnhem's flak defences. It is true that the first Arnhem lift encountered only moderate flak and did not lose a single aircraft to enemy action, but this was not because there was no flak at Arnhem. It was because the RAF took the most meticulous care to route 1st Airborne around the majority of known flak concentrations. To bring an immense formation of vulnerable transport aircraft flying at slow speed and low altitude safely across nearly 100 miles of enemy-occupied territory was an outstanding feat, and one of the most remarkable achievements of the Market Garden air plan. Surprisingly, however, few officers from 1st Airborne appear to have had any understanding of the exceptional measures taken on their behalf by the Allied air forces.

In addition to evasive routing there was also the extensive flak suppression effort, to which both the RAF and the USAAF contributed, and these operations shed some light on the true nature of the air defences over central

Arnhem on 17 September. According to the most vivid account left by one of the squadrons involved,

> At first the job sounded rather [like] a suicide affair, being a wing attack on heavy flak positions at Arnhem ... ignoring all opposition and pressing home the attacks no matter what came up at us ... The first types over Arnhem received a very hot reception from heavy flak which the later arrivals could see from some miles away.[10]

Of course, the aircraft involved enjoyed an immeasurable advantage over troop carriers and glider tugs in that they were fast and highly manoeuvrable: Mosquitos and Typhoons would typically fly at speeds of between 300 and 400 mph while attacking ground targets, whereas, during an airborne drop, Dakotas flew at 120 mph while maintaining straight and level flight in formation below 500 feet. Nevertheless, the ground-attack squadrons did not emerge unscathed. Three Mosquitos were shot down over Arnhem on 17 September and several others were hit; an RAF Mustang was also lost.[11] At the same time, the German anti-aircraft batteries evidently sustained considerable damage. The diarist of B Flight, 247 Squadron, recorded that 'not one target escaped its load'.[12] On 18 September the commanding officer of 4 Parachute Brigade discovered a wrecked flak train at Wolfheze railway station, dangerously close to the landing areas. The train had been 'destroyed by own air sp [support] [which] indicated threat to B[riga]des arrival happily averted'.[13]

There were mercifully few examples early in Market Garden that demonstrated the acute vulnerability of low-flying air transport formations to anti-aircraft fire. But on the first day of the operation, while crossing the front line, 101st Airborne Division lost 23 aircraft and a further 143 sustained damage. Later, the situation changed somewhat: as XXX Corps advanced, aircraft in the south of the corridor encountered rather less opposition, whereas 38 Group and 46 Group, operating at its northernmost extreme, became far more vulnerable to interception. On 17 September the effective combined strength of the two groups amounted to 371 aircraft; by 25 September they had lost 55 aircraft, and 350 more had been damaged. In other words, the number of aircraft destroyed or damaged actually exceeded their original first-line strength. Comparable figures for 9th TCC record some 1,173 aircraft committed to Market Garden on 17 September and total casualties (aircraft destroyed or damaged by 25 September) amounting to 932, of which 87 were listed as 'destroyed or missing'.[14] There could be no clearer illustration of the severity of the flak threat over Holland during the operation, nor any better justification for the Allied air forces' insistence on employing as many counter-measures as possible.

The myth that there was 'no flak at Arnhem' is often propagated alongside another claim to the effect that Urquhart was 'overruled' by Hollinghurst in the selection of the Arnhem DZs and LZs. Strident protests from 1st Airborne about the 'distant' landing areas are said to have been peremptorily brushed aside. Although the precise facts may never be established, this depiction of events is unquestionably exaggerated. The key decisions concerning the location of the landing areas were apparently taken on 11 September. No official record of the decision-making process survives, but Urquhart's version of events is as follows:

> I should have liked to put in troops on both sides of the river and as close as possible to the main bridge. This was unacceptable to the RAF, however, because of the flak barrage which bomber crews on their nightly visits to the Ruhr reported as extremely heavy in the Arnhem area. It was also considered that the tug aircraft, in turning away after releasing their gliders in this area, would either have run straight into the flak over Deelen airfield some seven miles to the north or into a mix-up with the aircraft involved in the Nijmegen airlift. Furthermore, the intelligence experts regarded the low-lying polderland south of the bridge as unsuitable for both gliders and parachutists.[15]

In at least one published account this passage is transformed into a record of a specific meeting at which Urquhart's proposals 'encountered strong opposition from the commander of 38 Group RAF, Air Vice-Marshal Leslie Hollinghurst'.[16] The reader is left with the impression of a major confrontation between the two officers. Yet in reality Urquhart never maintained that any such thing had happened. He did not even record that he proposed alternative landing areas; he merely stated that he would have preferred them. It is certainly very difficult to believe that he would seriously have advocated parachute drops or glider landings north of the river onto an urbanized area.

Generally speaking, as a historical source, Urquhart's recollections are far from satisfactory. He did not describe particular deliberations on any precise date with Hollinghurst or any other named RAF officer, and he conveyed the utterly false impression that the issues involved were entirely novel. He avoided any mention of the fact that the Wolfheze DZs and LZs had already been selected for Comet – something that would obviously have exerted an important influence on any decisions taken for Market Garden. Given that on 11 September it was still expected that the operation might be launched as early as the 14th, there would inevitably have been very strong grounds for adhering to the established plan.[17] Beyond this, Urquhart's assertion that the intelligence on German anti-aircraft defences was based purely on the observations of RAF bomber crews appears almost calculated to mislead, suggesting as it does a far more approximate intelligence acquisition process than was actually employed. It also conflicts with Urquhart's own after-action report, in which he stated specifically that the flak assessment was prepared by both RAF and Army intelligence staff.[18] Furthermore, as he must have known, their main source was a very substantial quantity of air imagery gathered during the preceding days. Here at least some official records have survived: the photographic interpretation reports are still liberally scattered through the files and are also frequently referred to in minutes, memoranda and correspondence.[19]

Major confrontations between senior operational commanders are normally well recorded in the official records. For example, Hollinghurst's opposition to Operation Comet is so recorded, along with the subsequent disagreements over 101st Airborne Division's tasking around Eindhoven.[20] If Urquhart genuinely believed that the success of his mission was being jeopardized by the location of 1st Airborne Division's DZs and LZs at Wolfheze, he had a duty to raise this issue not merely with Hollinghurst, but at higher levels of his command chain. He had plenty of time to do so between the initiation of Operation Comet on 4 September and its expansion into Market Garden a week later. Yet there is absolutely no record that he took any such action.

By far the most likely explanation for this is that there was actually very little disagreement over the location of the landing areas. Neither in his memoirs nor at any other time did Urquhart claim to have challenged the RAF's stance. In correspondence with the Cabinet Office historian in 1952 he went so far as to say that their objections to a landing south of the bridges were entirely justified: 'The RAF, I think, quite rightly were not prepared to fly into this defended zone.'[21] On the basis of the intelligence available, Urquhart's senior subordinates apparently took a similar view. As he put it, 'Generally, the brigadiers appeared not unhappy with the task confronting us.'[22] The recollection of Major General Sosabowski, commander of the Polish Parachute Brigade, was identical. 'I remember Urquhart asking for questions and nobody raised any', he recalled. 'Everyone sat nonchalantly, legs crossed, looking bored.'[23] Equally, according to Frost's memoirs, the plan was not challenged at battalion level.[24]

After the failure of Market Garden it was convenient for 1st Airborne to argue that the division had fallen victim to the RAF's unfounded fear of German flak. Everyone, it seems, appreciated that they were landing too far away from their objectives; everyone recalled arguing strenuously that different landing zones were needed. This is typical of the way that soldiers respond to the failure of any undertaking to which they have been committed, and it should not give much cause for surprise. Far more remarkable is the fact that historians have attached so much credence to the parochial recollections of junior officers and NCOs who inevitably had little grasp of the many diverse and complex factors that shaped the operation plan.[25]

The only more senior officer who (many years later) recalled making specific high-level representations about the landing area was the Glider Pilot Regiment commander, Colonel Chatterton. But Chatterton's approach was made not to the RAF but to Browning, and was concerned not with the general airlift but with the cancelled *coup-de-main*. Chatterton did not suggest attempting a full-scale glider assault south of the road bridge. Moreover, Browning refused to pass on Chatterton's proposals to the RAF. He merely cited RAF opposition to a daytime *coup-de-main* as the reason for its cancellation and informed Chatterton that it was too late to introduce further revisions to the airlift, as indeed it probably was.[26] If this was the channel through which objections to the Arnhem DZ/LZ locations were raised, then the issue of their rejection would appear to have had as much to do with Browning as with the RAF.

In this regard, it is important to understand that Browning's position in the British command chain left divisional commanders like Urquhart with far less influence over operation plans than their American counterparts. As we have seen, Browning secured overall control of the two British airborne divisions at the end of 1943 as Commander Airborne Troops, while, by contrast, the Americans chose not to appoint an equivalent commander in Europe until August 1944. Hence, in the top-level planning meetings that preceded Neptune, such as the Airborne Air Planning Committee, the US airborne would usually be represented by at least one and sometimes two divisional commanders, whereas Browning invariably spoke for the British airborne divisions, which were rarely represented by their own commanders or even by their staff.[27] And, while American divisional representation at such committees continued even after the formation of XVIII Corps HQ, British practice similarly remained unchanged. Thus, not one single 1st Airborne Division officer went to the initial First Allied Airborne Army conference on Market Garden on 10 September, whereas the meeting *was* attended by the commander of 82nd Airborne and by the Deputy Commander of 101st Airborne. As usual, the British airborne voice was that of Lieutenant General F.A.M. 'Boy' Browning alone.[28]

The total absence of British divisional representatives at such crucially important gatherings can only be considered extraordinary. It suggests either that the division commanders were completely confident of Browning's ability to promote their interests, or, far more probably, that he actively discouraged their attendance or even prohibited it altogether. Some such action would have been entirely consistent with his acute sensitivity regarding his relations with the divisional commanders, and with his determination to emphasize his seniority and absolute authority within the British airborne hierarchy, as well as his personal responsibility for directing British airborne operation plans. Furthermore, the documents demonstrate that he was intimately involved in the development of 1st Airborne Division's plans at Arnhem from the very beginning, and that this involvement extended to the issue of DZ/LZ selection.* If Urquhart had been doubtful about any aspect of the plan, he would have been unable to approach Brereton (as American divisional commanders like Taylor did), nor would he have enjoyed direct access to other senior British officers such as Dempsey or Montgomery himself. Literally everything had to be channelled through Browning.

* * *

Apart from the intelligence on German flak and the terrain south of the Arnhem bridges, there were three factors that may to some extent have made the landings at Wolfheze appear less daunting than historians have invariably supposed. Firstly, it is important to remember that 1st Airborne had objectives in Arnhem other than the bridges over the Lower Rhine. Buckingham asserts that 'The Arnhem portion of Market Garden failed … because the bulk of 1st Airborne's first lift did not manage to reach the Arnhem road bridge at all.'[29] Yet 1 Air Landing Brigade – one of the two brigades conveyed by the first lift – were never even tasked in the area of the bridges but were instead directed to form part of a perimeter line to the west of Arnhem, not far from the landing area itself. As for 4 Parachute Brigade, who were brought in by the second lift, they were not assigned to the bridges either but were instead to establish the northern section of the perimeter line. In point of fact, of the nine battalions of 1 and 4 Parachute Brigade and 1 Air Landing Brigade, only two were actually ordered to capture the road bridge. For the remainder, the distance from the landing grounds to the bridges was largely irrelevant when the operation plan was being devised.

Secondly, it is necessary to reiterate that the landing areas were at first selected not for Market Garden but for Comet, and that they were chosen *before* the Allies received the first intelligence reports mentioning the arrival of II SS Panzer Corps in the area.[30] Indeed, at the time, Allied intelligence indicated that only three enemy divisions of very limited capability were present in the entire corridor area. Arnhem was thought to be protected by nothing more than its anti-aircraft batteries.[31] On this basis (and given the exceptional depth of the operation), it was entirely logical that the airlift plan should have paid more heed to the threat from German flak than to any subsequent confrontation between 1st Airborne and enemy ground forces. Afterwards, of

* See Chapter 2.2.

course, the ground intelligence picture deteriorated, but, for reasons already examined, British intelligence officers from 21st Army Group down to 1st Airborne Division tended to understate the potential threat. By contrast, the worsening flak situation was taken very seriously by Allied air planners.

Thirdly, there was the all-important *quid pro quo* of a daylight airlift carefully routed away from German anti-aircraft defences. Although Urquhart's forces were to be landed further from the road bridge than he might have wished, the daytime lift offered immense compensating advantages in terms of accuracy, concentration and assembly on the ground. The true significance of this factor has so frequently been overlooked that it is worth considering in some detail. It can best be illustrated by comparing Market Garden with earlier Allied airborne operations. The first glider assault on Sicily – Operation Ladbroke – initially delivered just 73 personnel to the Ponte Grande out of 2,075 who took off from Tunisia; 69 of the 144 gliders involved landed in the sea. Of 3,405 US paratroops assigned to the Piano Lupo, only 200 reached their objective. At Gela, out of an entire regiment, only 37 officers and 518 other ranks could be assembled in the first 24 hours of the operation. And, at the Primasole Bridge, 1 Parachute Brigade could initially muster only 12 officers and 283 other ranks out of the 1,856 personnel that took off from North Africa.

In the sole genuine airborne assault at Salerno in September 1943 only 15 of the 40 aircraft involved placed their paratroops within 5 miles of the drop zone. In the American sector in Normandy only 10 per cent of paratroops landed on their drop zones, and 45 per cent landed anything from 2 to 25 miles away. Of 49 gliders committed to the Chicago mission only 6 landed on the intended LZ. Of the 52 in the Detroit mission the number that landed 'on or near' the LZ was between 17 and 23, although the number on the LZ itself may have been as low as 8. In the Keokuk mission only 5 out of 32 gliders landed on their designated LZ; in Elmira half of the 76 gliders in the first echelon missed their LZ by more than a mile. Of the 13,000 US personnel airlifted into Normandy on the night of 5-6 June only around 4,500 were under divisional control after 24 hours. In the British sector only 8 out of 35 aircraft bound for zone K actually dropped their paratroops onto that DZ; at DZ V, the success rate was 17 aircraft out of 71; and of a total of 98 glider sorties dispatched on the night of 5-6 June, 40 were either abortive or else landed more than a mile from their intended LZ. In Operation Dragoon in August two of the three morning missions put no more than 40 per cent of their paratroops within a mile of their DZs, and even the third mission could only manage 60 per cent.

How did the Arnhem airlift compare with these past operations? On 17 September the 12 Stirlings of 38 Group responsible for dropping the pathfinders delivered them onto their DZs with perfect accuracy. The teams

1st Airborne Division's initial landings at Wolfheze on 17 September 1944

assembled quickly and their equipment was operating well before the main airborne formations began to arrive. In the glider lift some 39 aircraft were unable to reach the Arnhem area, largely because of a series of tow-rope break-ages, but the operation was otherwise brilliantly executed. Of 134 gliders destined for LZ S, 132 landed on or very near that zone, while 116 of the 150 remaining gliders bound for LZ Z landed on the zone and 27 were located very near it. The accuracy of the parachute drop was also nearly perfect.[32] Urquhart afterwards described the airlift as 'quite first class. It was easily the most successful and accurate of any previously achieved either in operations or on exercises.' Moreover, in complete contrast to earlier experience, 'all units were able to move off to their tasks practically at full strength and in a very short time after landing'.[33]

The level of concentration achieved was not merely a matter of space but also of time. As in western Normandy in Neptune, Market Garden employed two air routes, in part to reduce the length of the air transport streams and the time involved in completing the airlifts. Along both routes the parachute aircraft serials were massed in up to three parallel lanes one and a half miles apart. Additionally, the 38 Group and 46 Group glider tugs flew on the northern route to Arnhem at 1,000 feet above the USAAF troop carriers, effectively adding a fourth lane. The spacing between serials was furthermore reduced to four minutes for troop carriers and seven minutes for glider tugs; six- and ten-minute intervals had been employed in Normandy. This too was only possible because the airlift took place in daylight rather than in darkness or twilight, when there was a far greater risk of mid-air collision. Thus, for Market Garden as a whole,

> By these means, the use of two routes, each with three or four lanes for traffic, and the closer spacing of serials, 1,055 planeloads of paratroops and 478 gliders were to be delivered in the initial lift within 65 minutes, the same time it took to bring in the 369 sticks of paratroops for 82nd Division in Neptune.[34]

To sum up, then, on 17 September the Allied air forces handed to 1st Airborne Division an immense advantage over the airborne forces committed to earlier operations – an advantage that should easily have made up for the fact that the landing area was at most seven miles rather than five miles from the Arnhem road bridge. Why, then, were they unable to exploit it?

As we have noted, Lathbury's 1 Parachute Brigade, consisting of 1, 2 and 3 PARA, were given the job of capturing the Arnhem road bridge, while 1st Airborne's other component brigades were to form a perimeter line around the town (see Map 15), north of the Lower Rhine. Lathbury devised a plan of advance that gave 2 and 3 PARA the task of capturing the bridge. The two battalions were to approach their objective along different and completely separate routes ('Tiger' to the north, 'Lion' to the south) and were not to provide mutual support until they reached their objective. The only other troops sent directly to the road bridge were drawn from the divisional Reconnaissance Squadron, which had the task of operating ahead of 1 Parachute Brigade as a *coup-de-main* party using specially equipped jeeps. The task of 1 PARA was to occupy high ground in northern Arnhem, which was to be reached via a third route to the north of 'Tiger', code-named 'Leopard'.[35] Thus, having been gifted the most accurate and concentrated airlift in Allied airborne history, Lathbury's plan required his brigade's three battalions to disperse and then advance into Arnhem along different routes without assisting one another. In this way, he ironically imposed on 1 Parachute Brigade many of the same handicaps that Allied airborne troops had suffered from in the past as a result of inaccurate or dispersed night-time airlifts.

The rationale behind Lathbury's plan has never been firmly established. He himself claimed that it was entirely founded on the belief that his troops would

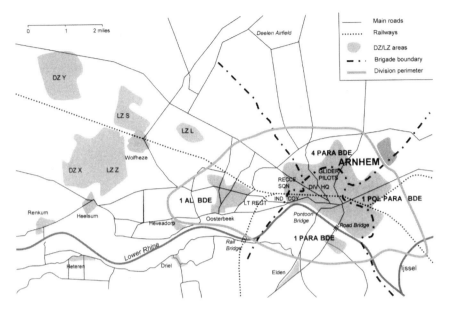

Map 15: Planned 1st Airborne Division dispositions at Arnhem

encounter minimal opposition in western Arnhem.[36] Yet it is notable that Urquhart's later defence of 1 Parachute Brigade's plan was founded on different arguments. In his view, the wooded and suburban terrain to the west of Arnhem would have seriously impeded any attempt by the three battalions to support one another; in such an environment 'the more avenues of approach that could be used the better'.[37] More recently, research on 1st Airborne Division's reconstitution during the spring and summer of 1944 has found little evidence of larger formation training or exercises by either 1 or 4 Parachute Brigade. The bulk of their training was allegedly restricted to company and platoon-level activity, and was mainly of a very routine nature.[38] If this was so, it would certainly help to explain why Lathbury was drawn to a battle plan in which each battalion performed quite separate and distinct tasks. The sole attempt by 1st Airborne to effect a co-ordinated multi-battalion assault during the battle of Arnhem (on 19 September) was poorly directed and wholly unsuccessful.

The impact of Lathbury's plan would have been serious enough under any circumstances, but unfortunately the disintegration of his brigade was then compounded by the failure of 1st Airborne Division's communications. So much has been written about this subject that it can serve no useful purpose to revisit the issues here. The key point is simply that the poor quality of British airborne radio equipment had been very firmly established before Market Garden. It had failed during the Oudna operation, the Bruneval Raid, Husky, and on a number of other occasions.[39] This handicap should thus have been very familiar to an officer of Lathbury's considerable experience. He nevertheless constructed a battle plan that was critically dependent on functional communications because of the geographical separation enforced upon the three participating battalions. Without communications they could only operate as entirely separate entities; there could be no prospect of effective brigade-level command and control.

Of the three battalions, 1 PARA were completely wasted. Tasked to take up positions in northern Arnhem, they were at first held in the DZ/LZ area as a reserve while Lathbury determined whether they would be required to support 2 or 3 PARA. Having lost precious time, they were then released to fulfil their original task. Employing 1 PARA in this haphazard fashion was a luxury that Lathbury could ill afford. They would afterwards be misled by an exaggerated appraisal (ironically provided by the Reconnaissance Squadron) of the strength of German positions near Wolfheze. In total, the SS training battalion, which had by chance been deployed there at the time of the landings*, numbered only around 400 personnel, predominantly equipped with infantry weapons and thinly spread along a three-mile line between the 'Tiger' and 'Lion' routes.[40] Attempts to bypass them took 1 PARA further to the north and into contact with other German units moving south into the Arnhem area. By the evening it was clear that the route to their objective was closed. A signal from Frost then requested reinforcements at the road bridge and consequently, having suffered heavy casualties, 1 PARA abandoned their original plan and marched south to offer their support to the remainder of the brigade.[41] This is unquestionably how they should have been tasked in the first place.[42]

Of the two battalions dispatched to the road bridge, 2 PARA duly reached it, demonstrating in the process that the success or failure of 1 Parachute Brigade operations on 17 September was not merely determined by the location of the landing areas. But 2 PARA could and should have arrived at the bridge in greater strength. Unfortunately, however, they were diverted from their primary goal by subsidiary tasking – the capture of the Arnhem rail bridge and of a German headquarters. In the event, the Germans demolished the rail bridge and the ill-conceived attack on the headquarters cost the battalion an entire company.[43]

In the meantime, 3 PARA were halted on the outskirts of Oosterbeek by elements of the same SS training battalion that 1 PARA had encountered further north. After their initial contact with the Germans they made no further progress throughout the afternoon: they were prepared neither to fight their way through nor to bypass the enemy by exploiting the more southerly

* See Chapter 2.3.

road into Arnhem employed by 2 PARA. Just one company were detached to find an alternative route to the road bridge, and only about half of this force ultimately reached it. When the remainder of 3 PARA finally entered Oosterbeek early in the evening, Lathbury and the battalion commander, Lieutenant Colonel Fitch, took the disastrous decision to halt for the night. At this point, according to Lathbury's own account, the battalion had sustained just four fatalities; otherwise, 35 personnel had been wounded. 'I was not worried about the situation', he wrote in the brigade diary.[44]

Throughout the evening very much stronger German blocking forces, including elements of 9th SS Panzer Division (battle-group Spindler), moved into Arnhem. When 3 PARA set out early the next morning they did not at first run into insuperable opposition. But when their lead company (B Company) encountered the first relatively light resistance near St Elisabeth's hospital, they were surprised to discover that the remainder of the battalion had disappeared. This force, which comprised A Company, the battalion headquarters company, all of their transport, three of their four anti-tank guns and the brigade and divisional communication vehicles, had effectively been left behind. When they finally entered western Arnhem they found that Spindler's troops had in the meantime closed the 'Lion' route.[45] From then on, there was minimal prospect of an Allied victory unless XXX Corps could reach the road bridge before 2 PARA surrendered.

* * *

The historiography of Operation Market Garden is replete with counterfactual arguments, which dwell interminably on what might have happened if only the Allied airborne plan had been different. The most commonly encountered proposition is that a landing south of the Arnhem road bridge would have allowed far more airborne troops to secure the objective before significant German opposition was encountered. It is often implied that this force would then have been able to hold the bridge until relieved by XXX Corps.

By any standards this is an extremely dubious assertion. Apart from the fact that 1st Airborne Division's battle plan actually assigned less than two battalions to the immediate vicinity of the bridge, Market Garden did not differ from earlier airborne operations by virtue of the fact that only a relatively small force (around 700 men) reached the primary objective. The key distinction was that the objective itself lay 64 miles behind the front line, and that 1st Airborne were consequently required to hold it for up to four days. Such an achievement was at this time unprecedented in the history of airborne warfare, and a number of successful operations would unquestionably have failed had the airborne not been relieved far more rapidly. Cosmetic tinkering with details of the Market Garden plan would not have compensated for its more fundamental shortcomings.

But the primary flaw in the counter-factual approach is that it fails to consider the German perspective on Allied actions. The reader is invited to believe that changes in the Allied operation plan would not have led to compensating adjustments in the enemy response. Would this really have been the case? Generally speaking, the German reaction to Market Garden was hugely impressive given the dire situation confronting their armed forces by September 1944. They nevertheless made two critical mistakes, which could potentially have cost them the battle. First, on the afternoon of 17 September, they neglected the defence of the Arnhem road bridge; second, they failed to demolish the road and rail bridges at Nijmegen, thus leaving the way open for a possible link-up between XXX Corps and 1st Airborne Division. Yet it is often forgotten that both of these errors resulted directly from their appreciation of Allied actions, and that they might have altered their priorities completely in different circumstances.

Consider, for example, the initial German failure to strengthen the defences at the Arnhem bridge. This resulted partly from confusion within their command chain and partly from the fact that the bridge was not immediately threatened. The main German counter-strokes following the airborne landings were directed towards western Arnhem because the landing areas lay to the west of the town. Otherwise, their focus was on Nijmegen. As General Bittrich, the commander of II SS Panzer Corps put it, 'Schwerpunkt is south!'[46] If the Germans secured Nijmegen, 1st Airborne Division could be cut off and destroyed at Arnhem.

When the bridge was captured by 2 PARA the Germans were caught completely off guard, and they were at first unable to mount any systematic or well-orchestrated counter-strokes. Poorly planned ad hoc attacks, such as that famously instigated by SS Captain Viktor Graebner on 18 September, were easily dealt with by Frost's men. Even on 19 September the fighting in western Arnhem remained the priority for the Germans. By contrast, in the words of one recent account, 'the first serious German counter-attack [on the road bridge] on Tuesday 19 September did not commence until late morning, when Kampfgruppe Knaust made its debut'. This was successfully repulsed and no further major attacks were launched until the arrival of two Tiger tanks in the evening.[47]

The limited nature of operations around the road bridge that day is confirmed by another recent account, which records:

Lieutenant Colonel Frost's men at the Arnhem road bridge passed Tuesday 19 September relatively quietly … SS-Hauptsturmführer Brinkmann [who was responsible for recapturing the bridge] probably wanted to hold his men in readiness in case the British broke through the Spindler line in his rear [in western Arnhem]. It is possible he even sent some of his tracked vehicles to help Hauptmann Bruhn at the climax of the 156th Parachute Battalion's attack on the Dreijenseweg position [north of Oosterbeek and west of Arnhem]: some of Bruhn's men claim to have seen Waffen-SS armoured units coming up from the rear to assist them.[48]

Hence it was not until 20 September, after 1st Airborne Division had been defeated in western Arnhem, that the Germans stepped up their efforts to recapture the road bridge – an objective that was then achieved within 24 hours. To this extent, the traditional view of the Arnhem battle, with its emphasis on three days of desperate fighting around the road bridge, clearly needs revision. German priorities initially lay elsewhere. It is certain, however, that the appearance of a larger airborne force at the road bridge on 17 September would have produced a very different German response. In particular, the troops actually sent into western Arnhem from the north (primarily battle-group Spindler) and into the DZ/LZ area from the west (Division Von Tettau) would have immediately been dispatched towards the bridge instead. Moreover, Division Von Tettau could potentially have been assembled between the Lower Rhine and the River Waal, southwest of Arnhem, before attacking eastwards into the notional alternative landing area south of the bridge.[49] This would have compelled 1st Airborne Division to hold a substantial force well south of the river pending the following day's airlift, in the same way that they actually held 1 Air Landing Brigade at Wolfheze. And the second lift would, in such circumstances, have been extremely hazardous: the area south of the bridge offered little cover and would have been very exposed to German fire from the north bank of the Lower Rhine and elsewhere. By contrast, extensive woodland gave valuable protection to the landing areas west of Arnhem.

In short, although more British troops might have reached the bridge had landing areas south of the river been selected, they would have faced far larger, earlier and more systematic counter-attacks from the Germans than were ever confronted by 2 PARA. Airborne casualties would have been high and inevitably limited ammunition stocks would rapidly have been exhausted by continuous and intensive combat. It is very unlikely that they would have held the bridge in these circumstances until the arrival of XXX Corps.[50]

Then, finally, there is the issue of the Nijmegen bridges. Even if the Germans had failed to recapture the Arnhem road bridge, they would still have been able to consider destroying the road and rail bridges to the south over the River Waal. This was in fact the course of action immediately recommended by Bittrich and the commander of 10th SS Panzer Division, SS Colonel Harmel, and would almost certainly have taken place but for the opposition of

Field Marshal Walther Model, commander of Army Group B – Bittrich's superior officer. According to Cornelius Ryan, Bittrich told Model on the afternoon of 17 September that the Nijmegen bridges should be 'immediately destroyed', and repeated his recommendation on the 18th, insisting that 'the Nijmegen bridge was the key to the entire operation ... Destroy it and the head of the Allied attack would be severed from its body.'[51]

Model remained adamant that no such action should be taken. German strategy in Holland in September 1944 involved holding a defensive line southwest of the Waal, and this would clearly have been impossible without the Nijmegen crossings. Nevertheless, his refusal was also based on the knowledge that the Arnhem bridge was only held by a small force of lightly armed paratroops, which he expected would soon be overwhelmed. Confronted by a more immediate and substantial threat at Arnhem it is entirely possible that Model would have acted very differently and that the Nijmegen bridges would have been demolished, so ensuring the ultimate defeat of 1st Airborne Division to the north.

Notes

1. Warren, *Airborne Operations*, pp. 226–227.
2. WO 171/341, XXX Corps intelligence summary 494, 7 September 1944.
3. AIR 37/1217, Operation Market, 1st Airborne Division Planning Intelligence Summary No. 2, dated 14 September 1944, prepared by G2 (I); see also AIR 37/1214, Appendix D, Headquarters Troop Carrier Command Intelligence Trace No. 4 for Operation Market.
4. AIR 37/1217, Operation Market, 1st Airborne Division Planning Intelligence Summary No. 2, dated 14 September 1944, prepared by G2 (I).
5. AIR 37/1217, Hollinghurst to Williams, 11 September 1944.
6. AIR 37/1217, Hollinghurst to Browning, 15 September 1944.
7. Hollinghurst papers, AC 73/23/49, comments on AHB monograph on the history of the airborne forces, p. 2.
8. War Diary of Luftflotte 3, September 1944, entry of 5 September 1944 (held at AHB).
9. Harclerode, *Arnhem*, p. 52.
10. AIR 27/1492, B Flight 247 Squadron F.540, September 1944.
11. AHB casualty archive, 17 September 1944.
12. AIR 27/1492, B Flight 247 Squadron F.540, September 1944.
13. WO 171/393, 1st Airborne Division War Diary, September 1944, Annexure 0.1, copy of diary of Brigadier J.W. Hackett.
14. Warren, *Airborne Operations*, pp. 226–227.
15. Urquhart, *Arnhem*, p. 18.

16. Harclerode, *Arnhem*, p. 51.

17. The anticipated 14 September launch date is recorded in AIR 37/1217, Hollinghurst to SASO, 11 September 1944; see also HQ 38 Group to HQ 46 Group, 11 September 1944.

18. 1st Airborne Division Report on Operation Market, 10 January 1945.

19. See for example WO 219/4998, HQ Airborne Troops interpretation report, 7 September 1944; SHAEF report on enemy defences in the area Arnhem–Nijmegen–Valkenswaard, 10 September 1944; HQ Airborne Troops interpretation report, 12 September 1944; HQ Airborne Troops interpretation report, 13 September 1944.

20. AIR 37/1217, Hollinghurst to Major General Paul Williams, Commanding General, IX Troop Carrier Command, 11 September 1944; WO 219/4997, memorandum by Lieutenant General Lewis Brereton, 11 September 1944.

21. CAB 106/1133, Urquhart to Harris, 22 November 1952.

22. Urquhart, *Arnhem*, p. 23.

23. Ryan, *A Bridge Too Far*, p. 95.

24. Frost, *A Drop Too Many*, p. 212.

25. See for example Middlebrook, *Arnhem*, pp. 64, 70. Middlebrook cites the alleged objections of Lieutenant Eric Vere-Davies, Staff Sergeant Alec Waldron, and Corporal Bob Allen.

26. Harclerode, *Arnhem*, pp. 51–52.

27. See for example the minutes of the Airborne Air Planning Committee, 31 December 1943, 14 January 1944, 27 January 1944, 14 April 1944, 28 April 1944, 18 May 1944, Notes on the Planning and Preparation of the Allied Expeditionary Air Force for the Invasion of North West France in June 1944, appendices.

28. WO 219/4998, minutes of a meeting called by Commanding General, First Allied Airborne Army, 10 September 1944.

29. Buckingham, *Arnhem*, p. 231.

30. Maps of the Comet landing areas are in AIR 37/979.

31. WO 205/850, Advanced Headquarters, IX Troop Carrier Command, Warning Order for Airborne Operation, 6 September 1944.

32. Warren, *Airborne Operations*, pp. 102, 112–114.

33. AIR 37/1217, Urquhart to Hollinghurst, 27 September 1944.

34. Warren, *Airborne Operations*, p. 90.

35. WO 219/5137, 1st Airborne Div Op Instr No. 10, Additional Notes on Operation Market, 13 September 1944, para 8 (a), (b) and (c).

36. CAB 106/1133, Lathbury to Harris, 5 April 1954.

37. L.F. Ellis, *Victory in the West, Vol. 2, The Defeat of Germany* (HMSO, London, 1968), p. 55.

38. Buckingham, *Arnhem*, pp. 41–45.

39. Frost, *A Drop Too Many*, p. 80; Harclerode, *Arnhem*, pp. 165–167; Buckingham, *Arnhem*, pp. 129–130; Otway, *Airborne Forces*, pp. 69, 131.

40. Kershaw, *It Never Snows in September*, pp. 72–73.

41. Middlebrook, *Arnhem*, pp. 137–142.

42. Lathbury himself acknowledged that it would have been better to retain 1 PARA as 3 PARA's reserve; see CAB 106/1133, Lathbury to Harris, 6 April 1954.

43. Middlebrook, *Arnhem*, pp. 146–148, 184–185.

44. WO 171/393, 1st Airborne Division War Diary, September 1944, Annexure N, Operation Market, Story of 1 Parachute Brigade.

45. Ibid.

46. Kershaw, *It Never Snows in September*, pp. 76, 137, 308–309.

47. Buckingham, *Arnhem*, p. 190–191. Buckingham's account states incorrectly that the Tigers arrived on 18 September.

48. Harvey, *Arnhem*, p. 137.

49. This force was partly formed from units withdrawn from a German defence line on the Waal river. See Kershaw, It *Never Snows in September*, p. 111. As these units were presumably brought across the Lower Rhine by ferries or bridges west of Arnhem, it would equally have been possible to move units north of the Lower Rhine to the south bank of the river to link up with the troops moving up from the Waal.

50. Kershaw, *It Never Snows in September*, pp. 307–309.

51. Ryan, *A Bridge Too Far*, pp. 190, 272, 274.

3.3. The Airlift

ONE OF THE most difficult issues facing the Market Garden planners was that insufficient aircraft were available to convey all three airborne divisions into Holland in a single airlift. This is not to say that there was a shortage of aircraft. On the contrary, the scale of the lift was unprecedented: the USAAF deployed nearly 1,200 transport aircraft on the first Market Garden lift, while the RAF's 38 Group and 46 Group mounted 371 sorties.[1] The problem was the enormous scale of airborne demands, which extended not only to approximately 35,000 personnel but also to colossal quantities of equipment and supplies. More than 3,500 aircraft would have been needed to transport all three divisions simultaneously, but the intermittent requirements of the Allied airborne forces could not possibly have justified the creation of such a force. For this reason, Allied airborne planning by the summer of 1944 assumed that operations would be mounted using consecutive lifts, as they were, for example, in Neptune and Dragoon.

In Market Garden three main lifts had to be organized and it was ultimately decided that they should be scheduled over a 45-hour period from 'H-Hour' – the time the first airborne troops would land on Dutch soil. The landings would take place between 13.00 and 14.00 on 17 September; the second lift would reach its objectives at 10.00 on 18 September and the third lift at 10.00 on the 19th. Historians portray this timetable as the second critical failing in the Market Garden air plan. It is said to have significantly slowed the build-up of airborne troops, and to have exerted a particularly serious impact on 1st Airborne Division because of their exposure at the northern end of the corridor and because of the distance between their landing areas and the Arnhem road bridge. Instead of moving all available forces towards the road bridge after the landings on 17 September, Urquhart was allegedly compelled to leave 1 Air Landing Brigade at Wolfheze to defend the DZs and LZs, pending the second day's lift and the arrival of 4 Parachute Brigade. Many American troops had also to be assigned to the task of landing zone defence. It is common to read that viable alternative courses of action were available. Buckingham describes the lift schedule as a 'serious and needless error' in the air plan.[2] Harclerode goes further and reproduces a diary note from an unnamed air force officer asserting that all three lifts could have been completed within the space of twelve hours.[3]

All of these arguments are open to objection on a number of counts. To begin with, the standard critique of the airlift plan is rarely if ever accompanied by any detailed analysis; there is little close scrutiny of the parameters within which the plan was formulated – the constraints and operating limitations that confronted the Allied air forces. Such issues as range and aircraft endurance, meteorology and visibility and their link with navigation, aircraft maintenance and aircrew training are invariably given only the most cursory consideration, if they are covered at all. Parallel air operations to protect the airborne armada from flak or enemy fighters are similarly ignored. This is partly because historians prefer to approach Market Garden almost exclusively from a land perspective, despite the fact that an airborne operation is as much an air as a land undertaking. But it also once again reflects the influence of senior 1st Airborne Division officers on the historiography of the operation; needless to say, none of these officers properly understood the key air planning issues.[4]

Secondly, the delay involved in the airlift timetable is consistently overstated through the simple technique of expressing the schedule in days rather than hours. By recording that the airlift was spread over 'three days', it is possible to convey the impression that it spanned 72 hours, rather than the 45-hour (two-day) period actually envisaged by the planners. On this basis, the allegedly detrimental impact of the airlift schedule can also be exaggerated, relative to the various notional alternatives that are consistently proposed. The aim of this chapter is to reassess the story of the Market Garden airlift, employing as many of the surviving documents as possible to explain the decisions taken by the Allied air planners. Ultimately, it is suggested that the whole issue of the airlift schedule is something of a red herring, but there is a need to consider far more closely how the available lift was utilized.

* * *

In most accounts, the story of the Market Garden airlift begins after Browning's return to England on the afternoon of 10 September. Yet the airlift plan can in fact be traced to the abortive Operation Linnet, originally scheduled for the end of August 1944, and involving the carriage of 1st, 82nd and 101st Airborne and the Poles into the Tournai area of Belgium. The salient features of Linnet were described earlier in this book. Three lifts were planned over a twenty-four-hour period, but the overwhelming majority of airborne troops were to be infiltrated early in the morning or before dusk on the evening of the first day. This was to be achieved through the so-called double-towing of American gliders. The third lift (the following morning) would have been a small-scale affair comprising only the Poles and some 150 American gliders. Linnet was then cancelled and replaced by Comet, which was very much more limited in scale and therefore required different air transport arrangements. However, when Montgomery enlarged Comet into Market Garden he made the assumption (presumably on Browning's advice) that the Linnet airlift plan would be resurrected.[5] Incredibly, he did so without consulting Brereton or any of his senior troop carrier commanders. Consequently, no consideration at all was given to some of the most elementary air planning issues raised by the new venture – particularly the fact that more distant objectives were involved. From the majority of British air transport bases the difference exceeded 100 miles in each direction.[6]

On 10 September Browning presented his outline plan to the assembled Allied airborne and troop carrier commanders (as we have seen, 1st Airborne Division were not represented at this meeting). The plan stated that the airlift schedule would be 'in principle as for Linnet'.[7] As so little time was available (given the 14 September launch originally envisaged) decisions were required immediately and, once taken, they had to be adhered to rigidly. So the First Allied Airborne Army planners sprang into action, examining Browning's outline, the number of aircraft available and the potential combinations of the three airborne divisions that might be infiltrated in any given period with the resources available. Within hours they had become concerned over the prospect of achieving two daylight lifts on the same day:

> With the shortening of the days at this time of the year, and complications of turn-around, it is believed that future plans should be made on the basis of one lift per day, with all US aircraft available. This will permit an operation to be carried through in spite of a late start due to bad weather, whereas tight schedule plans based on two lifts per day could not be met if early morning weather were bad.[8]

By 12 September Williams (who had overall command of the airlift) had accepted this advice. At another planning meeting,

> General Williams pointed out that owing to the reduced number of hours of daylight and increase in distance, it would not be possible to consider more than one lift per day.[9]

Williams had a long-standing and deserved reputation for close co-operation with the airborne forces.[10] He had commanded the US troop carriers in Husky, Neptune and Dragoon, and was thus one of the most experienced of all the Allied airborne commanders. He had nonetheless faced considerable criticism after Normandy, much of which was entirely unwarranted. He was in no way responsible for the strategic decisions that resulted in the breakneck expansion of 9th TCC in the months before June 1944, and he had been left with no alternative to the night-time airlift on D-Day. Many of his aircrew had had to confront a radical change of routing and objectives only days before the operation, and they had all been faced by weather conditions on the night of 6 June itself that would probably have precluded airborne operations altogether in different circumstances. Nevertheless, when the lift went wrong, US Army officers from Bradley downwards predictably decided to blame 9th TCC.[11] This experience, together with painful memories of Sicily, would inevitably have influenced Williams' outlook when he drew up the Market Garden airlift plan. At the same time, however, it should be remembered that Eisenhower himself had attached particular importance to improving the standard of troop carrier navigation when he created First Allied Airborne Army.

The problems Williams confronted as he considered the lift timetable were of a somewhat technical character, which is presumably why so few histories address them in any detail. They concerned the time involved in turning aircraft around for the second and third lifts, the range from UK troop carrier bases to their objectives in Holland, weather and visibility conditions and the co-ordination of the airlift with fighter escort and flak suppression operations. All of these factors were, to a greater or lesser extent, interlinked.

1. The turnaround. The difficulty with the turnaround between the airlifts had its origins in the American decision to build an immense multi-division airborne force. American industry might just have been capable of producing the transport aircraft that this force required, but generating sufficient quantities of trained manpower to fly and maintain them was another matter entirely. We have already considered the unfortunate consequences in terms of aircrew training. But it is also a fact that the phenomenal expansion of the American front-line troop carrier force before D-Day was not accompanied by any equivalent enlargement in the number of ground crew to service, refuel and repair them. In aircraft and crews, the troop carrier groups were enlarged to one third above their normal establishment, whereas the number of ground personnel was not increased at all. Moreover, by September the situation may well have been worse, for 9th TCC's front-line strength had increased further: on the night of 5/6 June the command had planned 925 sorties, but the first Market Garden lift was to involve 1,173 sorties.[12] Effectively, then, USAAF troop carrier groups were established to mount a single airlift at full strength, followed up in the short term, as in Normandy, by subsidiary lifts of more limited proportions. The maximum size of the follow-up lift would ultimately be dictated by the time available to turn around the aircraft back in England; the more time available, the larger that lift could be.[13]

It was for this reason that, on 10 September, Williams' staff briefly considered the possibility of conducting lifts at substantially less than full strength.[14] For planning purposes they used figures for the lift possible at half strength and at full strength; the rationale here was presumably that the actual lift available would fall somewhere between these two yardsticks. Clearly, they would have been certain of their ability to turn around at least half of their force for the second lift in accordance with the Linnet timetable, but not the whole force. As well as factoring routine maintenance, refuelling and glider marshalling into their calculations, they had also to consider the repair or replacement of damaged or lost aircraft. Across the entire Allied troop carrier and glider tug force some 320 aircraft were destroyed or damaged on the first day of Market Garden; on the second day the figure was 303 aircraft.[15] These losses were high enough in themselves but the predictions were substantially greater.

The planners were apparently confident of 9th TCC's ability to regenerate their entire front-line force within a period of 20–24 hours. But any follow-up lifts conducted within a tighter schedule would have been executed below full strength. Consequently, at these reduced intervals, it would have been necessary for First Allied Airborne Army to organize three or possibly four follow-up missions to infiltrate the same quantity of troops and equipment conveyed by the two full-scale missions planned for Market Garden on 18 and 19 September. In other words, if the first lift had been timed for the early morning, the full airlift would still have been drawn out over at least two whole days (from the morning of the first day to the evening of the second), and a final lift might have been required on the third day.

2. Range factors. The inability of 9th TCC to match the projected Linnet turnaround timetable in Market Garden stemmed directly from the increased range involved in the Arnhem, Nijmegen and Eindhoven lifts. The longer transit between the English air bases and the three airborne objectives left far less time for the turnaround if the lifts were to be mounted in daylight and at full scale. The greater distance also substantially reduced the absolute amount of lift available, because 9th TCC's Dakota tugs did not have sufficient endurance to double-tow gliders from the UK to the Market Garden corridor. Thus glider serials that had been included in the first and second lifts planned for Operation Linnet had to be shifted back into the third lift for Market Garden.[16] The first Linnet lift would have conveyed 240 gliders, whereas the first lift into Holland brought only 120; the second Linnet lift – the main American glider operation – was to have hauled no fewer than 1,760 gliders, whereas for the second Market Garden lift the figure was only 904.[17] In other

A USAAF C-47 (Dakota) 'double-towing' two Waco gliders

words, over the two lifts the American divisions lost nearly 1,000 glider sorties, which had now to be flown on the third day of the operation.

Most historians avoid analysis of the range factor. Consider, for example, Middlebrook's selective quotation of 38 Group's after-action report on Market Garden to support his forthright denunciation of the airlift plan. He freely cites a paragraph that states that 'In future ... it may be found necessary to complete the entire lift within a matter of hours, landing every essential unit or load before the enemy can assess the situation',[18] but he ignores the next paragraph, which adds a crucial caveat. 'It would be necessary either to reduce the scale of operations, or to transfer the air forces to continental bases from which a quick turn-round could allow two or more closely-timed lifts, perhaps without refuelling.'[19] At the beginning of September 1944 Brereton had of course warned Eisenhower that it would be very difficult to stage an airborne operation as far east as the River Rhine from bases in the UK.[20]

3. Weather and visibility factors. Successful airborne operations in the Second World War were dependent on a number of favourable weather and visibility factors. Weather conditions had to be sufficiently fine to allow aircraft to take off, transit to their objectives, deliver their paratroops or gliders, complete return journeys and land safely. Overcast conditions rendered glider operations all but impossible. Tow-rope breakages were a regular occurrence when tug and glider combinations flew through cloud, either because the glider pilot lost sight of the tug and the two aircraft got out of alignment or because, in assuming the recommended position for bad weather conditions, the glider inadvertently passed through the tug's slipstream. Operations executed in darkness or half-light had largely proved unsuccessful. Therefore, by September 1944, the majority of air planners within First Allied Airborne Army were convinced that future operations should be conducted in daylight and in the best possible visibility conditions.

Obtaining two or more successive days of clear and calm weather across three weather systems (the UK, the North Sea and Continental Europe) in mid-September was always going to be problematic. But, by that time, the planners had been able to observe the way in which adverse weather had caused the postponement of both Linnet and Comet, and had evidently concluded that they were most likely to obtain favourable conditions by avoiding the dawn lifts that had been proposed for both operations. Hence, as the records show, the attraction of scheduling successive lifts slightly later in the morning was not only that they could be flown at full strength but also that they could exploit the best available periods of visibility. The alternative was to mount smaller follow-up lifts using a schedule that was potentially more vulnerable to weather or visibility problems.[21] Such reasoning would have been reinforced by the prevailing weather conditions in the week leading up to Market Garden, which were characterized by early morning fog on every day except the 16th.[22]

During the early hours of the morning of 17 September the Allied air transport bases in central southern England and the West Country once again became shrouded in fog, which reduced visibility to 200 yards. This would have completely ruled out any attempt to stage a dawn lift (on a timetable similar to that devised for Linnet) and, consequently, the entire operation would have been thrown into confusion.[23] However, by 09.00 the fog was clearing so that ultimately, under the Market Garden schedule, the lift could take place as planned, with the vast majority of aircraft reaching their objectives in Holland between 13.00 and 14.00. On the following day, morning fog in England and adverse weather conditions over Holland would again have halted any attempt to stage a dawn lift and even the later lift planned for Market Garden was delayed for several hours, although it was otherwise successfully completed.[24] On the third day, First Allied Airborne Army's luck ran out: the weather deteriorated and the lift timetable broke down irretrievably. But it would have broken down sooner and with more serious results had any attempt been made to replicate the Linnet timetable.

The following table helps explain the advantages of the Market Garden plan in terms of both simplicity and results. It draws on the lift plan for Linnet and on the plan for Market Garden, and illustrates the impact of early morning fog and other adverse weather factors on 17 and 18 September. Clearly, the

Linnet schedule commended by so many historians would actually have been far more vulnerable to weather disruption than the Market Garden schedule because of its dependence on two dawn lifts. Neither plan would have executed a third lift before the weather broke on 19 September, but the consequences would potentially have been much more serious under Linnet-type arrangements because of the larger total number of lifts involved.

Linnet-type timetable	Market Garden timetable
Day 1: 1st lift planned for dawn, grounded by fog until 09.45	Day 1: 1st lift executed 09.45-13.00
Day 1: 1st lift executed 09.45-13.00	Day 2: 2nd lift planned for morning at full strength delayed by weather until midday
Day 1: 2nd lift planned early evening at less than full strength, delayed until next morning due to delayed 1st lift	Day 2: 2nd lift executed at full strength at midday
Day 2: 2nd lift re-planned for dawn, strength unclear, delayed by weather until midday	Day 3: airlift breaks down due to adverse weather
Day 2: 2nd lift executed midday	
Day 2: 3rd lift planned in evening at less than full strength, delayed until next morning due to delayed 2nd lift	
Day 3: airlift breaks down due to adverse weather	

Finally, it must be remembered that the Linnet airlift plan was drawn up at the end of August, whereas the Market Garden plan was prepared for mid-September. It is impossible to establish exactly how much daylight was lost in the intervening period, but enquiries submitted by the Cabinet Office historians to the Royal Greenwich Observatory after the war elicited a response that there was at least half an hour less daylight by 17 September than there had been on the 8th.[25] Assuming a similar rate of change in the preceding week, the First Allied Airborne Army planners would have had an hour less daylight at their disposal for Market Garden than for Linnet. Under the Linnet plan no fewer than 24 of the 43 serials in the second lift would have reached the Tournai area after 8 p.m.[26] On 17 September sunset occurred at 6.11 p.m. and nautical twilight ended at 7.26 p.m.[27] Hence, if the same full-scale lift arrangements had been applied that day to the more distant Market Garden objectives, well over half the aircraft involved would have had to find their landing areas after nightfall – probably with no more success than they had achieved in the past. The airborne troops would then have been confronted with a protracted night assembly task, which, judging from earlier experience, would have extended over many hours even if the airlift had been accurate.

4. Fighter escort and flak suppression operations. The Market Garden airlift, extending deep into enemy-occupied territory, had to be co-ordinated with an enormous fighter escort and flak suppression effort. This involved aircraft from RAF Bomber Command, Air Defence Great Britain (ADGB – formerly Fighter Command), Coastal Command, Second TAF and the USAAF's Eighth and Ninth Air Forces. On the first day of the operation alone, Bomber Command Lancasters and Mosquitos struck German fighter airfields and flak batteries; there were several RAF attacks on German positions in Arnhem, and 852 Eighth Air Force B-17s attacked 117 targets along the two airborne routes. They were followed by Ninth Air Force and ADGB fighters and fighter-bombers, the first of which arrived approximately thirty minutes before the first transport aircraft. They maintained a continuous presence over the Market Garden area to suppress German flak until the last airborne serials had left. Protecting the airborne formations from the Luftwaffe posed particularly acute problems, as Allied radar coverage did not yet extend into eastern Holland or northwest Germany. Consequently, it was necessary for two Eighth Air Force P-51 Mustang fighter groups to fly barrier patrols east of the corridor. Behind the barrier no fewer than six P-51 fighter groups mounted area cover above the southern airborne route, while 18 Spitfire squadrons and two P-51 fighter groups protected the northern route.

The air formations committed to escort and flak suppression were directed from six separate command headquarters, two in France, the remainder in England, all of which had to work closely with First Allied Airborne Army's Troop Carrier Command Post at Eastcote (northwest London). They were deployed over a huge geographical area incorporating different time and weather zones, and the vast majority of aircrew involved had not previously flown in support of an airborne operation.[28] Ultimately, they mounted more than 8,000 sorties during Market Garden, most of them between 17 and 19 September, and their role in the success of the first two airlifts was absolutely critical. Yet in the majority of histories these operations receive only the most cursory acknowledgement. Moreover, because the effort involved is so massively underestimated, it is simply assumed that the arrangements were flexible and could easily have been scheduled differently.

In truth, this is a very unrealistic contention. It should be obvious from the foregoing account that that there would not have been any prospect of organizing this enormous and highly complex air effort twice in the daylight hours of a single day. Synchronizing the deployment, withdrawal, turnaround, redeployment and second withdrawal of more than 3,000 combat and troop carrier aircraft would have posed monumental command and control problems and, as with the troop carriers, it is not established that the combat aircraft involved could have been turned around in the time available. Some such feat might have been achieved in Linnet or Comet because the supporting air missions were more limited in scale than those organized for Market Garden. This was partly because the flak assessment for Linnet was only moderate, and the estimates undertaken for Comet were more positive than those produced later for southern and eastern Holland. But Linnet also required less support because the objectives were far closer to the UK and lay within range of Allied radar, while Comet was, of course, a significantly smaller operation; moreover, both employed only a single air route.[29]* The worsening flak intelligence picture, the use of two separate routes and Market Garden's combination of both depth and scale imposed a very much greater burden upon Allied combat air power.

Beyond this, the escort and flak suppression operations would have become far more difficult to co-ordinate with the airlift in the event of weather disruption. This is illustrated by events on and after 19 September, when poor weather set back the lift programme and caused it to fragment in such a way that effective escort and counter-flak cover began to break down – particularly in the most northerly part of the corridor. The two RAF transport groups suffered their heaviest losses from 19 to 22 September and on the 21st their aircraft were intercepted by the Luftwaffe. The Polish glider lift on 19 September also encountered formidable flak, and the later Polish parachute lift faced opposition from both anti-aircraft artillery and fighters.[30]

Another key consideration was Market Garden's dependence on Eighth Air Force fighters for barrier patrol and area cover: they ultimately flew more than 3,000 fighter and fighter-bomber sorties.[31] Eighth Air Force personnel were trained solely for daytime operations. From the outset this pointed towards a daylight lift, as Browning himself noted in his outline plan for Market Garden on 10 September.[32] On the 11th Hollinghurst told his senior staff officer that

---

* Two routes were devised for Comet for the sake of tactical flexibility, but it was only ever intended to employ one for each lift.

'the operation will be carried out in broad daylight (because the Eighth Air Force cannot operate their fighters at early dawn or dusk)'.[33] The planning constraints that this imposed were, however, offset by the fact that several hours of daylight would now be available to execute counter-flak and other preparatory air operations before the airborne formations reached Holland.[34] This period was put to very good use.

* * *

The most elementary principle of military planning is simplicity. The more complex a plan is, the more interlocking and interdependent parts there are and the greater the scope for failure will be. On 10 September 1944 Williams learnt that an already challenging airborne plan had been imposed upon his command. His task then was to devise the airlift schedule that, on the basis of his extensive past experience, appeared most likely to deliver the airborne safely, accurately and as quickly as possible to their objectives. During the planning process there were no obvious rights and wrongs; there were only possibilities and probabilities, and significant risks were inherent in every available course of action. But Williams had to give particularly close consideration to the speed with which his transport aircraft could be turned around, the range between the UK airfields and the operational objectives in Holland, weather and visibility factors and co-ordination between the airlift and the escort and flak suppression effort.

Under all four of these headings the arguments favouring the launch of one lift per day during the morning hours were not merely persuasive but overwhelming. The alternatives were too complex and the turnaround timescales were too tight. The follow-up missions would have been smaller in scale than the three (planned) Market Garden lifts and, consequently, more would have been required in total; the effective suppression of German air defences would have been far more difficult, if not impossible. Williams' plan was also designed to minimize the danger of disruption due to weather and visibility factors, albeit by gambling on the continuation of fine weather over a three-day period. In this respect, it was demonstrably more successful on the first and second day of the operation than any notional alternative plan would have been, but on the third day it failed, just as any other plan would have failed. Finally, the plan in no sense placed the needs of the air forces above those of the men being delivered into battle.[35] Before September 1944 the Allies had consistently failed to pay sufficient attention to the difficulties of airlift planning; to that extent it could reasonably be argued that in Market Garden they finally got their priorities right. The airborne forces would hardly have benefited from yet another inaccurate or dispersed lift.

Throughout the Second World War only the Germans once attempted to stage two full-scale airborne lifts within the daylight hours of a single day – the first day of Operation Mercury, the invasion of Crete. The second lift went disastrously wrong, primarily because insufficient time was allowed to turn around the Luftwaffe's troop carrier fleet back in Greece. Nothing could illustrate more clearly the wisdom behind Williams' decision to avoid a similar airlift plan in Market Garden.

Beyond this, the operational logic behind Williams' airlift timetable was actually far more compelling than most accounts suggest. Both the initial landings and XXX Corps' offensive at the southern end of the corridor were scheduled for a period between 13.00 and 14.30 on 17 September. This synchronization was important. An earlier lift would have warned German forces at the southern end of the corridor of an impending ground operation to link up with the airborne, while an earlier attack by XXX Corps would have alerted the Germans further north. An earlier simultaneous assault would not have left time for preliminary air operations – particularly flak suppression – which required several hours of daylight. Losses to German anti-aircraft fire might thus have been considerable, causing the second lift to be delayed or reduced in scale. In the event, the Germans were to be confronted by a combined airborne and ground offensive, preceded by extensive air preparation. After this would come the second lift, scheduled for 10.00 on 18 September. At Arnhem, the plan promised to deliver the whole of 1st Airborne Division less than 24 hours after the initial landing and less than 24 hours after XXX Corps began their advance. In practice, weather conditions delayed the lift on 18 September so that the landings began at 14.00, but, as we have seen, these conditions would also have impacted seriously on any theoretical alternative lift timetable. It still proved possible to bring 1st Airborne into Holland in a period of about 25 hours.[36]

There is no record that British airborne commanders raised any objections to the Market Garden airlift schedule. In part, this was presumably because they realized that there was no practicable alternative if the airlifts were to be staged at full scale and in daylight. But it is not clear that a second lift on 17 September would have helped 1st Airborne significantly in any case. The units conveyed by the first airlift would not have arrived at Arnhem at 13.00, as they did in Market Garden, but soon after daybreak (assuming the weather had allowed them to take off). They would then have found themselves exposed in the field for the entire day, while the Germans mobilized against them. During this period it would still have been necessary to employ a substantial body of troops in the defence of the landing areas. Under the Comet lift plan the second lift would then have reached Arnhem at dusk; under the Linnet plan it could only have arrived after nightfall. Given the time required for unloading equipment and assembling personnel even in the most favourable circumstances imaginable (about one and a half hours for the first Market Garden lift), it is highly unlikely that the troops involved would have been usefully employed before the following day. Therefore, even if 1st Airborne Division had ever contemplated operations at full divisional strength, these could not have commenced until the morning of 18 September, 24 hours after the initial landing.

The only documented doubts to emanate from within the airborne forces were expressed by Gavin of 82nd Airborne, who complained that the revised timetable would delay a re-supply mission originally planned (under the Linnet schedule) for D+2; the D+2 lift would now bring in a glider infantry regiment and other glider-borne troops.[37] Gavin's concerns reflect the fact that the Market Garden lift plan actually penalized the Americans far more heavily than the British because it forced them to abandon their plans for double-towing gliders.

Responding to Gavin, Browning declared 'that if the ground situation proved as favourable as he anticipated, it might not be necessary to have a third lift of gliders but that re-supply might take the place of gliders'.[38] This remarkable statement provides a revealing insight into Browning's true thinking about the likely development of the operation. It does not support the view that the more extended airlift timetable was a source of great controversy between airborne and troop carrier commanders. The cancellation of Linnet, when the ground forces overran Tournai before the airborne arrived, was still prominent in the minds of all concerned. Anecdotal evidence suggests that Browning's confidence in XXX Corps' rate of advance was shared by the commander of 1st Airborne. Inspecting his division on 14 September, Urquhart allegedly told the assembled officers of 4 Parachute Brigade, who were scheduled to drop on the second day, that they 'would probably be just in time to see B Echelon of the Guards Armoured Division going through Arnhem'.[39]

One Army officer who did not share this optimism was none other than Field Marshal Montgomery. As Browning had effectively advised him that all three divisions could be conveyed to Holland in 2 lifts over about 11 hours, and that all 3 lifts would be completed in about 24 hours, he was predictably dismayed to learn that this was not to be the case. Browning, for his part, appears to have been reluctant to convey such disappointing news, so Montgomery only found out when a copy of the plan reached 21st Army Group headquarters; this may have been as late as 15 September. He responded by finally doing what he should have done at the very beginning of conceptual planning for Operation Comet: he approached Brereton directly (although still not in person), dispatching his acting chief of staff, Brigadier David Belchem, to England. Lacking any knowledge of the key determinants of the Market Garden airlift schedule, Belchem proposed a double lift for 1st Airborne Division on the first day of the operation, but he was reportedly told that it was far too late to change the established plan.[40] This was undoubtedly true, but it would in any case have been impossible to apply one lift plan to the British and another entirely separate series of arrangements to the Americans. Montgomery was comprehensively hoisted on his own petard. This was the result of his philosophy of 'leading the air down the garden path'.

* * *

The controversy surrounding the airlift timetable only really serves to divert attention from a far more fundamental problem, which concerned not the schedule itself but the very fact that Market Garden depended upon several consecutive lifts. In operations against 'shallow' objectives involving a rapid link-up between airborne and ground forces, multiple lift schedules were not open to objection in principle. But this approach was certain to be far more hazardous when employed to execute an airlift into an area deep within enemy-occupied territory, where German forces were known to be expanding their presence. The enemy reaction would begin immediately after the first lift, the later lifts would be mounted into an active battle zone and troops from the earlier lifts would have to be wastefully deployed in the defence of DZ/LZ areas. The fact that multiple lifts were required in Market Garden, despite the availability of very large numbers of transport aircraft and gliders, raises important questions about how the airlift was used by the airborne divisions.

On 17 September 1944, 1st Airborne Division were in fact the beneficiaries of a larger airlift than any other British airborne force had so far secured during the Second World War. That they needed a second substantial lift was primarily due to their massive requirement for glider capacity. In the aftermath of Operation Husky in 1943, the War Office and the Air Ministry had agreed that airborne division glider lifts should in future not exceed 430 aircraft for operations mounted from the United Kingdom.[41] No fewer than 576 glider sorties were required by 1st Airborne Division for their own purposes during the first two days of Market Garden; additionally, the Polish Parachute Brigade needed 80 glider and tug combinations. In all, on the first day, 1st Airborne were assigned 475 sorties (155 parachute and 320 glider sorties). On the night of 5–6 June, by contrast, 6th Airborne Division were conveyed to Normandy by only 364 sorties. The second Market Garden lift allocated a further 380 sorties to 1st Airborne's lift, 45 to the Poles and 33 to re-supply, whereas, in Normandy, 6th Airborne's second lift involved just 256 sorties.

In summary, then (and excluding the Polish and re-supply requirements), a total of 855 aircraft were assigned to 1st Airborne Division during the first two days of Market Garden. This amounted to 235 more than the 620 allocated to 6th Airborne's two lifts. Despite this, 6th Airborne were able to bring in two parachute brigades in their first lift, whereas 1st Airborne, with 111 more aircraft, brought in 1 Parachute Brigade and most – though not all – of 1 Air Landing Brigade. Moreover, on 18 September, 1st Airborne could only use their 380 aircraft allocation to carry in one additional parachute brigade plus the remaining half battalion of the Air Landing Brigade.

These figures disclose a substantial disparity in the way that the available airlift was employed by the two British divisions and completely undermine one common argument, to the effect that 1st Airborne were provided with insufficient airlift or an unreasonably slow reinforcement rate. In reality, if Urquhart had employed the available lift capacity in the same way as 6th Airborne, he could have brought a substantially higher proportion of his three combat brigades into Arnhem on 17 September and, if a second lift had still been deemed essential, he might have been able to assemble all three brigades *and* the Polish Parachute Brigade by the afternoon of the 18th. Why, then, did he not do so?

The answer lies partly in the division of tasking between the RAF and USAAF transport fleets after Normandy. By September, for administrative and basing reasons, the US troop carriers had been given responsibility for all Allied parachute operations (except Special Operations and pathfinder drops), leaving both 38 and 46 Group RAF to provide glider tugs for the British airborne forces. It appears that 1st Airborne were entirely content with this arrangement. Presumably, this was to some extent because they expected abundant US troop carriers to be available for their paratroops, but the primary reason was simply that the bulk of their lift requirement was for gliders. In the specific circumstances of Market Garden's first day, when the Allied airlift had to be spread across three airborne divisions, this allocation of air transport capacity meant that 1st Airborne received a substantial glider lift and sufficient American troop carriers to deploy one of their two parachute brigades.

On paper, there might appear to be no obvious objection to this arrangement: contrary to another popular myth, the British were given almost exactly the same amount of air transport as the American divisions. However, one of the great handicaps that resulted from the decision to launch Market Garden at virtually no notice was that the three divisions had to employ aircraft and glider loading plans originally drawn up for Operation Linnet.[42] There was simply no time to customize the lift to the specific (and very different) demands of the Arnhem mission, and there appear to have been no readily available contingency schemes for the airborne to operate on 'light scales,' with reduced equipment holdings or a leaner headquarters and support infrastructure. Consequently, a very large part of 1st Airborne's glider lift was used to carry divisional units, vehicles, weapons and equipment, rather than air landing infantry.

It is easily forgotten that only 5,850 of the 10,241 personnel conveyed by the first and second Arnhem lifts were members of 1st Airborne's two parachute brigades or 1 Air Landing Brigade. Of the remainder, the Glider Pilot Regiment numbered 1,262 personnel, leaving a balance of 3,129 additional to the three brigades.[43] Otherwise, the two lifts brought in 96 artillery pieces and 863 further items described in the available record as 'other vehicles'.[44] A total of 86 gliders provided the equipment lift for the two parachute brigades; the Light Regiment, Royal Artillery, required 57 gliders; the two anti-tank gun batteries 48 in total; the divisional headquarters 29; the Royal Engineers 26, and the 17-pounder battery 22. The Light Composite Company, Royal Army Service Corps, absorbed 41 glider and parachute sorties, while the divisional Reconnaissance Squadron absorbed 30.[45] On average, each glider sortie mounted for 1st Airborne on 17 September carried just 8 personnel, whereas the standard British Horsa glider was designed to carry 25.[46]

These figures illustrate the extent to which airborne warfare had been transformed since 1940. The German forces that attacked Scandinavia and Holland had predominantly consisted of combat units and had carried with them only the barest minimum of weaponry, equipment and stores. By contrast, despite their modest beginnings, the Allied airborne had by September 1944 assumed the proportions of a veritable Frankenstein's monster. The consequences were

Artillery being loaded onto a Horsa glider

all too evident in the enormous demand for airlift generated by the three airborne divisions in Market Garden. To make matters worse these mounting lift demands could only be realized by sacrificing much of the flexibility of the original airborne concept, because of the more complex and protracted lift arrangements involved and the DZ/LZ defence requirement. Unloading gliders and marshalling stores was also a time-consuming process; it is notable that 1 Parachute Brigade took longer to move off from their landing areas on 17 September than the American parachute regiments, which dropped that day with very little equipment.[47]

Only the experience of their defeat at Arnhem (and a captured German assessment of the battle[48]) would lead the Allies to conclude that a single lift should be staged for Operation Varsity in March 1945. This did not involve a very substantial enlargement of the Allied air transport force, but it did necessitate a marked reduction of airborne requirements (as well as far less ambitious airborne tactical objectives). Varsity was restricted to two rather than three divisions, and 6th Airborne Division based their deployment plans on a total glider lift of some 440 aircraft. It is interesting to note, however, that even this figure made provision for a 'liberal scale of insurance' in case some glider cargoes were lost or damaged (as indeed many were).[49] The inclusion of some such allowance in 1st Airborne Division's plans the previous September may perhaps have been another factor in their high overall airlift requirement.

Notes

1. Warren, *Airborne Operations*, pp. 226–227.
2. Buckingham, *Arnhem*, p. 231.
3. Harclerode, *Arnhem*, p. 163.
4. For a good example of their tendency to oversimplify the issues involved, see Frost, *A Drop Too Many*, p. 200.
5. WO 219/4998, Operation Sixteen Outline Plan, 10 September 1944.
6. Figure based on Map 6, Operation Market Routes of Initial Troop Carrier Missions, in Warren, *Airborne Operations*, p. 92.
7. WO 219/4998, Operation Sixteen Outline Plan, 10 September 1944.
8. WO 219/4998, memorandum by Lieutenant Colonel Thomas Bartley, 10 September 1944.
9. WO 219/4998, First Allied Airborne Army memorandum to Brigadier General Ralph Stearley, 12 September 1944.
10. Harclerode, *Arnhem*, p. 49.
11. Warren, *Airborne Operations*, p. 58.
12. Ibid., pp. 19, 224–226.
13. In Normandy, Allied planning was based on the assumption that a large-scale follow-on airlift could not be mounted before D+6 or D+7, i.e., 12 or 13 June

1944. See Minutes of the Ninth Meeting of the Airborne Air Planning Committee, 28 April 1944, Appendix V/39, Notes on the Planning and Preparation of the Allied Expeditionary Air Force for the Invasion of North West France in June 1944.

14. WO 219/4998, memorandum by Lieutenant Colonel Thomas Bartley, 10 September 1944.
15. Warren, *Airborne Operations*, pp. 226–227.
16. Ibid., p. 89.
17. Air 37/509, No. 11 Group Operation Instruction No. 39/1944, 2 September 1944; Warren, *Airborne Operations*, p. 226.
18. Middlebrook, *Arnhem*, p. 443.
19. 38 Group Report on Operation Market Garden, 1 January 1945 (held at AHB).
20. WO 219/2186, Brereton to Eisenhower, 1 September 1944; WO 219/2121, memorandum by SHAEF planning staff, 4 September 1944.
21. WO 219/4998, memorandum by Lieutenant Colonel Thomas Bartley, 10 September 1944.
22. AIR 27/2017, 542 Squadron F.540, September 1944. This unit diary records weather conditions at Benson in Oxfordshire daily throughout this period; identical conditions would certainly have affected the British air transport bases, which were nearly all located in central southern England.
23. Stan Cornford and Squadron Leader Peter Davies, 'Arnhem: The Weather', *Air Clues*, Vol. 48, No. 10 (October 1994), p. 396; AIR 37/13, An Account of the Organization, Training and Operations (and Lessons Learned) of 46 (Transport Support) Group, Royal Air Force, during the Invasion of Hitler's Europe, p. 70.
24. Warren, *Airborne Operations*, p. 117.
25. CAB 106/1133, HM Nautical Almanac Office, Royal Greenwich Observatory, to Lieutenant Colonel G.W. Harris, 28 January 1954.
26. AIR 37/509, Field Order No. 3 for Operation Linnet, 31 August 1944.
27. CAB 106/1133, HM Nautical Almanac Office, Royal Greenwich Observatory, to Lieutenant Colonel G.W. Harris, 28 January 1954.
28. Cox, 'Air Power in Operation Market Garden', pp. 194, 231.
29. On radar cover for Linnet, see AIR 37/509, Wing Commander A.H.D. Livock to Commanding General, First Allied Airborne Army, 2 September 1944.
30. Warren, *Airborne Operations*, pp. 131–139.
31. Report by First Allied Airborne Army, Operations in Holland, September to November 1944, 22 December 1944.
32. WO 219/4998, Operation Sixteen Outline Plan, 10 September 1944. 'Will probably have to accept morning [lift] due to Eighth Air Force support.'
33. AIR 37/1217, Hollinghurst to SASO, 11 September 1944.
34. CAB 44/254, p. 8.

35. This claim is made in Buckingham, *Arnhem*, p. 83.
36. Warren, *Airborne Operations*, p. 117.
37. WO 219/4998, First Allied Airborne Army memorandum to Brigadier General Ralph Stearley, 12 September 1944.
38. Ibid.
39. Middlebrook, *Arnhem*, p. 63.
40. Harclerode, *Arnhem*, p. 50. Montgomery's chief planning officer later recalled that he had only seen the Airborne Corps plan for Market on D-2, i.e., 15 September; see Lamb, *Montgomery in Europe*, p. 220.
41. Extract from Joint War Office/Air Ministry Report on the Employment of Airborne Forces, Appendix V/18, Appendix D, Notes on the Planning and Preparation of the Allied Expeditionary Air Force for the Invasion of North West France in June 1944.
42. Warren, *Airborne Operations*, p. 89; Report by First Allied Airborne Army, Operations in Holland, September–November 1944, 22 December 1944. The glider-loading manifests in many cases had the operation names 'Linnet' and 'Comet' crossed out and 'Market' written in; see AIR 27/1574, 271 Squadron F.540, September 1944.
43. Middlebrook, *Arnhem*, pp. 455–460.
44. Warren, *Airborne Operations*, p. 227.
45. Middlebrook, *Arnhem*, pp. 455–460; see also Urquhart, *Arnhem*, p. 217.
46. Warren, *Airborne Operations*, p. 227. The breakdown for 17 September was 359 glider sorties and 2,908 personnel, or 8.1 personnel per glider.
47. Buckingham, *Arnhem*, p. 128.
48. After Market Garden the Germans produced their own written assessment of what had happened, the reasons for their ultimate victory and how the battle might influence the future conduct of airborne and counter-airborne warfare. Among other things, the Germans concluded that they would have been far more vulnerable if the Allies had been able to deploy more airborne troops against key objectives on the first day of the operation and they were critical of the Allies for using so many troops to defend landing areas pending follow-up airlifts. This document was captured by the Allies in December 1944 and used to inform planning for Operation Varsity. See 38 Group RAF Report on Operation 'Varsity', 20 May 1945 (held at AHB).
49. Otway, *Airborne Forces*, pp. 304–305, 318; Warren, *Airborne Operations*, pp. 157–158. The first Market lift involved 1,544 aircraft, while the Varsity lift involved 1,596. Some 74 C-46 transports were used in Varsity, which had twice the capacity of the Dakota; otherwise, lift capacity was increased by 'double-towing' American Waco gliders – a technique made possible by basing some of the American air transport wings at forward airfields in France.

3.4. Air Support Operations

THE THIRD COMMON critique of air power's role in Market Garden concerns the more general offensive air support provided for the operation. History variously alleges insufficient fighter cover for airborne troops on the ground, the absence of an air plan to isolate the Market Garden battle area in the way that Normandy had been cut off from the rest of France before June 1944 and, most of all, a failure to provide 1st Airborne Division with direct support during the battle of Arnhem.[1] This line of argument dates back to Major General Urquhart's after-action report, in which he claimed that more of his troops might have reached the Arnhem road bridge on 17 September had Allied fighter-bombers been made available.[2] Urquhart's critique has since been extended in the innumerable published histories of Market Garden so that it is now common to read that air support for the operation was deficient at almost every level. Stephen Badsey has gone so far as to argue that the Allies fought Market Garden with 'air inferiority, which was self-inflicted'.[3]

And yet only the most cursory attempts are made to explain why the airborne forces should have received this supposedly diminutive assistance. No historical perspective has ever been introduced into the story, which apparently begins on 17 September 1944 and ends nine days later, and events in Holland are invariably considered in near total isolation from other parts of the struggle to liberate Europe, as if no fighting was taking place anywhere else. Through such questionable means it is possible to construct an unfair and misleading argument that implies (if it does not state overtly) that the Allied air forces in general and the RAF in particular provided wholly inadequate backing for Montgomery's offensive.

Needless to say, the reality is very different and more complex. To understand the problems encountered by the Allied air forces in Market Garden, it is necessary to examine the broader question of how air power had been employed in support of Allied ground forces since the Normandy landings. Command and control was also a critically important influence, as was Montgomery's position within the Allied command chain and his relationship with other Allied commanders. Issues of resource allocation, logistics, aircraft technology and meteorology were no less significant, and there is a need to consider historical factors relating to the structure of the Allied airborne forces, as well as their more specific preparation for Market Garden. If the application of air power is viewed from these various perspectives it is only possible to draw one conclusion: beyond the basic fighter escort and flak suppression tasks executed in support of the airlifts, there was never much prospect that the Allied air forces would exert a decisive impact on the outcome of the operation. For this, however, they were not primarily to blame.

The task of providing air support for Montgomery's 21st Army Group in the Normandy campaign was formally assigned to Second TAF, under Air Marshal Sir Arthur Coningham. Coningham had at his disposal two groups of fighters and fighter-bombers – 83 and 84 Group – which were steadily deployed to advance landing grounds in Normandy throughout June and July 1944. It was particularly important for the RAF's Spitfires and Typhoons to be brought forward in this way. Both aircraft boasted only limited endurance, as they had originally been designed as home-based interceptor fighters. In Normandy, for example, Typhoon missions rarely exceeded one hour in duration. Consequently, to provide optimal cover to ground forces, they had to operate from bases immediately behind the front line. A third group of longer-range medium bombers, 2 Group, remained based in the UK. Offensive air operations in support of the campaign were also undertaken by Bomber Command. Before June, these primarily targeted the French transportation system to isolate the Normandy landing area, although there were numerous attacks on German coastal defences as well. After D-Day, efforts continued to maintain Normandy's isolation, but Bomber Command also provided direct support to British and Canadian ground forces in operations such as Charnwood, Goodwood, Totalize, Tractable and Bluecoat.[4]

Montgomery originally expected that after the Normandy landings Allied forces would gradually advance through northern France and up to the Rhine. On the basis of this plan, Second TAF had intended to construct a substantial number of airfields in the open country to the south of Caen, positioned to support British and Canadian ground forces as they moved from Normandy up to the River Seine.[5] In the event, Montgomery's inability to overcome the German defences around Caen caused Second TAF's deployment to be drastically revised. Although 83 Group's move to Normandy was only slightly delayed, 84 Group were compelled to operate from southern England for much of June and July. By the time enemy resistance collapsed in mid-August, the two groups and the whole of their support infrastructure had been crammed into a small area of northern Normandy between Caen and Bayeux, which was no more than 12 miles from the coast at any point.[6]

After Falaise, the Allied ground forces drove flat out across northern France while Second TAF, through no fault of their own, were left massively over-committed to northern Normandy. Coningham was compelled to adopt the most radical measures in order to ensure that at least some of his squadrons kept up with the advance of Montgomery's more forward units.

> It was decided that not more than three forward operational airfields should be used at any one time. Certain Wings were left behind temporarily and their transport used to move petrol and ammunition to the forward Wings ... There was not sufficient time to construct airfields to keep pace with the advance. Therefore captured airfields were cleared of mines and booby traps and were reconditioned as soon as possible up to the minimum standards acceptable for fighter bombers. Air lift for the carriage of personnel and equipment was used whenever possible, and the forward airfields were moved by bounds each of approximately 100 miles ... The rapidity of the advance was such as to make it largely impossible to provide more than a meagre scale of landline communications, and it was only by the use of the [insecure] radio telephone circuits that it was possible to obtain the necessary speech communications ... The Airfield Construction Groups RE [Royal Engineers], which were only 50% mobile when fully established, were assisted by a pool of vehicles obtained from other [RAF] Airfield Construction Groups which were immobilized for the purpose, in order to keep them working on the repair of enemy airfields as far forward as possible ... Night reconnaissance Wellington aircraft of No 34 Strat/R Wing had to be employed, during this period, for ferrying petrol to their forward airfield in order to keep the other two squadrons in the air.[7]

Coningham was one of many senior Allied officers who were appalled by the grounding of large numbers of transport aircraft in this period, pending some future airborne operation that never seemed to materialize.[8] He did every-thing in his power to ensure that Second TAF continued to provide effective fighter cover and close support to 21st Army Group, but it was inevitable in the circumstances that, in mid-September, only a limited proportion of his first-line aircraft should have been available for operations in Holland. On the eve of Market Garden, 83 Group had 29 fighter and fighter-bomber squadrons located at airfields around Brussels and Antwerp, a force that had been doubled in size since 10 September through a truly remarkable feat of expeditionary logistics and also through the expedient of crowding squadrons onto the few available airfields. All the Typhoons were based either at Brussels Melsbroek or (from 17 September) at Antwerp Deurne.[9]

These squadrons would have to be spread across the Market Garden corridor, and would have to meet the separate and distinct support requirements of XXX Corps and the three airborne divisions, as well as the two other Second Army corps committed to the operation. Moreover, their potential value would be limited by the fact that their airfields were more than 100 miles from Arnhem, which marked the limit of the Typhoons' effective operational radius.[10] They would be left with minimal time to identify and attack targets in the area before fuel constraints compelled a return to base, and recovery could itself be problematic as there were so few functional bases. The closure of airfields on, say, weather grounds (a common occurrence during the Second World War) had the potential to place airborne squadrons in an extremely hazardous situation, and Antwerp Deurne also lay well within range of German artillery to the northwest.[11] Beyond this, the fact that Second TAF radar cover did not yet extend into eastern Holland to cover Arnhem and Nijmegen meant that it would inevitably be very difficult to protect these locations from attack by the Luftwaffe.[12]

The rapidity of the Allied advance from Normandy was by no means the only factor to influence the amount of air support available for Market Garden. Montgomery's strategy for the breakout involved pushing Dempsey's Second Army northwards towards Belgium to the maximum possible extent, while

83 Group Typhoons outside a well-camouflaged former Luftwaffe hangar at Brussels Melsbroek

A Type 15 mobile radar, typical of the equipment used by Second TAF in 1944

First Canadian Army were assigned the less glamorous and far more difficult task of securing the French coastal plain, with its vital channel ports. All the ports – Le Havre, Boulogne, Calais, Dunkirk – were strongly defended, whereas First Canadian Army had been weakened by heavy losses in the fighting in Normandy. Moreover, as they advanced up the coast, they were soon confronted by the same logistical problems that hampered the progress of other Allied ground formations. They simply did not have the resources to fulfil the formidable task Montgomery had given them.[13] Air power was therefore employed to offset their relative weakness. First, they were permanently assigned the whole of 84 Group, leaving 83 Group to work with Second Army; second, they were allocated a very substantial proportion of Bomber Command's resources to assist in the capture of the channel ports.[14]

Throughout September, therefore, Second TAF and Bomber Command were operating in support of Montgomery's forces. But they were for the most part working with First Canadian Army in France rather than Second Army in the Low Countries. It would have been impossible to employ Second TAF in any other way in this period; Montgomery could hardly have denied tactical air support to half his army group, and in any case the majority of 84 Group's squadrons were based too far south to participate in Market Garden.[15]

It might have been feasible to re-deploy Bomber Command, but, again, this would largely have halted Canadian operations around the channel ports.

Between 5 and 11 September Bomber Command flew some 2,500 sorties against Le Havre; on 17 September the Command mounted 762 sorties against Boulogne (as well as 596 over the nights of 16/17 and 17/18 September in support of Market Garden); between 20 and 25 September they flew 1,700 sorties against Calais.[16] All these operations required extensive preparation, and Bomber Command squadrons also spent some considerable time in September waiting in a state of inactivity, either for the completion of ground assault preparations by the Canadians or for the clear weather conditions that were required to target the channel port defences accurately. In other words, the channel ports actually tied up Bomber Command resources for considerably longer than the bare sortie statistics suggest.[17] There was a brief five-day interval between the assaults on Le Havre and Boulogne, but it is highly unlikely that even a moderately effective campaign to isolate the Market Garden area could have been planned and executed in so short a period, and 21st Army Group did not at any time request operations of this nature.

To sum up, on the eve of Market Garden the total air power available to 21st Army Group was as follows: there were the Eighth and Ninth Air Force and ADGB formations that flew in support of the airlifts; there were other RAF elements such as 2 Group, Coastal Command, and various home-based reconnaissance squadrons that also contributed to Market Garden; and there were the two formations more broadly committed to 21st Army Group operations – Second TAF and Bomber Command. Beyond this, there were of course the troop carriers and glider tugs of First Allied Airborne Army. In all, on 17 September, this would have meant that a very substantial majority of the aircraft under Eisenhower's control were assigned in some way to Montgomery's forces. Hence, it cannot reasonably be contended that he lacked air support when Market Garden was launched, despite his later ridiculous claim to the contrary.[18] However, while there was clearly ample scope for organizing a formidable air effort to protect the airlifts, the potential for using air power effectively to provide offensive support for operations on the ground was, from the outset, far more limited. Only Second TAF's 83 Group were in a position to operate in Holland continuously from 17 September, but their fighter-bombers were based too far away from Arnhem and their fighters lacked the all-important assistance of radar.

To confront the potential problems inherent in this situation the closest possible liaison between Montgomery and Coningham was essential, but their relationship had unfortunately broken down in the later stages of the North African campaign and had never recovered. The failure of Montgomery's initial plans in Normandy again exposed their very fundamental differences. As Tedder's diarist wrote on 5 July, 'Situation is that Monty thinks Air is not sufficiently vigorous in support of immediate battle, [while] Coningham is highly critical of the slow progress of the Army.'[19] Working with the CIGS, Montgomery then sought to have Coningham sacked. He failed but, according to his own account, he found no further grounds for complaint against Second TAF's commanding officer. 'His attitude has been very different,' Montgomery wrote in July, 'and his advances almost an embarrassment.' Sadly, these well-intentioned efforts were not reciprocated. Although Montgomery was told to work directly with Coningham, he consistently refused to do so.[20]

Early in August Coningham deployed Second TAF's headquarters forward into Normandy to a location just south of Bayeux, near to 21st Army Group. The intention was clearly that the two headquarters should collaborate closely and, to this effect, regular morning meetings were held between senior Army and RAF officers so that the campaign could be properly directed along truly joint lines. Yet Montgomery chose not to attend, preferring instead the parochial seclusion of his tactical HQ.[21] This acutely unsatisfactory situation could have resulted in disaster in Normandy, but the more harmonious relations established between Montgomery's and Coningham's subordinates –

Air Vice-Marshal Broadhurst of 83 Group with Lieutenant General Dempsey of Second Army

officers such as Dempsey and Air Vice-Marshal Broadhurst of 83 Group – fortunately helped to fill the vacuum.[22] This was nevertheless far from ideal, for it meant that there was no interface at the very top of 21st Army Group and Second TAF. The disaster was merely postponed until September. Montgomery 'went over my head', Coningham recalled after the war. 'Month after month he did that; until he had his failure at Arnhem. Then they made him listen. [He] violated all command channels....'[23]

The most rational air support plan for Market Garden, given the depth of the objectives, would have involved the assignment of as many Second TAF resources as possible to the three airborne divisions, mirroring German practice earlier in the war; miles inside enemy territory, they would otherwise lack firepower. Second Army – primarily XXX Corps – would in contrast be able to call on their organic artillery, self-propelled guns, tanks and heavy mortars. They should not have required anything like the same level of air support. The officer with responsibility for both Second Army and the airborne, by virtue of his position as commander of 21st Army Group, was of course Montgomery. He should at this stage have worked through Coningham to clarify the broader tactical air support requirements of his operation, but instead he did nothing. By 14 September Second TAF were based near to 21st Army Group headquarters in Brussels but, unfortunately, this had effectively become 'a rear headquarters, used for administrative purposes rather than being intimately involved in the day-to-day fortunes of the battle'.[24] Montgomery, true to form, remained at his tactical HQ.[25] Consequently, after Market Garden was formally authorized, Dempsey as usual approached Broadhurst and succeeded in ensuring that 83 Group's fighter-bomber squadrons were overwhelmingly monopolized by XXX Corps on the crucial afternoon of 17 September.[26] Dempsey had no responsibility for the airborne forces until they were relieved by XXX Corps, nor was he in a position to make representations on their behalf.

The only perverse logic in this arrangement stemmed from the fact that the Allied airborne in general – and the British airborne in particular – would probably not have been well placed to exploit tactical air power even if it had been made available. Isolated from the mainstream of military experience, they had largely ignored the development of close air support techniques, tactics and procedures. And yet the need for close control and co-ordination between ground troops and their tactical air support was particularly critical in airborne operations. As Ian Gooderson has written,

This was because pilots could not be expected easily to distinguish friend from foe on the ground and in a battle taking place beyond the established front lines, and were thus reliant upon the airborne troops indicating their own and the enemy's positions by pre-arranged signals or radio communications.[27]

The absence of such facilities had been identified as a potential handicap before the Normandy campaign, and both US and British airborne troops came under attack from Allied aircraft on D-Day.[28] Nevertheless, when Market Garden was sanctioned in September I Airborne Corps as a whole had no air support facility in their signals organization; they were not linked into the general army-air signals net.[29] Part of the problem was that the radio then used by the British Army for requesting air support was not air-portable, while the standard radio equipment of the British airborne was unsuitable for air support purposes. But it is also difficult to escape the conclusion that British airborne commanders were not very interested in the application of tactical air power, particularly if it necessitated specialized training and preparation. As one of the Market Garden after-action reports put it, 'with all other training commitments in an airborne unit, it is not possible to give wireless crews sufficient training in air support working'.[30] Unfortunately, however, it was never likely that any other formation would be capable of furnishing trained air support personnel or radios at short notice when resources were stretched to the absolute limit by the intensity of operations in France. The task of creating an air support organization should have been embraced by the airborne forces during their preparations for Neptune in the first six months of 1944. Instead, tentative steps were only initiated in August by American elements within the newly created First Allied Airborne Army, who (in their words) were compelled to 'beg, borrow or steal' to obtain the minimum of staff and equipment.[31]

Only days before the launch of Market Garden First Allied Airborne Army allocated two US air support parties to each airborne division and to I Airborne Corps headquarters. Between them they were supposed to operate an air support signals net and ground-to-air radios. They had no experience of working with the British airborne and they were under-trained and unfamiliar with some of their radio equipment; moreover, there was no opportunity to conduct trials or exercises to determine whether they could function effectively.[32]

Given the general tendency of the airborne to neglect air support issues, it is hardly surprising to discover that after Market Garden was authorized they were appallingly slow to approach Second TAF. This was largely Browning's responsibility, as he was the officer in command of the three airborne divisions committed to the operation. At 83 Group headquarters, Broadhurst was thus left in near-total ignorance of their needs. It was not until 16 September, the day before Market Garden was launched, that First Allied Airborne Army belatedly woke up to the problem, following the receipt of intelligence suggesting the presence of German armour to the east of Nijmegen.[33]

Lieutenant Colonel Laroque of their operations staff then flew to Brussels and spent the day meeting Coningham's senior staff officer, Air Vice-Marshal Groom, Broadhurst and a number of their executives. However, when Laroque asked for air strikes against several targets selected by 1st and 82nd Airborne, 'Groom said that he couldn't commit the 83rd Group on these additional tasks as they were supposed to be in support of the Second Army ... 84 Group would not be available on account of the range entailed.' At 83 Group headquarters, Laroque was again told that the additional targets 'were beyond their capabilities' given their already extensive commitments.

Over dinner that evening, Broadhurst agreed to accept some of the new targets nominated by the airborne on the basis that they could be attacked the following morning, leaving the afternoon free for operations in support of XXX Corps. Ostensibly this might appear to have been a very laudable and co-operative gesture, but it actually left Broadhurst's Typhoon pilots with virtually no time to plan or prepare for these missions, and the number of aircraft that could be assigned to them was clearly limited in relation to the number of attacks requested – an important consideration given the inaccuracy of air-to-ground weaponry in the Second World War.[34] Incredibly, Laroque was still finalizing his arrangements with 83 Group in the early hours of the morning of 17 September. His concluding observation on this lamentable episode could hardly be more telling:

> I feel very strongly that in any future operation someone must be sent at an early date to tie up all details with the air forces in support. Second TAF and 83 Group had no information as to detailed timing and were very co-operative in accepting missions which considerably stretched their capabilities. The air end of all these operations must be determined well in advance of D-Day, and all air formations operating must be personally briefed well beforehand.[35]

*   *   *

In addressing the issue of air support in Market Garden, historians have largely ignored the fact that the operation was launched before half of Second TAF's deployed force was available, and the very existence of First Canadian Army has conveniently been forgotten; equally, there has been little or no consideration of Montgomery's steadfast refusal to work with Coningham. By contrast, one particular aspect of Second TAF's marginalization in September 1944 has received an inordinate amount of attention: this was the stipulation made by First Allied Airborne Army that Coningham's squadrons should not operate over the Market Garden corridor at the same time as American aircraft engaged in fighter escort and flak suppression missions for the troop carrier and glider formations. It is maintained that this had the effect of barring Second TAF from the operation, so denying air power to the Allied ground forces. As events turned out, adverse weather repeatedly delayed the airlifts, and 83 Group's Typhoons had thus to be held on the ground pending their completion. As 83 Group's flying was also disrupted by bad weather and poor visibility in the Low Countries, there was often very little time left for offensive air activity in support of XXX Corps or the three airborne divisions.[36]

In the week that preceded Market Garden there was no opposition to First Allied Airborne Army's proposals. Second TAF were represented at the main air planning meetings in England,[37] but they did not raise any objections; nor did anyone else suggest alternative arrangements. Nevertheless, the decision to hold Second TAF outside the battle area until the airlifts had been completed is now commonly presented as another major blunder – a further critical flaw in the air plan. How valid is this judgement?

The Allied air formations that participated in the campaign to liberate Western Europe were not subject to highly centralized command and control during the summer of 1944. The authority of Leigh-Mallory's AEAF headquarters was heavily circumscribed and he functioned more as an adviser and co-ordinator than as a commander.[38] As soon as victory in Normandy was assured he received notice that his position was to be abolished and his headquarters disbanded.[39] Hence, even his quite limited powers were waning by September, although the SHAEF air staff did not formally replace the AEAF until October.[40]

Market Garden thus coincided with a transitional phase in Allied air command and control as the temporary machinery created for the Battle of Normandy was replaced by more robust and enduring arrangements. But although this was hardly ideal, air resources were in most respects logically allocated and co-ordinated during the operation. A prominent role for the USAAF fighters and fighter-bombers (and for ADGB) was inevitable, as 83 Group had insufficient resources to provide escort and flak suppression for the airborne lift, as well as tactical air support for both Second Army and the airborne forces. Indeed, on the day Eisenhower authorized Market Garden, 83 Group were operating only 15 squadrons from the Brussels area; the remainder were still in northern France.[41] Moreover, the USAAF's P-51s and P-47s were in many respects better suited to the Market Garden escort and counter-flak tasks, which involved protracted operations extending from England across southern Holland and into western Germany. By a considerable margin, they were superior in endurance to the RAF's Typhoons and Spitfires, and the Eighth Air Force's fighters worked predominantly as escorts for the US strategic bomber force, whereas Second TAF – as a tactical air force – had only limited experience of escort work. In short, it is impossible to maintain that the apportionment of tasking between the USAAF formations and Second TAF was incorrect.

Yet the commitment of so many aircraft into a restricted area over Holland inevitably posed massive airspace management problems. The northern sector of the airborne corridor, bordered to the west by Point Ellis, to the east by Nijmegen and to the north by Arnhem, was no more than 30 miles wide and 30 miles deep at any point. Into this small box, on each of the first two days of the operation, it was necessary to fly nearly 1,000 troop carriers and glider combinations, together with hundreds of American bombers, fighters and fighter-bombers. On 17 September some of the aircraft involved in the first lift were still leaving Dutch airspace when the Typhoons arrived to support XXX Corps, and a Typhoon squadron diarist would later write of 'the narrow escapes our chaps were having, trying to fly in an atmosphere positively charged with mad careering aircraft of all shapes and sizes'.[42]

Beyond the broad issue of airspace management lay a further problem, which would today be described as combat identification. There was deemed to be a high risk that unfamiliar but friendly fighter and fighter-bomber formations might be misidentified as Luftwaffe interceptors and attacked. The potential for misidentification was especially marked where Second TAF's Typhoons were concerned. As Chris Hobson has pointed out in his pioneering study of air 'blue-on-blue' incidents in the Second World War, fratricide was a 'significant cause of Typhoon attrition with a total of at least 12 aircraft being shot down in three years of service'.

> Most of the reports of these incidents suggest that the Typhoon was being confused with the Focke-Wulf FW190 … The two aircraft are superficially similar in shape; the FW190 has a radial engine in a circular cowling and, although the Typhoon has an in-line engine, the large circular air intake under the propeller spinner gave it the appearance of a radial engine from a distance. Also, in plan, the two aircraft have the same general proportions … with a distinctively short nose forward of the wing leading edge.[43]

Of the 12 Typhoons known to have been downed by friendly aircraft fire, it is established that at least 7 were lost to American fighters. However, the number actually lost tells us very little about the numerous occasions upon which Second TAF aircraft came under attack, or the threat of attack. Minimal investigation of the records is required to produce evidence of the problem. Take, for example, one of the most famous of all Typhoon missions, namely the destruction of Panzer Group West's headquarters at La Caine in Normandy on 10 June 1944. Approaching their critically important target, 247 Squadron were fired on by a P-51, 'which had been hovering suspiciously in the vicinity for some time'. The attack caused the Typhoons to scatter and lose sight of the headquarters; its location was only re-established after it was rocketed by other aircraft. The diarist of 247 Squadron continued:

Our fun for the trip was far from over, for about 10 miles off Cherbourg four [USAAF P-47] Thunderbolts flew up our rear and looked really menacing until the CO gave [orders for] a break. It's high time these types pulled their heads out and had a good look at the other kites in the sky – or as an alternative if they must fly to within 10ft of another machine before recognising same, then circle overhead instead of making quarter attacks.[44]

For general airspace management purposes and to reduce the scope for 'blue-on-blue' engagements, it was necessary to segregate the missions assigned to the various Allied fighter and fighter-bomber formations. Thus, in operations against the German counter-offensive at Mortain on 7 August, Ninth Air Force put up a fighter screen to ward off enemy aircraft, while their fighter-bombers targeted enemy troop movements outside the immediate battle area; Mortain itself was left to Second TAF. Equally, in the fighting around Falaise in the middle of August, a clearly defined boundary was established to dictate the areas over which Second TAF and the Ninth Air Force could operate.[45] Hence, when First Allied Airborne Army sought to bar Second TAF from the Market Garden corridor while American fighters were in the area, they were not proposing a new or revolutionary course of action but one that had been accepted and regularly practised since the Normandy landings. Indeed, had Operation Linnet been executed at the beginning of September, both Second TAF and the Ninth Air Force would have been excluded from the battle area while Eighth Air Force fighters escorted the airlift.[46]

This segregation appears to have been applied quite successfully throughout the later stages of 1944, but combat identification became increasingly difficult as the Allied air forces converged during the final months of the war. On 24 December a 439 Squadron Typhoon was shot down by USAAF P-47s near Duren in Germany; on 1 January 1945 a 183 Squadron Typhoon fell victim to a USAAF P-51. On the 14th another was brought down by P-47s over Germany; on the same day P-47s shot down a 174 Squadron Typhoon over Holland. On 22 February a Hawker Tempest (a fighter developed directly from the Typhoon and very similar in appearance) was shot down by P-51s and on 2 March yet another Typhoon was mistakenly intercepted by American fighters during a rocket attack on shipping on the Rhine. Over the same period USAAF fighters also shot down three Spitfires. Five pilots were killed in these unfortunate incidents.[47]

In Market Garden some kind of clear division between Second TAF, the airborne lift and the Eighth and Ninth Air Force fighters and fighter-bombers was therefore essential; there was never any realistic prospect that Second TAF would enjoy total freedom of action until the airlifts had been completed. In other words, the impact of their exclusion from the corridor during the airlift was probably not nearly as great as historians have tended to suggest. The difference was not between exclusion and non-exclusion; it was between exclusion and some notional alternative demarcation arrangement. If the range and weather factors that restricted Second TAF operations are then also taken into consideration, it will be seen that, at best, only some slight expansion of their activities might have been possible.

But it is important not to assume that an alternative demarcation plan would necessarily have proved more successful, for Second TAF's periodic exclusion from the Market Garden battle area was not in itself the fundamental problem. Rather, the critical difficulty lay in the Allies' widely dispersed air command and control structures, which, with the primitive communications technology of the day, proved incapable of co-ordinating repeated short-notice changes in airlift arrangements with Second TAF operations on the continent. It is theoretically possible that different demarcation provisions might have created more scope for Second TAF to intervene. However, the underlying shortcomings in Allied command, control and communications might then simply have manifested themselves in other ways – for example, by leaving the troop carriers with more limited protection, so increasing their vulnerability to German air defences.

After Market Garden, Coningham proposed a solution: in future, airborne operations and the supporting application of air power should be placed under the command and control of the air formation responsible for the projected battle area.[48] This approach had also, of course, been recommended after Operation Husky but was never properly applied. In 1945 Second TAF were therefore put in charge of all air planning, command and control during Operation Varsity – the Rhine crossing – with very successful results.

Yet it is not clear that a similar procedure could have been employed in Market Garden, for the offensive was mounted at the north-eastern extremity of Second TAF's area of responsibility, and their communications infrastructure could not have supported an operation extending from England into western Germany.[49] By contrast, by March 1945, many more Second TAF squadrons were suitably positioned to support Varsity. Moreover, Allied radar coverage had been extended well across the German frontier, many of the Allied troop carrier formations had been deployed forward to bases in France (together with First Allied Airborne Army's headquarters) and the majority of other transport squadrons had been moved to southeast England. In the intervening months the Luftwaffe had virtually been eliminated as a fighting force, and the operation involved only a very brief Allied incursion into enemy airspace in any case, as the airborne objectives were only four miles east of the Rhine. Finally, while planning for Varsity began five months before the operation was launched, Market Garden had to be scrambled together in less than a week.[50] Hence, Second TAF faced a far simpler command and control task in Varsity than confronted First Allied Airborne Army in Market Garden.

In short, Second TAF's exclusion from the Market Garden area during the airlifts was not in any sense a cause of the operation's failure. Rather, it was a symptom of a far broader command and control problem, which stemmed overwhelmingly from the decision to launch the operation at exceptionally short notice when the entire Allied troop carrier and glider force and First Allied Airborne Army's headquarters were still based in the UK. This cardinal error was then compounded by the selection of objectives that lay too far inside enemy territory and beyond the operational radius of more than half of Second TAF. Montgomery did not understand the difficulties that would be involved because he chose not to consult any senior air force officers about his plans. His sole airborne adviser – Browning – had absolutely no knowledge of air power.

Notes

1. On interdiction see Karel Magry (ed.), *Operation Market-Garden Then and Now*, Vol. 2, p. 711, and Kershaw, *It Never Snows in September*, p. 305. On close air support see Middlebrook, *Arnhem*, p. 444, and Harclerode, *Arnhem*, pp. 168–169.
2. 1st Airborne Division Report on Operation Market, 10 January 1945.
3. Stephen Badsey, *A Bridge Too Far: Operation Market Garden* (Osprey, Oxford, 1993), p. 84.
4. For a broad survey of RAF operations in Normandy see Hilary St George Saunders, *The Royal Air Force, 1939–45, Vol. 3, The Fight is Won* (HMSO, London, 1975), Chapter 6.
5. D'Este, *Decision in Normandy*, pp. 222–223.
6. John Terraine, *The Right of the Line* (Hodder and Stoughton, London, 1985), p. 638; for Second TAF's main dispositions see Man, *The Penguin Atlas of D-Day and the Normandy Campaign*, p. 87.
7. AIR 20/1593, report by Air Marshal Sir Arthur Coningham on operations carried out by Second Tactical Air Force from D-Day 6 June 1944, to VE Day, 9 May 1945, pp. 22–23.
8. Ibid.
9. WO 285/9, Dempsey diary, 10 September 1944, 15 September 1944. For Typhoon squadron dispositions, see Christopher Shores and Chris Thomas, *2nd Tactical Air Force, Vol. 2, Breakout to Bodenplatte*, July 1944 to January 1945

(Classic Publications, Hersham, 2005), p. 289; see also 245 Squadron diary, entry of 17 September 1944 (held at AHB).

10. WO 285/9, Dempsey diary, 10 September 1944.

11. 245 Squadron diary, entry of 23 September 1944. 'The Hun shelled the 'drome until an Auster took off to spot for the RA, who soon shut them up.'

12. Air Ministry, *The Second World War, 1939–1945, Royal Air Force, Signals, Vol. 4, Radar in Raid Reporting* (unpublished official narrative, 1950), p. 446. The effective range of Second TAF radar was in the order of 50 miles.

13. Lamb, *Montgomery in Europe*, pp. 257–258.

14. Air Historical Branch, *The Liberation of North West Europe Vol. 4, The Breakout and the Advance to the Lower Rhine*, pp. 132–139.

15. WO 219/4998, memorandum by Lieutenant Colonel J. Larocque, Air Corps, Assistant G3, to Brigadier General Stearley, 18 September 1944.

16. Martin Middlebrook and Chris Everitt, *The Bomber Command War Diaries: An Operational Reference Book, 1939–1945* (Viking, Harmondsworth, 1985), pp. 577–579, 585–589.

17. Air Historical Branch, *The Liberation of North West Europe Vol. 4, The Breakout and the Advance to the Lower Rhine*, p. 138.

18. Montgomery, *Memoirs*, p. 298.

19. Orange, *Coningham*, p. 202.

20. Ibid., pp. 199, 203–204; Terraine, *The Right of the Line*, pp. 610–611.

21. Orange, *Coningham*, pp. 199, 206–207.

22. D'Este, *Decision in Normandy*, p. 220.

23. US Army Military History Institute Papers, Supreme Command, Forrest Pogue Interviews, interview with Air Chief Marshal Sir Arthur Coningham, 14 February 1947.

24. Hamilton, *Monty*, p. 402.

25. Saunders, *The Royal Air Force 1939–45, Vol. 3, The Fight is Won*, p. 200; AIR 20/1593, report by Air Marshal Sir Arthur Coningham on operations carried out by Second Tactical Air Force from D-Day 6 June 1944, to VE Day, 9 May 1945.

26. WO 285/9, Dempsey diary, 10 September 1944.

27. Gooderson, *Air Power at the Battlefront*, p. 95.

28. AIR 37/1214, Allied Airborne Operations in Holland, September–October 1944, Appendix G, Air Support Notes on Operation Market; Index E, Air Support and Ground-to-Air Signalling; Warren, *Airborne Operations*, p. 46; Crookenden, *Drop Zone Normandy*, p. 217.

29. Gooderson, *Air Power at the Battlefront*, p. 96.

30. AIR 37/1214, Allied Airborne Operations in Holland, September–October 1944, Appendix G, Air Support Notes on Operation Market; Index E, Air Support and Ground-to-Air Signalling.

31. WO 219/2865, memorandum by Lieutenant Colonel J. Larocque, Air Corps, Assistant G3, to Brigadier General Stearly, 11 November 1944; see also Captain R.S. Barnard, Headquarters United States Strategic Air Forces in Europe, to Commanding General, First Allied Airborne Army, undated, enclosure 7E.

32. Ibid.; Cox, 'Air Power in Operation Market Garden'. p. 230.

33. AIR 37/615, Major M.E. Stuart to Commanding General, British Airborne Corps, 15 September 1944.

34. WO 219/4998, memorandum by Lieutenant Colonel J. Larocque, Air Corps, Assistant G3, to Brigadier General Stearley, 18 September 1944.

35. Ibid.

36. Harclerode, *Arnhem*, pp. 168–169; Buckingham, *Arnhem*, pp. 117-118.

37. AIR 37/615, ASP 1 to SASO, 13 September 1944.

38. Terraine, *The Right of the Line*, pp. 607–610.

39. Orange, *Tedder*, p. 280.

40. Air Historical Branch, *The Liberation of North West Europe Vol. 5, From the Rhine to the Baltic, 1 October 1944 to 8 May 1945* (unpublished official narrative), p. 12 (held at AHB).

41. WO 285/9, Dempsey diary, 10 September 1944.

42. AIR 27/1492, B Flight 247 Squadron F.540, September 1944.

43. Chris Hobson, 'Air-to-Air Blue-on-Blue: A Preliminary Study of Air-to-Air Fratricide Incidents Involving Royal Air Force Aircraft during the Second World War', *Royal Air Force Air Power Review*, Vol. 2, No. 2, Summer 1999, p. 46.

44. AIR 27/1491, A Flight 247 Squadron F.540, June 1944.

45. Air Historical Branch, *The Liberation of North West Europe Vol. 4, The Breakout and the Advance to the Lower Rhine, 12 June to 30 September 1944*, pp. 85, 105–106.

46. WO 219/2186, HQ AEAF to Advanced AEAF HQ, 2 September 1944.

47. Hobson, 'Air-to-Air Blue-on-Blue', p. 56.

48. AIR 37/706, report by the Air Officer Commander-in-Chief, Second TAF, 5 January 1945.

49. Hollinghurst papers, AC 73/23/49, comments on AHB monograph on the history of the airborne forces, p. 3.

50. Warren, *Airborne Operations*, pp. 156–161.

3.5. The Air Battle

ALTHOUGH HISTORIANS HAVE often alleged that the airborne forces received inadequate air support during Market Garden, such arguments have never been based on careful or detailed analysis of the air battle. The aim of this chapter is to address this further deficiency in the historiography, drawing on both British and German records to trace the course of air operations and measure their contribution to the Allied defeat, relative to events on the ground. Two basic tasks confronted the Allied fighter and fighter-bomber squadrons committed to Market Garden. The first and most important was clearly the protection of the Allied troop carrier and glider fleets involved in the airlifts; the second was the provision of air cover and offensive support to Allied ground forces, including XXX Corps and the airborne.

Where the first of these tasks was concerned, much depended on the Luftwaffe's response to the airborne assault. By September 1944, Germany had effectively lost the air war over Western Europe. The Luftwaffe's day fighter formations were massively outnumbered and were suffering from increasingly desperate shortages of trained aircrew, spare parts and fuel.[1] On 8 September, one Jagdkorps in the Western European theatre had 323 serviceable aircraft available, but 'only 56 could be sent on operations during the day owing to the fuel shortage'.[2] During Market Garden, they did enjoy certain compensating advantages over the Allies. They had a number of airfields close to the battle area, whereas the nearest Allied bases were around Antwerp and many Allied fighters flew from England. There was thus the potential for the Luftwaffe to reach eastern Holland more rapidly than Eighth Air Force formations, and they were quite well placed to exploit gaps in Allied fighter cover at fairly short notice. Arnhem, at the most northerly tip of the airborne corridor, was their easiest target; conversely it was the most difficult point in the corridor for the Allies to protect.[3] The Luftwaffe also benefited from radar coverage across Holland and were warned of incoming aircraft by visual observation posts on the coast;[4] by contrast, as already noted, the Arnhem and Nijmegen areas lay beyond the range of Allied radar.

However, few of the German airfields closest to eastern Holland could quickly be made suitable for day fighter operations.[5] Consequently, although the Germans diverted more than 300 fighters to airfields in the northwest after 17 September, almost doubling the number already positioned there, few if any of these aircraft became involved in the air battle over Holland until 23 September. The Luftwaffe mounted 75 day sorties on the 17th, 303 on the 18th, 210 on the 19th and 107 on the 21st. Operations on the 20th and 22nd were restricted to a few reconnaissance missions. All of these sorties were conducted by Luftflotte 3 – which was responsible for Western Europe – with aircraft already available on 17 September.[6] It was only on the 23rd that the presence of other aircraft was noted in the Allied records: US fighters operating over Holland encountered approximately 185 German aircraft that day, whereas Luftflotte 3 mounted only 44 sorties.[7] Until then the Luftwaffe succeeded in flying, on average, around 116 sorties per day.

Moreover, despite their closer proximity to Arnhem and Nijmegen, the Luftwaffe actually found few opportunities to intervene in the battle area unopposed. This was partly because of the large number of American fighters deployed to provide air cover for the various airlifts and re-supply missions, but it was also due to the very extensive and historically neglected efforts of 83 Group's fighter squadrons. Strangely, even the official Market Garden after-action reports record only the 1,300 offensive support and reconnaissance sorties flown by 83 Group during the operation. For reasons unclear, the 1,755 fighter sorties mounted by the Group from 17 to 25 September were omitted from First Allied Airborne Army's account.[8] With so many fighters normally airborne, any gaps in Allied air cover that did appear were either very fleeting or else occurred in periods of adverse weather, which inevitably hampered Luftwaffe operations too.

It is true that the Luftwaffe achieved high flying rates during the crucial early days of Market Garden – on 18 and 19 September – when, potentially, their intervention might have had a significant operational impact. But it must be remembered that the total German effort would have been divided between ground attack and interception tasks, and between different locations. Hence, of the 303 sorties mounted on 18 September, 110 were dispatched in the afternoon in an entirely futile attempt to intercept the incoming troop carriers. Not one Allied transport aircraft was attacked let alone shot down by a German fighter.[9] As for the morning mission, this is said to have been used primarily to provide fighter cover over German troop movements. A few 'low level attacks were made on troops near gliders but the effects could not be observed.'[10] Recording broadly the same events, the 83 Group diary describes how the Germans expended much of their effort on 'derelict gliders of yesterday's landings', an observation later confirmed by troops on the ground. Fighters from 83 Group intercepted the German formations and claimed to have shot down four enemy aircraft for the loss of one of their own.[11] It is quite obvious from these accounts that Luftwaffe activity on 18 September did not exert any tangible effect on the land battle.

The Luftwaffe's lack of success on the 18th may well have been responsible for a change of tactics the following day, when they assigned their main effort to intercepting the airlift and mounted only 48 ground-attack sorties. Again, the units assigned to the intercept role at no stage even threatened an Allied airlift that was, in any case, far smaller than originally planned. Indeed, most of them only reached the Market Garden area after the lift had been completed; they were then engaged by USAAF fighters that had been providing cover for the transport aircraft.[12] The morning mission targeted 82nd Airborne in the Nijmegen area and was apparently unchallenged; the Second TAF fighters that should have been on patrol were grounded by the weather all morning. However, poor weather conditions evidently affected the Luftwaffe as well, for they recorded executing just four low-level attacks near Groesbeek. Again, the impact would have been minimal. On the 20th the Luftwaffe did not mount any fighter or fighter-bomber sorties in the Market Garden area, and the outcome of the operation was already beyond doubt by the time they renewed their offensive missions on the afternoon of the 21st.[13]

From the foregoing account, it is possible to draw only one conclusion: in the period from 17 to 20 September – the decisive phase of Market Garden – Luftwaffe daytime operations would barely have been noticed by the vast majority of Allied troops at Arnhem and Nijmegen. It is absurd to suggest that the Allies somehow inflicted 'air inferiority' on themselves, nor can it be argued that Luftwaffe activity influenced the outcome of the fighting in and around Arnhem. The fact that the Luftwaffe periodically launched missions into south-eastern Holland came as no surprise at all to the Allies and some such response was indeed anticipated. Allied intelligence predicted that the Luftwaffe would mount around 300 single-engined fighter sorties within the first 24 hours of Market Garden; the actual figure was 268. The intelligence estimate for the following three days of between 100 and 150 sorties per day was again very accurate.[14]

The Luftwaffe enjoyed one notable daytime success in Market Garden but it contributed nothing to the German victory. On the afternoon of 21 September the Polish Parachute Brigade's lift and a re-supply mission bound for Arnhem were, in desperation, launched without fighter escorts; the Eighth Air Force and ADGB airfields were fogbound for much of the day. The Eighth Air Force's 56th Fighter Group ultimately got airborne, but they were unable to reach Holland in time for their scheduled rendezvous with the transport aircraft. Meanwhile, the Luftwaffe dispatched 107 fighter-bombers to Arnhem and Nijmegen for ground-attack operations; the effort expended to mount this operation was such that they were unable to launch any further day missions in the Market Garden area for 48 hours.

As luck would have it, they reached their objective at precisely the same time as the Allied air transports. The troop carriers committed to the Polish airlift clearly came under attack but the USAAF official history records that their only losses were caused by anti-aircraft fire, and even then only five aircraft were destroyed (although 33 others were damaged). Moreover, the losses were predominantly inflicted *after* they had made their drop. The RAF re-supply mission suffered far heavier attrition. The Luftwaffe claimed to have shot down 20 transport aircraft, but the total losses incurred by 38 Group and 46 Group that day amounted to 23 destroyed and 61 damaged out of 117 dispatched. The tables were only turned when the Eighth Air Force fighters appeared and shot down 13 German aircraft.[15]

The episode did not have any impact on the subsequent activities of the Polish Parachute Brigade on the ground, which had already been doomed to failure by the course of the fighting in Arnhem. And the sad fact is that, even if the re-supply mission and all other re-supply missions flown to Arnhem had succeeded, they would not have changed the outcome of the battle. Even if they had reached 1st Airborne Division the supplies would at best have made life marginally easier pending their withdrawal across the lower Rhine, but most of the canisters fell directly into German hands. With hindsight, it has to be admitted that the destruction and damage of large numbers of Allied transport aircraft in these futile ventures had only the most symbolic operational justification.

An Allied report drawn up after Market Garden summed up the Luftwaffe's daytime operations in the following terms:

> The support given by the German Air Force to the ground troops, either in intercepting transports and gliders en route, or dealing with troops that had already landed, was small. Its part in combating the Allied airborne landings has been a minor one, was largely ineffective, and has contributed little to the outcome of these operations.[16]

All of the surviving documentary evidence supports this conclusion. Anecdotal accounts of how airborne soldiers came under attack from one or two German fighters may capture some of the fear and panic that strafing and light bombing can instil among inexperienced ground troops, but they do not provide an accurate measure of the overall operational impact of Luftwaffe activity.

In fact, the Luftwaffe's most important intervention in the land battle during Market Garden occurred at night rather than in daytime. It was not mounted to influence the fighting at Arnhem directly but was instead aimed at impeding XXX Corps' advance north. The attack occurred on the night of 19/20 September, when German bombers of Fliegerkorps IX targeted Eindhoven, causing considerable damage and destroying an Allied supply column. This was Fliegerkorps IX's last operation of the war; on 22 September they were relegated to the status of a training command for the conversion of bomber pilots to fighters – a curious irony given their success in Market Garden relative to the day fighters' failure.[17]

The events are not in doubt. Far more questionable is any proposition that the raid came as a surprise, that it should somehow have been prevented or that it had a significant impact on the outcome of Market Garden. In fact, the documents demonstrate quite clearly that a threat from German night bombers was identified before the operation. First Allied Airborne Army thought that the Luftwaffe might be capable of mounting between 100 and 150 sorties within the first 24 hours of the operation, followed by (on average) 50-100 sorties over the next three days. As events turned out, these estimates were excessive not in their assessment of the number of aircraft available, but in their supposition that the Luftwaffe's dire logistical position would permit consecutive operations on this scale.[18]

The threat posed by night bombing resulted in an ill-fated attempt to deploy a glider-borne RAF ground-control intercept (GCI) team to Arnhem on 18 September. After coming under attack immediately upon landing, they were forced to destroy their equipment to prevent it falling into enemy hands, the result being that RAF night-fighters were unable to operate over the corridor with the benefit of GCI until Second TAF radar facilities were established at Eindhoven on the 21st.[19] In the intervening period they worked on a 'freelance' basis, with only an outside chance of actually intercepting enemy aircraft. Even with GCI, however, they might at best have shot down a few of the German bombers airborne on the night of 19/20 September. They could hardly have beaten off the entire raid.*

As for the impact of the Luftwaffe attack, it may have held up traffic for some hours on 20 September, but there is no documentary evidence that these delays were in any way decisive. The raid was understandably a traumatic event for the inhabitants of Eindhoven and sadly there were many civilian casualties,

---

* Coningham would later claim that Second TAF could have provided GCI coverage over Arnhem from the first day of Market Garden. However, he appears to have been mistaken on this point, for the records show that Second TAF GCI coverage did not extend as far as Arnhem on 17 September. Indeed, No. 15053 Fighter Direction Post was afterwards specifically deployed forward from Boechout (near Antwerp) to Eindhoven to bring Arnhem within range. See Air Ministry, *Radar in Raid Reporting*, p. 446.

but there is good reason to doubt its effectiveness from a purely military perspective. To begin with, it involved only 75 relatively light twin-engined bombers; by the standards of autumn 1944 this was a puny force.[20] Secondly, although nearly 9,000 buildings are said to have sustained some damage in the attack, the fact that such widespread damage was inflicted by so small a force strongly suggests that the bombing was dispersed across the city and was not effectively concentrated on Eindhoven's vital arteries. Only 228 premises were actually destroyed. Blockages along the main road through the centre of the city caused northbound traffic to be diverted along different routes, but there is nothing to indicate that XXX Corps were brought to a complete standstill.[21]

However, there were other documented hold-ups that day, which clearly had a far more important impact on the course of the operation. The most significant was an attack launched by Panzer Brigade 107 between Eindhoven and Son. When the attack began at 06.30, XXX Corps vehicles were still moving up from Eindhoven, but the destruction of several ammunition lorries by German shelling then effectively blocked the corridor until 11.00; the congestion extended right back through the city and beyond, towards Valkenswaard. The 43rd (Wessex) Division, en route to Nijmegen, spent the whole of the morning stationary in this area as a direct result. Further north, too, the road became heavily congested because only a single narrow bridge had been secured across the Maas-Waal Canal at Heumen.[22] The cumulative effect of these delays led to the postponement of the Waal River crossing for several hours; the 82nd Airborne troops assigned to this unenviable task were left waiting on the southern bank of the river while their assault boats were laboriously brought forward from Eindhoven. Yet even then it should be noted that the capture of the Nijmegen bridges that day was the result of a combined action in which the Guards Armoured Division ultimately seized the road bridge, and there is no evidence that British ground forces were hampered by specific shortages of manpower or materiel that day. Indeed, they expended no fewer than 3,400 rounds of 25-pounder artillery shells, as well as an unspec-ified quantity of tank, mortar and small arms ammunition.[23] The impact of congestion on the road north was felt only after the bridge was taken, when it proved impossible to exploit this critical breakthrough immediately.

Overall, then, there is no reason to believe that the Luftwaffe played an important part in the failure of Operation Market Garden. Unimpeded by the RAF and the USAAF, Luftflotte 3 posed only a minimal threat to Allied ground forces; against concerted opposition their prospects were even more limited. Fighter-bomber attacks at the northern end of the corridor were far too light and scattered to be effective, and German fighters stood little chance of pene-trating the Allied fighter screen to intercept incoming troop carriers. Beyond their one chance interception of the 21 September mission to Arnhem, their only notable achievement in Market Garden was the bombing of Eindhoven on the night of the 19th, which briefly slowed but did not halt XXX Corps' northward advance.

With the Luftwaffe thus largely excluded from the battle, why were the Allies unable to exploit their air superiority to influence ground operations decisively? The truth is that there was actually very little scope for doing so. Generally speaking, Allied ground-attack aircraft had, since the Normandy landings, proved most effective as defence or pursuit weapons. Their role in blunting German counter-attacks after 6 June and most famously in halting German armour at Mortain on 7 August was crucial; they gave the Allied armies an immense advantage by rendering all but impossible the open assembly and movement of enemy ground forces in daylight.[24] But in the offensive support role their record was far less impressive. Neither Second TAF nor the US 9th Tactical Air Command provided the key to the final breakout from Normandy. Instead, the critical air contribution came from the strategic bomber forces operating in support of consecutive ground offensives in late July and early August. This same pattern would emerge in Market Garden after the first day of the operation. In fact, between 18 and 25 September the vast majority of air strikes executed by Second TAF were of a defensive nature, targeting enemy forces seeking to cut the corridor, troops threatening 1st Airborne Division at Arnhem and German rail traffic bound for eastern Holland.

The first day of the operation was different: RAF Typhoons played a decisive part in breaking German resistance, enabling XXX Corps to commence their initial advance towards Valkenswaard and Eindhoven. But it is important to understand clearly why the role of tactical air power that day should have been so exceptional. To begin with, all the available 83 Group resources were concentrated on a single mission. Although heavily committed to ground attacks around Arnhem and Nijmegen on the morning of 17 September (along with the Mosquitos, Bostons and Mitchells of 2 Group),[25] after H-Hour their squadrons were entirely assigned to the support of XXX Corps. This was fully in accordance with the requests Dempsey submitted to Broadhurst shortly after Market Garden was authorized. However, as we have seen, Dempsey gave no thought whatever to the air support requirements of the airborne forces and no representations were made on their behalf until the very last moment.

Secondly, the support that 83 Group provided for XXX Corps on the afternoon of 17 September could hardly have been more carefully choreographed; this was not 'impromptu' or 'on call' close air support. The task confronting XXX Corps' leading elements – the Irish Guards (part of the Guards Armoured Division) – involved a northward advance up a single narrow road along which enemy troops were known to be deployed in some strength. The advance was therefore preceded by a heavy rolling artillery barrage commencing at 2.15 p.m. and extending across the German positions ahead of the Guards' tanks and supporting infantry. Following the barrage the Typhoon squadrons of 83 Group maintained 'cab rank' relays above the leading ground units, with eight aircraft arriving every five minutes during the first half hour or so, and every ten minutes thereafter. They were to be tasked against specific targets by a forward air controller operating what was known as a Visual Control Post (VCP) – normally an armoured car or tank equipped with ground-to-air radio. As soon as the Irish Guards ran into serious opposition, the Typhoons were called down to execute a series of low and extremely accurate attacks, some of which were no more than 100 yards ahead of the Guards' tanks.[26] The techniques employed were (by Second World War standards) very sophisticated. They were the product of close collaboration between the Army and the RAF stretching back to the North African campaign and encompassing numerous operations and exercises, as well as much specialized training.

Beyond this, the general area over which the Typhoons operated that day was well established in advance, and the positions occupied by the Germans would have been patently obvious from the air, even if their precise aiming points were only clarified after the battle began. They were largely sited in forested areas contrasting very sharply with the more open farmland that otherwise characterized this section of the corridor. Finally, at this stage, there was still a clear front line – a precise boundary between the Allied and German forces – which meant that, beyond a specific point on the road north, any ground troops were certain to be hostile. The Guards also employed reflective panels and yellow smoke to indicate their location to the Typhoon pilots. The VCP worked very effectively, both to guide aircraft onto potential targets and to prevent fratricide. Thus, despite the very close proximity of British and German ground forces and the relative inaccuracy of rocket projectiles, only one of the Guards' vehicles fell victim to friendly fire from the air.[27] The weather was fine and visibility good until the end of the afternoon.[28]

Had such conditions prevailed throughout Market Garden, close air support might have played an equally vital role later on. Unfortunately however, the operational environment changed dramatically. After 17 September, 83 Group tasking was dispersed across the entire corridor area and beyond in a vain attempt to satisfy the requirements of a veritable plethora of Second Army and airborne units; there were also many interdiction missions against enemy troop and rail movements. The weather deteriorated sharply, almost completely grounding 83 Group's Typhoon squadrons on 18 and 19 September. Having flown 319 offensive support sorties on the first day of the operation, they succeeded in mounting only 62 on the 18th. And very few of the aircraft that managed to take off were able to find targets in the areas to which they were sent. A Typhoon flight dispatched to Groesbeek obtained no guidance from friendly ground forces and the only troops they observed were American; of the attacks executed in support of XXX Corps (and XII Corps, covering XXX Corps' left flank), only one showed any signs of success. A pre-planned mission against four German airfields outside the Market Garden area was also delayed by the weather until the very end of the afternoon, and was then unsuccessful.[29]

This experience was typical of the remainder of the operation. No longer was there any scope for preliminary planning or choreography; all air support had to be conducted on a responsive and ad hoc basis. The difficulties were exacerbated by consistently poor weather, the absence of a clear front line, the Typhoon's endurance limitations and the failure of ground-to-air radio equipment. To make matters worse, much of the fighting took place in environments where combat identification was hugely problematic from the air, and where there was ample cover for hostile ground forces – within towns such as Nijmegen and Arnhem, or heavily wooded areas like Oosterbeek.

It was on the 18th that, in different circumstances, effective close air support might have made an important difference to events on the ground. In the popular mythology, the primary cause of XXX Corps' slow progress that day was the demolition of the bridge across the Wilhelmina Canal at Son, just north of Eindhoven. In actual fact, they only reached the bridge at 7 p.m. and, given that they stopped for the night at a similar time on the previous evening, it is unlikely that they would have advanced further even if it had been intact. Their slow progress had little to do with events at Son; rather, they were held up at the village of Aalst – between Valkenswaard and Eindhoven – attempting to overcome German resistance along the north bank of a small stream called the Tongelreep.[30] The possibility that minor water obstacles in this area might seriously impede the advance had, of course, been recognized in the original Market Garden plan, which had proposed dropping 101st Airborne Division both to the north and south of Eindhoven.

When the Irish Guards called for air support to help clear the German positions, they were advised that the Typhoon squadrons had been grounded by the weather.[31] Conditions over the Market Garden corridor itself were apparently not entirely unfavourable, but the official sources confirm that the weather at 83 Group's airfields was very different. According to 182 Squadron's record it was a day of 'poor visibility and rain showers'; the 247 Squadron diary states that the 'weather [was] extremely bad today, and visibility [was] less than 1,000 yards'.[32] The very obvious hazards involved in flying a fighter-bomber at between 300 and 400 mph in such conditions were magnified by the absence of alternative landing options in the event of airfield closure.

Given the fundamental importance of the Typhoons' intervention on 17

September it would be very easy to assume that their absence on the 18th was central to the Guards' disastrous failure that day. Yet the Guards' performance must be considered in context. Historically, of course, their regiment enjoys a formidable fighting reputation, but their relatively brief experience of armoured warfare between 1941 (when the Armoured Division was formed) and 1945 (when it was disbanded) is not widely considered to have been a happy one. Deficiencies in both doctrine and training, which they shared with other British armoured formations, were exacerbated in some respects by a regimental culture inevitably better suited to their traditional infantry role than to one so much more dependent on the exploitation of technology. They arrived in Normandy early in July 1944, lacking any effective grasp of armour-infantry co-operation and wedded to the concept of the set-piece attack. Instead of maintaining constant pressure on the enemy, it was envisaged that initial contact would be followed by a lengthy period of preparation before the main assault began. A timetable drawn up by the 5th Guards Armoured Brigade for one exercise in November 1943 provided for a three-hour gap between the first contact with the enemy and the launch of the brigade attack.[33]

Such practices were all too evident in their subsequent approach to live hostilities. At a critical stage during Operation Goodwood (Montgomery's offensive to the southeast of Caen, launched on 18 July 1944) the Guards were confronted with the task of capturing the village of Cagny. Cagny had been very heavily bombed and was by no means strongly defended, but a battery of four 88 mm anti-aircraft guns, having survived the bombardment, had been re-deployed in the anti-tank role and had destroyed an isolated and exposed squadron of tanks belonging to 11th Armoured Division. Otherwise, the village was only held by a handful of German infantry.

The Guards outnumbered the German units at Cagny by a very substantial margin and could almost certainly have overrun them quickly, but their advance instead came to a halt at around midday. They then spent several hours organizing an attack and did not finally suppress German resistance in the village until the early evening, after which their forward elements bedded down for the night, just as they did at Valkenswaard on the first evening of Market Garden. The next day, they made little further progress between Cagny and Frenouville and only secured this second objective on 20 July, having belatedly discovered that the Germans had evacuated it.[34] Early in August the Guards were halted during another failed offensive – Operation Bluecoat.[35] Following the collapse of German resistance in Normandy they swept across northern France with remarkable speed, reaching Brussels barely a week after crossing the Seine, yet this feat was possible because they encountered only weak and ineffective opposition along the way. The Irish Guards' war diary for 3 September records an advance of 82 miles in 13 hours. 'The populace cheered and established plum apple and beer points along the road; the sun shone hotly and everyone enjoyed themselves enormously.'[36] They would afterwards fight gallantly in a series of actions around the Albert and Meuse-Escaut canals, but their rate of advance slowed dramatically and in their most notable offensive action – the Irish Guards' capture of the Neerpelt bridgehead on 10 September – they were faced by confused and leaderless opponents who were taken completely by surprise; only three of their number became casualties.[37]

On the first day of Market Garden the Guards were confronted by a German battle group occupying prepared positions. Although some of their number were recent recruits of low quality, they also included veteran paratroops, elements of II SS Panzer Corps (which had been moved to the front from Arnhem), and a battery of ten Russian-made anti-tank guns. The Germans knew full well that an Allied ground offensive was imminent and were bracing themselves for the onslaught.[38] Yet, as a cohesive entity, this force was effectively eliminated in the subsequent fighting. The German units that halted the Guards at Aalst on 18 September were a motley assortment scrambled together and thrown into the line on the day itself. The first hold-up in the Guards' advance – extending from 7 to 10 a.m. – was caused by a report suggesting that the road to Aalst was covered by three German self-propelled guns. In fact, there was but a single Sturmgeschutz III, which, according to one account, had already been abandoned. Having finally dealt with this obstacle, the Guards then ran into the main German blocking force just north of the village, which comprised at least two but no more than four 88 mm guns covering the bridge over the Tongelreep, plus supporting infantry. There were afterwards repeated exchanges of fire, but it is nevertheless clear that the Guards again broke contact with the enemy during the afternoon. This may be inferred from the fact that, when the Germans eventually withdrew, their departure went entirely unnoticed. At about 5 p.m., the battalion headquarters at Valkenswaard received a visit from the divisional and brigade commanders 'to find out the situation and give further orders'. It may be surmised that they were not entirely happy with the situation. Soon afterwards it was finally established that the Germans had abandoned their positions and the advance resumed, but the Guards were 24 hours behind schedule by the time they reached Eindhoven. On the 19th the role of lead battalion was transferred from the Irish Guards to the Grenadiers.[39]

It should not be forgotten that the Guards were confined to an extremely narrow axis of advance in this engagement. There was very little room to manoeuvre, and the general topography of the area very obviously favoured their opponents. But it is still hard to avoid the conclusion that at this stage of the operation they had not fully grasped the critical importance of maintaining a forward impetus, even if this meant taking greater risks. Their overnight halt at Valkenswaard has itself sometimes been seen as evidence that this was so, but far more telling are the Commonwealth War Graves Commission records, which suggest that the Irish Guards incurred just one fatality on 18 September; the Guards Armoured Division as a whole lost only one tank.[40] For a front-line armoured formation fighting in the vanguard of a major offensive, such casualty rates can only be considered minuscule. The Guards had of course taken heavier losses the day before, but it is worth noting that virtually all their casualties were inflicted during the initial German ambush rather than in the subsequent advance to Valkenswaard.[41] It is of course possible that tactical air support might have helped the Guards to overwhelm German resistance on the road to Eindhoven on 18 September, but clearly some much more fundamental issues lay behind their halt at Aalst that day.

Are there stronger grounds for contending that the Typhoons might have decisively influenced the fortunes of the airborne troops further north – particularly at Arnhem – as Major General Urquhart himself maintained?[42] This also seems doubtful. Urquhart's critique was inevitably very parochial. He did not acknowledge that the Typhoons played a vital part elsewhere in the Market Garden corridor on the first day of the operation, and he appears to have been unaware that the weather was largely responsible for grounding 83 Group on 18 and also 19 September, when 'heavy ground mist covered the airfield and no flying was possible, according to 182 Squadron'.[43] As the Battle of Arnhem was effectively lost on the 19th, this means that there was actually no real opportunity for tactical air power to intervene in time to make any difference.

But even if the weather had been more favourable, it is highly unlikely that 83 Group would have been able to change the outcome of the fighting. The general failure of 1st Airborne Division's communications meant that until 20 September there was literally no information about the course of the battle or the dispositions of British and German troops in the town. Writing on 18 September, 83 Group's diarist could only record that 'The Arnhem division had not reported, though it was known that the bridge over the Neder Rijn was intact.' On the 19th he wrote that 'Still there was no news from Arnhem.' Hence it was not until the 20th – the day on which resistance at the bridge was overwhelmed – that 83 Group finally got some idea of 1st Airborne's plight, and they received only the vaguest insight into the location of friendly and enemy ground forces then. The two American air support teams belatedly assigned to 1st Airborne enjoyed no more success with their untested radio equipment than the other signallers at Arnhem. They proved unable to contact the rest of the Corps air support net, and no ground-to-air communication was established with 83 Group aircraft either. In any case, both teams quickly fell victim to enemy action.[44]

The resulting total absence of targeting information would have been a particular handicap because of the terrain across which so much of the battle was fought. The key actions either occurred in the streets of western Arnhem itself or in the dense woodland that extends from the edge of the town out to Wolfheze. Until 20 September the fighting was also very dispersed, with separate actions breaking out right across the area from the road bridge to the landing zones. Even with effective forward air control provisions it would have been very difficult to bring air power to bear in such a situation; with no guidance at all from the ground it would have been impossible. And, as the 83 Group Typhoons could spend very little time loitering over the more northerly reaches of the Market Garden corridor, the scope for finding targets of opportunity would also have been extremely limited.[45]

Moreover, for the Typhoon pilots there was the ever-present risk that apparently hostile troops might turn out to be friendly. For much of the operation they possessed no bomb line information other than that supplied by 1st Airborne before 17 September, and this ultimately bore no relation to the dispositions of British or German troops; the original line was in fact well outside the town.[46] The idea that German airmen were somehow unaffected by such considerations is entirely without foundation.[47] Luftwaffe fighter-bombers had obvious hostile targets in the glider-strewn landing grounds near Wolfheze but, even then, German ground troops at Arnhem are said to have taken cover whenever they heard an aircraft overhead. In his account of the German perspective on Market Garden, Robert Kershaw describes how one Luftwaffe attack initially targeted the German stronghold of Elst rather than Polish paratroops at Driel, and also records that German pilots actually visited forward ground positions to draw maps of the British defences for use in subsequent bombing attacks. They evidently had no other means of pinpointing potential targets.[48]

The difficulties confronting 83 Group in Market Garden are amply illustrated by the events of the following day. On 20 September they were at first grounded by morning fog, but by midday this had lifted, allowing at least some Typhoons to fly armed reconnaissance missions during the afternoon. They were instructed to target infantry, artillery and 'tanks north of the Neder Rijn in the Arnhem area'. However, over Arnhem, the Typhoon pilots found '10/10ths cloud at 1,000 feet'. There was no radio contact with 1st Airborne, no movement was observed and no attacks were executed; one aircraft was lost during a transit north that should probably not have been attempted in the first place. The 21st was very similar. Although more Typhoons took to the air, they found thick low cloud over Arnhem, which prevented all but one attack from being prosecuted; this resulted in the destruction of a single German truck and the loss of another aircraft.[49] No further air-to-ground strikes were even attempted, despite a number of specific requests for air support.

Historians have once again tended to view tactical air power as the critical missing ingredient on the 21st. Recalling the events of 17 September, they argue that with the RAF's help XXX Corps (again spearheaded by the Irish Guards) might well have been able to overwhelm German resistance between Nijmegen and Arnhem.[50] This may be true, but it is once again important to understand that the conditions which prevailed north of Nijmegen that day were very different from those that allowed air power to be exploited to such devastating effect at the beginning of the operation. Then, as we have noted, the Typhoons' support for the Irish Guards had been pre-planned down to its smallest detail well in advance. By contrast, on the 21st, there is no evidence that 83 Group received any prior warning of the Guards' requirements. Indeed, when the call for support first came through, such aircraft as might theoretically have been provided were already airborne and committed to armed reconnaissance missions.[51] Nowhere do the group, wing or squadron records indicate that the Typhoons were expecting to work with the Guards' VCP that day, and this may well partly explain why the VCP was unable to reach them (although, at the time, the Guards blamed faulty radio equipment).

It would in any case have been very difficult to arrange air support for them because the timing of their advance remained uncertain until the very last moment. It was evidently hoped that they might move off from the Nijmegen bridgehead early in the morning, but they did not actually receive the order to strike north until 11 a.m., and they did not execute the order until 1.30 p.m. In these circumstances it proved hard enough to secure the services of nearby artillery units, which did not become active until late in the afternoon; obtaining tactical air support from airfields more than 100 miles distant was inevitably going to be far more difficult.[52] The Typhoons ultimately recovered to their airfields to undergo routine maintenance and refuelling, and the Guards then submitted a further request for assistance. But by this time the afternoon's airlift was imminent, and 83 Group were therefore unable to respond until the transport aircraft and their escorts had left the Arnhem area.[53] Well before this – indeed, before the Guards even set out from the Nijmegen bridgehead – any lingering chance of an Allied victory in Market Garden had disappeared.[54]

The following day, almost inevitably, the weather cleared and the Typhoon squadrons were for the first time since 17 September able to play a full part in the operation. In total they flew some 260 offensive support sorties. Yet this considerable effort had still to be dispersed across a range of different tasks such as armed reconnaissance in the Arnhem area, pre-planned attacks on targets in Arnhem, interdiction of German troop movements outside the Market Garden corridor and support for ground forces inside the corridor; there was no scope for concentrating force at any single decisive point.

Moreover, the difficulties encountered over the preceding days by no means disappeared entirely. The interdiction task in the Reichswald Forest area was hampered by poor visibility, and the armed reconnaissances over Arnhem were again conducted outside the bomb line – a reflection of the fact that 83 Group had still not received detailed and up-to-date intelligence on the Arnhem battle. At least one pre-planned attack targeted a 'factory to the south of the town', which was almost certainly the brickworks on the south bank of the Lower Rhine.[55] On 19 September 1st Airborne troops moving into Arnhem on the opposite side of the river had been ambushed from the brickworks, but it was of little tactical significance by the 22nd.

The Typhoons' most important task on 22 September was executed much further south near the town of Veghel, where the Germans were seeking to cut the corridor. The fighting at Veghel reproduced the conditions in which tactical air power had proved most effective in Normandy; in taking to the offensive the Germans were for once compelled to assemble and manoeuvre in open terrain in daylight. Yet Typhoon operations were far from straightforward even at Veghel. The absence of a clearly defined front line again proved a particular handicap and there was a protracted delay while XXX Corps established a bomb line.[56] As a result, by the time the Typhoons arrived, the original targeting intelligence with which they had been supplied was no longer accurate and they were effectively left to find targets of opportunity.[57] These at least were easily located, and 83 Group ultimately claimed to have damaged or destroyed 9 tanks and 71 other vehicles that day, although they lost 3 more Typhoons in the process.[58]

Subsequent operations by 83 Group involved little more than damage limitation to shore up a vulnerable corridor leading nowhere, and to relieve pressure on 1st Airborne Division. In certain respects the Typhoon squadrons' task was simplified during the final stages of Market Garden. Eindhoven airfield, severely damaged by Bomber Command earlier in the month, had been sufficiently patched up by 22 September to permit 83 Group to deploy several squadrons forward, more than halving their transit time to Arnhem and allowing them to spend considerably longer in the target area searching for enemy forces. Moreover, they now at last began receiving specific and accurate intelligence on German positions around the 1st Airborne perimeter via a radio link that had been established with 64 Medium Regiment, Royal Artillery, and a VCP began operating on the south bank of the Lower Rhine.[59]

Yet considerable difficulties remained. Requests for air support passed back from 1st Airborne had to be routed from 64 Medium Regiment to I Airborne Corps Headquarters, who then passed them to XXX Corps, who then passed them on to Second Army, who then finally submitted them to 83 Group. It is hardly surprising that this convoluted chain was not particularly responsive.[60]

*83 Group Typhoons at Eindhoven airfield, following their deployment
on 22 September 1944*

The weather worsened again on 23 September so that only 80 offensive
support sorties could be flown, and once more these were spread across a large
area and dispersed over a variety of tasks. These included the interdiction of
German forces almost anywhere between Veghel and the Reichswald Forest,
direct support for 1st Airborne and strikes on German rail traffic heading for
Arnhem or other parts of eastern Holland.[61]

The following day, 83 Group mounted some 228 offensive sorties, although
weather conditions were still relatively poor; on the 25th they flew 191. Their
missions were broadly divided between the interdiction of German rail traffic,
direct support for 1st Airborne Division and support for Second Army
elements – notably XII Corps. The interdiction task was unquestionably the
most rewarding and, in one instance, 'the destruction of one train led to a
second colliding with it'. On the 25th, Typhoons from 181 Squadron and 247
Squadron demolished a German strongpoint in a factory at Best, which was
blocking XII Corps' advance. But sadly, at Arnhem, 1st Airborne Division were
by this time confined to such a small area that 'it was difficult to locate targets
close to them and not easy to assess results'.[62]

The periodic reluctance of 83 Group to accept air support requests in such
circumstances has been the subject of some criticism; it has been pointed out
that 64 Medium Regiment, positioned south of the Waal near Nijmegen,

succeeded in laying down artillery fire with pinpoint accuracy very close to 1st Airborne's perimeter.[63] This line of argument invariably fails to clarify precisely how it was possible to deploy the artillery to such remarkable effect. Recently, however, a full explanation has been provided by Denis Falvey, who served with 64 Medium Regiment during Market Garden. Falvey points out the crucial role played by 1st Airborne's artillery staff – by Lieutenant Colonel R.G. Loder-Symonds and perhaps most of all by the trained observation officers who served under him. They became the 'eyes' of the artillery:

> So began a remarkable collaboration with men and guns they had never seen, which was made effective by adherence to common and well-used procedures. We merely carried out the fire orders they issued … So I suggest we need to adjust our perspective and give more credit to the airborne OP officers, and less to the artillery.[64]

By contrast, as we have seen, 1st Airborne arrived in Arnhem on 17 September with literally no experience of air support tactics, techniques and procedures (which they had completely ignored) and with two untried American air support teams equipped with inoperable radios. The difference could hardly be more telling. Loder-Symonds and his subordinates provided expert guidance for 64 Medium Regiment while the Typhoon squadrons received hardly any guidance at all.

Notes

1. Air Ministry, *The Rise and Fall of the German Air Force, 1933–1945* (St Martin's Press, New York, 1983), p. 339.
2. War Diary of Luftflotte 3, September 1944, entry of 8 September 1944.
3. AIR 37/706, report by the Air Officer Commander-in-Chief, Second TAF, 5 January 1945.
4. Kershaw, *It Never Snows in September*, p. 230.
5. Air Ministry, *The Rise and Fall of the German Air Force*, p. 340.
6. War Diary of Luftflotte 3, September 1944, entries of 17–25 September 1944.
7. War Diary of Luftflotte 3, September 1944, entry of 23 September 1944; US Strategic Air Forces in Europe Air Intelligence Summary for week ending 24 September 1944 (held at AHB); US Strategic Air Forces in Europe Air Intelligence Summary for week ending 15 October 1944.
8. Calculated from AIR 25/698, 83 Group F.540, September 1944.
9. Warren, *Airborne Operations*, p. 118.
10. War Diary of Luftflotte 3, September 1944, entry of 18 September 1944.
11. AIR 25/698, 83 Group F.540, September 1944. For the ground perspective

see WO 171/393, 1st Airborne Division War Diary, September 1944, Annexure 0.2, 1 Air Landing Brigade diary.

12. Warren, *Airborne Operations*, p. 128.

13. War Diary of Luftflotte 3, September 1944, entries of 19 and 20 September 1944; AIR 25/698, 83 Group F.540, September 1944.

14. WO 219/4998, memorandum by AC of S G2, 12 September 1944; War Diary of Luftflotte 3, 17–21 September 1944. Figure of 268 combines operations on the afternoon of 17 September and the morning of 18 September.

15. Warren, *Airborne Operations*, pp. 137–138, 227; War Diary of Luftflotte 3, September 1944, entries of 21–23 September 1944. The Luftflotte 3 War Diary records that 13 aircraft were lost; the 56th Group pilots claimed 15 for the loss of 2 of their own fighters.

16. WO 205/693, report entitled 'German Air Force Reaction to Airborne Landings in Holland', by Colonel J. Cella, GSC, AC of S, G2, First Allied Airborne Army, 2 October 1944.

17. Air Ministry, *The Rise and Fall of the German Air Force*, p. 340.

18. WO 219/4998, memorandum by AC of S G2, 12 September 1944.

19. Air Ministry, *Radar in Raid Reporting*, pp. 445–446.

20. Margry, Karel (ed.), *Operation Market-Garden Then and Now*, Vol. 2 (Battle of Britain International, London, 2002), pp. 396, 400.

21. Ibid.

22. Ibid., pp. 346–347, 520, 528–529; WO 171/341, XXX Corps to Second Army, sitrep as at 202330.

23. WO 171/376, Guards Armoured Division War Diary, 20 September 1944.

24. D'Este, *Decision in Normandy*, p. 155.

25. Warren, *Airborne Operations*, p. 100.

26. WO 171/1256, War Diary, 2nd Irish Guards (Armoured Battalion), 17 September 1944.

27. Ibid.; WO 205/872, 21st Army Group report on Operation Market Garden, 17 September 1944.

28. AIR 27/1492, B Flight 247 Squadron F.540, September 1944.

29. Ibid.; AIR 25/698, 83 Group F.540, September 1944.

30. Margry, Karel (ed.), *Operation Market-Garden Then and Now*, Vol. 1 (Battle of Britain International, London, 2002), p. 254. 18 September 1944. The stream is incorrectly identiüed as the River Dommel in the Irish Guards' War Diary.

31. Ryan, *A Bridge Too Far*, p. 253.

32. AIR 27/1136, 182 Squadron F.540, September 1944; AIR 27/1489, 247 Squadron F.540, September 1944.

33. Timothy Harrison Place, *Military Training in the British Army* (Frank Cass, London, 2000), pp. 108, 117, 121–122.

34. Daglish, *Operation Goodwood*, pp. 42, 156, 168, 181.

35. Wilmot, *The Struggle for Europe*, p. 441.
36. WO 171/1256, War Diary, 2nd Irish Guards (Armoured Battalion), 3 September 1944.
37. Margry (ed.), *Operation Market-Garden Then and Now*, Vol. 1, p. 56.
38. Kershaw, *It Never Snows in September*, pp. 26–30, 45; WO 171/1256, War Diary, 2nd Irish Guards (Armoured Battalion), 17 September 1944.
39. Kershaw, *It Never Snows in September*, pp. 26–30, 45; WO 171/1256, War Diary, 2nd Irish Guards (Armoured Battalion), 17 and 18 September 1944; Margry (ed.), *Operation Market-Garden Then and Now*, Vol. 1, pp. 248–260. There are a number of discrepancies between the various sources; for example, Kershaw places the Russian anti-tank gun battery between Valkenswaard and Aalst. However, the Irish Guards did not record encounters with anti-tank guns (or with anything other than the Sturmgeschutz III) in this area and speciücally noted the elim- ination of the Russian battery during the üghting on 17 September. The Guards recorded that they ran into four 88 mm guns north of Aalst on 18 September but Margry, who comes from Aalst and was able to draw heavily on local eyewitness accounts (as well as the oüicial British records), concluded that there were only two.
40. WO 171/376, Guards Armoured Division War Diary, 18 September 1944. The sole Irish Guards fatality of 18 September in the Commission's database is Lance Sergeant Cyril Joseph Richardson of the 3rd Battalion. However, the fact that he is buried at the Commonwealth War Cemetery at Leopoldsburg in Belgium strongly suggests that he became a casualty somewhere to the south of Valkenswaard during the ürst day's üghting (or perhaps earlier still) and was then evacuated to a base location for medical treatment.
41. WO 171/1256, War Diary, 2nd Irish Guards (Armoured Battalion), 17 September 1944. The diary states that they lost nine tanks in the ambush, but later records that 'the day's üghting cost us in all 9 tanks'.
42. 1st Airborne Division Report on Operation Market, 10 January 1945.
43. AIR 27/1136, 182 Squadron F.540, September 1944.
44. WO 219/2865, memorandum by Lieutenant Colonel J. Larocque, Air Corps, Assistant G3, to Brigadier General Stearly, 11 November 1944.
45. The 'up' and 'down' times recorded in the squadron diaries indicate a typical sortie duration of one hour; much of this would have been spent in transit.
46. Cox, 'Air Power in Operation Market Garden', p. 230.
47. This unfounded proposition appears in Harvey, *Arnhem*, p. 185.
48. Kershaw, *It Never Snows in September*, pp. 230, 267.
49. AIR 25/698, 83 Group F.540; AIR 27/954, 137 Squadron F.540; AIR 27/1136, 182 Squadron F.540; AIR 27/1489, 247 Squadron F.540; AIR 27/1492, B Flight 247 Squadron F.540; all entries from September 1944.
50. Gooderson, *Air Power at the Battlefront*, p. 91.

51. AIR 25/698, 83 Group F.540, September 1944.
52. WO 171/1256, War Diary, 2nd Irish Guards (Armoured Battalion), 21 September 1944. According to the diary, an artillery observation ofücer did not join them until 15.00 and there was no actual üre support until 17.00.
53. AIR 25/698, 83 Group F.540, September 1944.
54. Kershaw, *It Never Snows in September*, pp. 221–227, 310.
55. AIR 25/698, 83 Group F.540, September 1944.
56. Ibid.
57. AIR 26/184, 124 Wing F.540, September 1944. The original location supplied to 124 Wing was E.5736, but no targets were found there; the main Typhoon attacks were executed at E.5536, E.5834 and E.5633, in the area around Erp and Gemert.
58. AIR 25/698, 83 Group F.540, September 1944.
59. Ibid; AIR 27/1134, 181 Squadron F.540; AIR 27/1136, 182 Squadron F.540; AIR 27/954, 137 Squadron F.540; AIR 27/1489, 247 Squadron F.540; AIR 27/1492, B Flight 247 Squadron F.540; AIR 24/1504, 2 TAF Operations Daily Log; all entries from September 1944.
60. Cox, 'Air Power in Operation Market Garden', p. 230.
61. AIR 25/698, 83 Group F.540, September 1944.
62. Ibid; AIR 27/1134, 181 Squadron F.540; AIR 27/1489, 247 Squadron F.540; both entries from September 1944.
63. Cox, 'Air Power in Operation Market Garden', p.230.
64. Denis Falvey, *A Well-Known Excellence: British Artillery and an Artilleryman in World War Two* (Brassey's, London, 2002), p. 197.

Part 3: Conclusion

TWO BROAD THEMES are common in the familiar critique of the Allied air forces' role in the failure of Market Garden: first, it is maintained that airmen exerted too much influence over the entire operation plan; second, the air plan is said to have failed in part because it ignored earlier airborne practice. The first contention is quite simply unsustainable; indeed, the reverse is true. Excluded completely from the conceptual planning process, the RAF and the USAAF then effectively had Market Garden imposed upon them. Neither the air transport commanders nor Coningham, the key tactical air force commander, were given any opportunity to influence the operation before Montgomery submitted it to Eisenhower for approval, and they were allowed only three clear days for detailed planning and preparation, despite the enormous complexity of the air task. They were thus left to do the best they could in exceptionally difficult circumstances. This was an entirely unnecessary and avoidable situation, which would not have arisen at all if the correct command channels had been observed.

As for the assertion that the Market Garden air plan was flawed because it neglected established airborne tactics and doctrine, this could hardly be more misleading; in reality, of course, the entire Market Garden concept was at odds with past practice and with previously identified airborne lessons. Furthermore, there would only have been good grounds for mimicking earlier airlift plans if they had been successful and this was manifestly not the case. Indeed, it is impossible to understand many of the air planning decisions taken in the days preceding Market Garden without acknowledging the extent to which past airborne ventures had gone very badly wrong, primarily because of a series of inaccurate and dispersed night-time airlifts. It was for this reason that Eisenhower attached top priority to improving troop carrier navigation when he appointed Brereton to command First Allied Airborne Army, and the actions of Williams, Hollinghurst and their staffs in planning the Market Garden lift were entirely consistent with Eisenhower's directive. Their determination to avoid the acute problems encountered in Sicily and Normandy ultimately ensured that the airlift was the most accurate and concentrated of the war.

Other aspects of the Market Garden air mythology may now also be dispensed with. For example, this study has demonstrated that the potential difficulties involved in finding landing areas close to the Arnhem and Nijmegen objectives did not suddenly emerge at a meeting between Hollinghurst and Urquhart some time after 10 September; they had actually been identified five days earlier. Browning had accepted their legitimacy and had alerted Second Army to the problem, and both he and Dempsey had subsequently recommended that the operational objective should be switched from Arnhem to Wesel. But Montgomery could not be persuaded to choose an alternative crossing point, nor was he sufficiently concerned to order First Allied Airborne Army to change their plans.

Equally, it must now be accepted that there were entirely genuine difficulties involved in planning airborne landings south of the Arnhem bridges. The sheer depth of the operation and the resulting importance of evasive routing narrowed the DZ/LZ options to some extent. The terrain features in this area are well documented and would have made large-scale glider landings exceptionally hazardous, as well as massively complicating the assembly and movement of personnel, vehicles and equipment. At the same time, Allied intelligence revealed such a substantial build-up in German flak defences at both Arnhem and Nijmegen during the first half of September that some officers came to suspect that the security of the forthcoming operation had been compromised. Given the inherent vulnerabilities of transport aircraft – particularly during airborne operations – Allied air commanders therefore took an entirely rational decision when they sought to exploit the intelligence at their disposal by avoiding the main anti-aircraft artillery concentrations. Information exploitation is, after all, a fundamental principle of operational planning.

This did not leave 1st Airborne to cope with landing areas that can reasonably be termed 'distant', and the unprecedented accuracy of their lift should in any case have helped to offset such handicaps as arose because the DZs and LZs were not immediately adjacent to the bridges. Sadly, however, they did not do so because 1 Parachute Brigade arrived at Arnhem with a deeply flawed plan and were badly led during the critical first 24 hours of the battle. As far as other elements of the division are concerned, it is quite wrong to assert that they did not concentrate near to the road bridge because of the location of the landing area near Wolfheze. The divisional plan never envisaged that either 4 Parachute Brigade or 1 Air Landing Brigade would deploy near the bridge. In any case, the supposition that the road bridge would have been held if more troops had landed in its immediate vicinity must be considered highly questionable. The heroic stand mounted by Frost and his troops only lasted for three days because, for much of this period, the Germans assigned their main effort to the battle in western Arnhem. Confronted by a different threat, they would have produced a different response. Their numerical and logistical advantage was such that 1st Airborne Division never stood much chance of success in the absence of prompt relief over land by XXX Corps.

As for the Market Garden airlift, it is now possible to dismiss the notion that Williams' 45-hour schedule was 'wrong' or that it represented 'a serious and needless error'. In fact, the rationale underpinning the schedule cannot be contested if the constraints confronted by his staff are taken into consideration. Williams' plan was constructed within very tight parameters but nevertheless provided for the carriage of more airborne troops within the first critical 24 hours of the operation than any other scheme would have done. It would not have been possible to stage two full-scale lifts during the daylight hours of a single day, and the weather would have defeated an attempt to mount two lifts on any scale on 17 September.

Thus, it was not the Market Garden airlift timetable that was 'wrong'. Rather, the critical error lay in the assumption made by all Allied army, airborne and troop carrier commanders that a multiple-lift operation could safely be launched against deep and defended objectives. The multiple-lift concept reflected the steady growth of the airborne forces throughout the war, their acquisition of enormous quantities of equipment and their dependence on extensive headquarters and support provisions. But the advantages conferred by these facilities should have been more carefully weighed against the high costs in terms of airlift planning and execution – the increasingly cumbersome and protracted timetables, the loss of tactical surprise and the extravagant DZ/LZ defence requirement. These drawbacks might potentially have been moderated if the airborne forces had possessed a range of contingency plans designed to cater for differing operational scenarios, including high-risk ventures requiring the fastest possible delivery of combat troops. But the only available 'off the shelf' lift plan on 10 September 1944 had originally been devised for Operation Linnet – a venture which (if it had been mounted) would not have faced strong German opposition. Nevertheless, Market Garden only happened at all within the timescales agreed between Montgomery and Eisenhower because the Linnet airlift plan already existed. There would not have been sufficient time for the planners to devise entirely new arrangements catering for Market Garden's specific and far more exacting needs.

The difficulties that arose with drop zone selection and airlift scheduling were consequences of the way in which the Allied air command chain was excluded from involvement in conceptual planning in September 1944. But the same fundamental lack of air force input was evident in the application of combat air power. It was very unwise to launch Market Garden at the northernmost extremity of Second TAF's area of responsibility, at the limits of 83

Group's operational radius, and with 84 Group out of range and pre-allocated to First Canadian Army. Bomber Command's prior assignment to the Canadians was equally problematic. The depth of the operation also influenced the way in which offensive air power was employed. Ideally the air forces should have been used to strike targets *ahead* of Allied ground forces, as they were in Normandy and later during Operation Varsity in 1945. But, because the Market Garden objectives lay so far inside enemy-occupied territory, much of the available air power had to be used merely to ensure the safe transit of Allied troop carrier and glider formations.[1] The situation was worsened by poor liaison. Montgomery refused to work with Coningham and had minimal contact with Brereton, while the airborne forces maintained hardly any links with Second TAF; the Allied air headquarters were geographically dispersed, and communications were fragile in the extreme. The complexities of airspace management and demarcation and several successive days of poor weather created still further difficulties, as did the absence of a clear front line in the battle area. Beyond all this, despite their desperate need for fire-power, 1st Airborne Division went into action on 17 September with virtually no knowledge of close air support procedures.

It is perhaps remarkable in these circumstances that the Allied air forces achieved as much as they did in support of Market Garden. They largely succeeded in keeping the Luftwaffe at bay, and their efforts to ensure the security of the airlifts were very successful. This was a considerable achievement, given the distance of the objectives from Britain, their proximity to Germany and the formidable ground-based air defences deployed in some parts of Holland. It also proved possible for Second TAF to conduct exceptionally effective close air support for XXX Corps on the first day of the operation through careful planning and adherence to well-established and thoroughly rehearsed techniques; and Coningham's squadrons mounted a large and very effective day fighter effort over Holland.

Yet the troops on the ground, ignorant of the constraints affecting Second TAF, were nevertheless disappointed by what they perceived to be a lack of air support. After Market Garden's failure the search for scapegoats predictably gave rise to the usual hackneyed complaints against the RAF. But although, in different circumstances, a more prominent role for tactical air power would obviously have been preferable, it is by no means certain that more air support would have turned the battle in the Allies' favour. Neither the past record of the Guards Armoured Division nor their performance south of Eindhoven on 18 September suggests that they were ever very likely to achieve their difficult 64-mile advance in time to relieve 1st Airborne Division. Nor would the Typhoons have stood much chance of changing the outcome of the Arnhem battle, given the strength of the German blocking lines and the lack of intelligence on their dispositions. Uninformed criticism of Second TAF may conveniently divert attention from events on the ground, but it cannot in itself provide a satisfactory explanation for the Allied defeat.

Notes

1. Kershaw, *It Never Snows in September*, p. 305.

General Conclusion

I T IS STILL commonly argued that Market Garden might have ended the war during 1944 if it had succeeded, and Montgomery's concept of mounting a narrow thrust into Germany remains remarkably seductive. Middlebrook even contends that Allied forces might have continued their advance, so beating the Russians into parts of Eastern Europe.[1] Sadly, such extravagant scenarios cannot be taken seriously. The Allies' logistical position in September 1944 was so precarious that a breakthrough at Arnhem would probably have been impossible to exploit; it is absurd to contend that British forces might have sustained an offensive into Germany or even Poland with a supply chain stretching back to the Normandy beaches. Montgomery apparently believed that victory at Arnhem would leave Eisenhower no alternative but to divert supplies away from the American armies further south, but this assumption reflected his isolated and parochial outlook, and his near total separation from the rest of the Allied command chain. On political grounds alone it would probably not have been feasible for Eisenhower to authorize such a measure, but in any case he did not believe the narrow thrust strategy to be practicable. Operations into the German heartland stood little chance of success unless the advance of British and American forces was properly co-ordinated and sustained by supplies shipped through Antwerp or the Channel ports.

It is also certain that continuing German resistance would have been a major obstacle to any eastward advance from Arnhem. The effectiveness of the German reaction to Market Garden itself lends weight to this view, as does the (largely forgotten) savagery of post-Market Garden operations in southeastern Holland. Only in the following months were German manpower reserves exhausted, primarily by the failure of the Ardennes offensive. Hence, when the Western Allies finally crossed the Rhine in March 1945 and pierced the thin crust of German defences on the eastern bank, they found little else standing in their way. A far more daunting challenge would have awaited any Allied penetration of the Rhine barrier during 1944.

It would be wrong to suggest that Market Garden achieved nothing at all. As Eisenhower had hoped, the operation completely thwarted German plans for establishing a defensive line along the Albert Canal and so removed any lingering threat to Antwerp from the north. It also disrupted German V2 launch plans for a limited period.[2] But the costs were very high. The Allies lost almost the whole of 1st Airborne Division and literally the entire mountain of arms and equipment that their gliders carried into Arnhem, along with much of the Glider Pilot Regiment; the German Fifteenth Army escaped across the Scheldt Estuary to fight another day, and operations to open up the estuary to Allied shipping were delayed until October. Even after the capture of Walcheren early in November a further three weeks of mine clearance were required, so that it was not until the 28th that the first Allied supply ship finally docked at Antwerp. Further to the northeast an extended and costly struggle was required to shore up the exposed eastern flank of the Market Garden corridor, and, if the Germans were afterwards stretched to defend the elongated front line that the operation created, the Allies of course faced much the same problem. The early disasters in the Ardennes were a direct result.

For the proponents of airborne warfare the consequences of Market Garden's failure were also deeply negative. Browning was soon afterwards replaced as deputy commander of First Allied Airborne Army and also as commander of I Airborne Corps; 101st and 82nd Airborne were for the rest of the war used as conventional infantry; and there would be no further opportunity to deploy airborne troops to decisive effect before Germany's final defeat. In the following March, Operation Varsity was in most respects successfully executed in conjunction with the Allied Rhine crossing (Operation Plunder), but Plunder would undoubtedly have achieved its aims without the supporting airborne assault. Indeed, Varsity was executed some hours *after* the leading Allied ground units reached the eastern bank of the river.[3] Hence, like some previous airborne ventures, Varsity apparently had more to do with creating employment for the airborne forces than with operational necessity.

On all of these grounds, therefore, Market Garden must be deemed the most lamentable failure of the Allied campaign to liberate Western Europe. The primary aim of this study has been to reconsider the operation and to dispel some of the more enduring myths that have for so long clouded historical judgements on the events of September 1944. Its central thesis should by this stage be sufficiently clear for further detailed reiteration to be unnecessary, but its broad thrust may now be summarized as follows.

First, Market Garden was not in any sense unusual because it failed or because it resulted in high casualties among the airborne forces. On the contrary, high casualties and at least partial mission failure had characterized the majority of earlier airborne ventures. In terms of the proportion of objectives achieved, the Allied airborne were actually more successful in Holland than they had been in Normandy or Sicily. There were, however, two critical differences between Market Garden and these previous operations. Not only was it was launched against far deeper goals, making the crucial link-up between airborne and ground forces infinitely more problematic; it also involved airborne missions that were interlinked and interdependent, so that a failure to capture just one objective could lead directly to the failure of the entire undertaking. Given that no large-scale airborne operation mounted by the Allies or the Germans had ever previously secured absolute mission success, there was always a strong probability that Market Garden would fail. The single critical airborne mission failure occurred not at Arnhem (where the key objective was captured late on 17 September and held for three days) but at Nijmegen, where the road and rail bridges across the Waal were not taken until the early evening of 20 September.

Second, it is not accurate to describe the joint airborne and ground offensive Market Garden as a brilliant conceptual plan ruined by faulty detailed planning at First Allied Airborne Army headquarters. Although originally conceived as a pursuit operation, by the time Market Garden was launched the enemy had long since stopped retreating. Yet it was by no means a set-piece offensive either, for on 17 September 1944 many of the pieces were still not in place. Nor did Market Garden emerge from a measured or rational examination of how airborne forces might usefully contribute to the Allied cause. Instead, it was a direct product of Montgomery's resolute determination to ensure that he beat the Americans into Germany, and of mounting pressure to find a use for the Allies' enormous and hugely expensive airborne army. In the three weeks preceding the operation this combination of circumstances led to the production of one airborne plan that was quite simply pointless (Linnet) and another that bordered on the suicidal (Comet).

A sound operational concept was never likely to emerge from this situation. It is therefore not surprising to learn that Market Garden was founded on flawed suppositions, massaged intelligence, the neglect of past lessons and the acceptance of innumerable risks, which substantially reduced its chances of success even before it was placed in front of Eisenhower. The very decision to target Arnhem was highly questionable. The town was not selected as the objective on operational grounds but because Montgomery was seeking to maximize the distance between his 'narrow thrust' and the American axis of advance. Yet by striking so far north he both opened his eastern flank to counter-attack and readily accepted the challenge of the Waal crossing, which could have been avoided by choosing a bridging point further south. This, of course, was where Market Garden ultimately came to grief. Beyond this, the idea of conducting a multiple-lift operation against deep and well-defended objectives was fundamentally unsound, while the assumed 24-hour airlift schedule can only be deemed a blunder of truly staggering proportions.

Finally, as it necessitated repeated daylight airlifts to destinations far inside enemy territory and more than 300 miles from most Allied air transport bases, the Market Garden concept established exceptionally restrictive parameters within which detailed operation plans had to be formulated. The First Allied Airborne Army staff were left with very few feasible options and with hardly any time, given the original execution date of 14 September. This course of events was by no means inevitable. Had the conceptual plans been devised on truly joint lines, the air issues that later caused so much controversy could easily have been addressed by the responsible commanders before Market Garden was authorized. As it was, despite the pivotal role assigned to them, the Allied air forces were not allowed to exert any prior influence; Montgomery placed the cart squarely before the horse.

It is in the air forces' exclusion that we can identify Market Garden's most valuable and enduring military lesson, namely the critical importance of bringing all key participants – air, land or maritime – into the planning process at the earliest possible stage. To plan in isolation is to court disaster. It might appear remarkable that a Field Marshal and Army Group commander with Montgomery's immense experience should have neglected this elementary principle, but his methods were notoriously unorthodox. Eisenhower's chief of staff, Bedell Smith, would later claim that Montgomery 'had never grown above corps or at most army commander level', and this point was echoed by Montgomery's former intelligence chief in an interview with Carlo D'Este in 1983. In his view, 'Montgomery thought of himself as an army group commander but ... acted more like an army commander. He still involved himself closely in the affairs of the Second Army, dictating precisely what was to be accomplished and leaving precious little initiative to his army commander.' His idiosyncratic leadership style also entailed the routine violation of established command channels, deliberate self-isolation at his tactical headquarters and the relegation of HQ 21st Army Group to the status of an administrative backwater.[4] Such methods were completely incompatible with the top-level command and control of an immense and highly complex joint operation like Market Garden, which required careful co-ordination of all participating land, air and airborne assets.

The Allied air forces were not primarily responsible for Market Garden's failure. Their stance ensured that the first two airlifts were immeasurably more successful than those mounted in earlier airborne operations. The RAF's position over the location of the Arnhem landing areas would be open to legitimate criticism in the absence of a sound rationale for avoiding the country south of the bridges, but abundant and up-to-date intelligence in fact provided an overwhelming case for landing elsewhere, particularly if a high degree of accuracy and concentration could be achieved. Equally, given the scale and depth of the operation and the prevailing assumption that multiple lifts could safely be mounted, the arguments in favour of Williams' airlift timetable were unanswerable. Despite all the uninformed criticism that this schedule has attracted since, no other plan could, in the circumstances, have provided for the deployment of so many troops within the first 24 hours of the operation.

Finally, it is quite wrong to assert that Market Garden received inadequate offensive air support or that it was executed with 'air inferiority'. Enormous air resources were assigned to the operation beyond those already at Montgomery's disposal; if the Allies had lacked air superiority over Holland the entire venture would simply have been impossible. That air power was unable to make the difference between defeat and victory does not reflect any lack of air effort or resourcing. Rather, it reflects the total absence of air input at the beginning of the planning process, the exceptionally ambitious nature of the Allied objectives and the fact that the operation was blighted by several consecutive days of poor weather.

Historians are fond of speculating about how, in different circumstances, Market Garden might have succeeded. Elsewhere in this study we have noted how the counter-factual arguments usually revolve simplistically around particular details of the airborne plan at Arnhem and do not come close to addressing the more fundamental issues. Any serious attempt to re-plan the operation would have to start at the very top by considering Eisenhower's position and the explicit warning he received from Brereton about the difficulty of mounting an airborne Rhine crossing from England. Events were to prove the validity of Brereton's case, and the Supreme Commander should certainly have considered his arguments very carefully before authorizing Market Garden. He might then have decided to postpone the operation until a substantial proportion of the Allied air transport fleet had been moved to mainland Europe.

However, if we assume Eisenhower was satisfied that the operational benefits of a Rhine bridgehead outweighed the risks Brereton identified, our attention would have to switch to the headquarters of 21st Army Group. Here, it would have been necessary for Montgomery to convene a meeting of the four senior participants in his forthcoming venture – Brereton, Coningham, Leigh-Mallory and Dempsey. They would each have required sufficient staff support to cover the component parts of the operation, namely the ground offensive, the airborne missions, the airlift, air support for the airlift and tactical air support for troops on the ground. Only on this basis would it have been possible to devise a conceptual plan in which all committed force elements were optimally employed to achieve co-ordinated, efficient and mutually reinforcing effects that were properly understood by all concerned.

The obvious initial task would have been to establish an appropriate Rhine crossing point on sound operational grounds. Given that intelligence had revealed the presence of II SS Panzer Corps near Arnhem and that the responsible Army commander (Dempsey) was therefore disposed to avoid Arnhem and Nijmegen, it is very likely that Wesel would have been chosen. Wesel lay no further behind the front line than Arnhem, and the various water obstacles to the north would have protected Second Army's left flank, while First Army covered their right. The problematic Waal crossing essential to the capture of Arnhem would have been avoided altogether.

If for any other reason Arnhem had been retained as the Rhine crossing point, the plan would have had to address precisely the two obstacles that an operation against Wesel would have avoided – II SS Panzer Corps and the Waal River. The arrival of II SS Panzer Corps in the Arnhem–Nijmegen area should have ruled out the multiple airlift plan completely. In such circumstances it was ridiculous to employ in the defence of landing areas troops that could have been dispatched directly to the key operational objectives. Market Garden should thus have involved just one lift to Arnhem and Nijmegen, carrying the maximum possible number of combat troops and the minimum of equipment and support units. This would pre-suppose the availability of some kind of ready-made general-purpose loading plan for deploying the airborne at light scales. Upon landing, the airborne forces should have moved in their entirety and as rapidly as possible to their assigned bridges. If any follow-up lifts were considered essential, alternative landing areas might have been employed to retain an element of surprise but the second lift should have been dispensed with if it could not be executed without diverting combat troops from their primary tasks. Airborne reinforcements could still have been sent to 101st Airborne's area of responsibility and employed to strengthen the Allies' hold on the corridor, while any additional airlift capacity could have been used to drop supplies further north.

Through this means, it might have been possible to deploy both 1 Parachute Brigade and 1 Air Landing Brigade near to the Arnhem road bridge before 9th SS Panzer Division's intervention. But it would be wrong to suppose that this achievement alone would have changed the outcome of Market Garden. In these hypothetical circumstances all the German troops actually sent to western Arnhem and the DZ/LZ area would have counter-attacked around the road bridge instead. The chances of 1st Airborne Division holding out until 21 September would still have been limited in the extreme. As with so many other airborne ventures in the Second World War, Market Garden was only likely to succeed if the airborne could be promptly relieved by conventional ground forces – in this case, XXX Corps.

A number of measures might have been taken to accelerate XXX Corps' advance. The critical delay in their progress occurred due to 82nd Airborne's initial failure to seize the Nijmegen bridges. Although XXX Corps reached

Nijmegen at midday on 19 September, they did not set off for Arnhem until the afternoon of the 21st. How, then, could the capture of the bridge have been expedited? It is beyond doubt that the Market Garden plan should have attached a far higher priority to the Waal bridges on the first day of the operation. The fundamental problem here lay in the over-tasking of 82nd Airborne, which left Gavin with too few troops to take the Groesbeek Heights and the Maas, Maas-Waal Canal and Waal bridges, and which diverted attention from the overriding necessity of securing a Waal crossing before the Germans strengthened their defences.[5] Having failed to take the bridges with just two companies on the 17th, 82nd Airborne had on the 18th to employ much of their available combat power in defence of their landing areas and the Groesbeek Heights. Even on the 19th only one battalion could be spared for the road and rail bridges. Obviously, there would have been no need to fight for the landing zones if only a single airlift had been mounted, but this would still have left the problem of the Groesbeek Heights. The Allies would probably have had to accept the risk of abandoning them to free up sufficient airborne troops for the bridges.

Otherwise, to judge from the Guards Armoured Division's overnight halt at Valkenswaard on 17 September and their desperately slow progress the next day against only very limited opposition, more could have been done at every level of command to emphasize the acute urgency of XXX Corps' task and the inevitability of quite heavy casualties. There is no evidence to suggest that Montgomery put senior subordinates such as Dempsey or Horrocks under anything like the pressure that Kesselring imposed upon Von Bock in 1940, when the Germans crossed Holland in the opposite direction. More thought might also have been given to the provision of infantry support for the Guards in the more northerly stretches of the corridor. They reached Nijmegen on 19 September with very few infantry, and relied heavily on 82nd Airborne in the fighting that afternoon. A shortage of supporting infantry likewise influenced their decision not to advance north immediately after the capture of the bridges on the 20th.[6]

Beyond revising the airborne missions and accelerating XXX Corps' advance, an alternative Market Garden plan would also ideally have used air power to disrupt the German response and slow their subsequent build-up. This would have been critically dependent on the persistence of clear weather conditions during the first days of Market Garden, whereas in actual fact the prevailing adverse weather between 18 and 21 September would, under any circumstances, have imposed severe constraints on the amount of offensive air support that could have been provided. It would also have been very difficult to isolate the battle area, given the limited time available. Normandy was only successfully cut off from the rest of France before D-Day after several months of bombing. But if, for the sake of argument, we attempt to establish how an alternative plan might have *sought* to exploit air power more effectively, the development of an effective interdiction strategy would have to be our primary focus. Montgomery would have had to secure Bomber Command's transfer from the Canadians to Second Army, and it might also have been difficult to find sufficient fighter escorts on 17 September, given that the Eighth and Ninth Air Forces and Air Defence Great Britain were already so heavily committed to Market Garden; but if only one airlift had been flown there would have been no shortage of fighters on subsequent days. On the assumption that fighter cover could have been provided, Bomber Command and perhaps other Allied formations might have targeted railways, roads and bridges to the north, east and southeast of Arnhem. Heavy bombing might also have been used to 'screen' the Allied offensive, as it was in operations like Goodwood, Totalize and Tractable in Normandy. Potentially, this could have offered a partial solution to enemy counter-offensive action around Groesbeek. The absence of follow-up airlifts would also have freed up the airspace over Holland, so creating at least limited additional scope for employing tactical air power in and around the battle area.

The attraction of some such approach to re-planning Market Garden is that it addresses all three main factors in the Allied defeat not as independent and disconnected issues but as symptoms of a deeper problem – flawed command and control. Only a revised command and control process could have resulted in the optimal use of all committed resources to maximize the effectiveness of the first airlift, to expedite the relief of the airborne troops by XXX Corps and to slow the German response to the 17 September landings. Needless to say, some of the proposed courses of action are open to objection, just as the plans actually adopted had both strengths and weaknesses. This is a reflection of the enormously challenging task the Allies set themselves and the extent to which Market Garden stretched their resources to the absolute limit. It might also be argued that no such comprehensive revision would have been justified, given that Market Garden so nearly succeeded. But this would overlook the possibility that relatively superficial adjustments in the Allied plan might have been countered by changes in the German response. Finally, as with so many other counter-factual attempts to re-plan military operations, this alternative vision of Market Garden doubtless depends too much on hindsight. Yet it does not require exceptional hindsight to suggest that a joint operation should involve genuine consultation between all participating services from the very beginning, that past operational lessons should be heeded and not ignored, that enemies should not be underestimated or that two broad rivers might potentially be more difficult to cross than one.

Notes

1. Middlebrook, *Arnhem* p. 442.
2. T.D. Dungan, *V-2: A Combat History of the First Ballistic Missile* (Westholme, Yardley Pennsylvania, 2005), p. 124.
3. Air Historical Branch, *The Liberation of North West Europe, Vol. 5, From the Rhine to the Baltic, 1 October 1944 to 8 May 1945*, p. 178.
4. Hamilton, *Monty*, pp. 402–403; D'Este, *Decision in Normandy*, p. 352.
5. Warren, *Airborne Operations*, p. 93.
6. Magry (ed.), *Operation Market Garden Then and Now*, Vol. 2, pp. 354–356, 504.

Bibliography

Books

Air Ministry, *The Rise and Fall of the German Air Force, 1933–1945* (St Martin's Press, New York, 1983)

Air Ministry, *The Second World War, 1939–1945, Royal Air Force, Signals, Vol. 4, Radar in Raid Reporting* (unpublished official narrative, 1950)

Air Publication 3231, *The Second World War 1939–1945, Royal Air Force, Airborne Forces* (Air Ministry official monograph, 1951)

Ambrose, Stephen, *Pegasus Bridge, D-Day: The Daring British Airborne Raid* (Pocket Books, London, 2003)

———, *D-Day June 6 1944: The Battle for the Normandy Beaches* (Pocket Books, London, 2002)

Badsey, Stephen, *A Bridge Too Far: Operation Market Garden* (Osprey, Oxford, 1993)

Beevor, Anthony, *Crete: The Battle and the Resistance* (Penguin, London, 1991)

Bradley, Omar N., *A Soldier's Story* (Henry Holt and Company, New York, 1951)

Brongers, Lieutenant Colonel E.H. , *The Battle for the Hague, 1940* (Aspekt, Soesterberg, 2004)

Buckingham, William, *Arnhem 1944* (Tempus, Stroud, 2004)

Chatterton, Brigadier George, *The Wings of Pegasus: The Story of the Glider Pilot Regiment* (Battery Press, Nashville, 1982)

Clarke, Lloyd, *Orne Bridgehead* (Sutton Publishing, Stroud, 2004)

Crookenden, Napier, *Dropzone Normandy: The Story of the American and British Airborne Assault on D-Day 1944* (Ian Allen, Shepperton, 1976)

Daglish, Ian, *Operation Goodwood* (Pen and Sword, Barnsley, 2004)

Dungan, T.D., *V-2: A Combat History of the First Ballistic Missile* (Westholme, Yardley Pennsylvania, 2005)

Eisenhower, Dwight D., *Crusade in Europe* (Heinemann, London, 1948)

Ellis, L.F., *Victory in the West, Vol. 2, The Defeat of Germany* (HMSO, London, 1968)

D'Este, Carlo, *Decision in Normandy* (Penguin, London, 2001)

Falvey, Denis, *A Well-Known Excellence: British Artillery and an Artilleryman in World War Two* (Brassey's, London, 2002)

Field Marshal the Viscount Montgomery of Alamein, *Memoirs* (Collins, London, 1958)

Foot, M.R.D. (ed.), *Holland at War Against Hitler: Anglo-Dutch Relations, 1940–1945* (Frank Cass, London, 1990)

Frost, Major General John, *A Drop Too Many* (Cassell, London, 1980)

Golley, John, *The Big Drop: The Guns of Merville, June 1944* (Jane's, London, 1982)

Gooderson, Ian, *Air Power at the Battlefront: Allied Close Air Support in Europe, 1943–45* (Frank Cass, London, 1998)

Hamilton, Nigel, *Monty: The Battles of Field Marshal Bernard Montgomery* (Hodder & Stoughton, London, 1994)

Harclerode, Peter, *Arnhem: A Tragedy of Errors* (Caxton Editions, London, 2000)

Harrison Place, Timothy, *Military Training in the British Army* (Frank Cass, London, 2000)

Hart, Stephen, *Colossal Cracks: Montgomery's 21st Army Group in Northwest Europe, 1944–45* (Stackpole, Pennsylvania, 2007)

Harvey, A.D., *Arnhem* (Cassell, London, 2001)

Hinsley, F.H., Thomas, E.E., Simkins, C.A.G. and Ransom, C.F.G., *British Intelligence in the Second World War: Its Influence on Strategy and Operations*, Vol. 3, Part 2 (Her Majesty's Stationery Office, London, 1988)

Major & Mrs Holt's Battlefield Guide, *Operation Market Garden* (Leo Cooper, Barnsley, 2001)

Kershaw, Robert J., *It Never Snows in September: The German View of Market-Garden and The Battle of Arnhem, September 1944* (Ian Allen, Hersham, 2004)

Kesselring, Field Marshal Albert, *The Memoirs of Field Marshal Kesselring* (William Kimber, London, 1953)

Lamb, Richard, *Montgomery in Europe 1943–45: Success or Failure* (Buchan & Enright, London, 1983)

Macdonald, C.B., *The Siegfried Line Campaign* (Office of the Chief of Military History, Washington, 1965)

Man, John, *The Penguin Atlas of D-Day and the Normandy Campaign* (Viking, London, 1994)

Margry, Karel (ed.), *Operation Market-Garden Then and Now*, Vol. 1 (Battle of Britain International, London, 2002)

Margry, Karel (ed.), *Operation Market-Garden Then and Now*, Vol 2 (Battle of Britain International, London, 2002)

Middlebrook, Martin, *Arnhem 1944: The Airborne Battle, 17–26 September* (Penguin, London, 1995)

Middlebrook, Martin and Everitt, Chris, *The Bomber Command War Diaries: An Operational Reference Book, 1939–1945* (Viking, Harmondsworth, 1985)

Murray, Williamson, *Strategy for Defeat: The Luftwaffe, 1933–1945* (Air University Press, Alabama, 1983)

Orange, Vincent, *Coningham: A Biography of Air Marshal Sir Arthur Coningham* (Center for Air Force History, Washington DC, 1992)

Otway, Lieutenant Colonel T.B.H., *Airborne Forces* (War Office official monograph, 1951)

Pallud, Jean Paul, *Blitzkrieg in the West Then and Now* (After The Battle, London, 1991)

Pissin, D.W., *The Battle of Crete* (USAF Historical Study 162, 1956) http://afhra.maxwell.af.mil

Ryan, Cornelius, *A Bridge Too Far* (Wordsworth Editions, Ware, 1999)

de Ste. Croix, Philip (ed.), *Airborne Operations: An Illustrated History of the Battles, Tactics and Equipment of the World's Airborne Forces* (Salamander, London, 1982)

St George Saunders, Hilary, *The Royal Air Force, 1939–45, Vol. 3, The Fight is Won* (HMSO, London, 1975)

Shores, Christopher and Thomas, Chris, *2nd Tactical Air Force, Vol. 2, Breakout to Bodenplatte*, July 1944 to January 1945 (Classic Publications, Hersham, 2005)

Terraine, John, *The Right of the Line* (Hodder & Stoughton, London, 1985)

Tugwell, Maurice, *Airborne to Battle: A History of Airborne Warfare* (William Kimber, London, 1971)

Urquhart, Brian, *A Life in Peace and War* (Harper & Row, New York, 1987)
Urquhart, Major General R.E., *Arnhem* (Pan, London, 1958)
Warren, John C., *Airborne Missions in the Mediterranean 1942–1945* (USAF Historical Division Research Studies Institute, Air University, 1955)
Warren, John C., *Airborne Operations in World War II, European Theater* (USAF Historical Division, Research Studies Institute, Air University, 1956)
Wilmot, Chester, *The Struggle for Europe* (Reprint Society, London, 1954)

Articles

Cornford, Stan and Davies, Squadron Leader Peter, 'Arnhem: The Weather,' *Air Clues* (October 1994)
Cox, Sebastian, 'Air Power in Operation Market Garden', *Air Clues* (April, May and June, 1985)
Lyall Grant, I.H., 'The German Airborne Attack on Belgium in May 1940', *Journal of the Royal United Services Institution*, Vol. CIII, February 1958
Greenacre, Major John, '"There is, I'm afraid, no alternative …" The Provision of Transport and Support Aircraft to British Airborne Forces during the Second World War', *Royal Air Force Air Power Review*, Vol. 10, No. 3, Autumn 2007
Hobson, Chris, 'Air-to-Air Blue-on-Blue: A Preliminary Study of Air-to-Air Fratricide Incidents Involving Royal Air Force Aircraft during the Second World War', *Royal Air Force Air Power Review*, Vol. 2, No. 2, Summer 1999

AHB Collections and Duplicates

1st Airborne Division Report on Operation Market, 10 January 1945
6th Airborne Division Report on Operations in Normandy, 6 June – 27 August 1944
38 Wing RAF Report on Training and Operations in North Africa and Sicily, May/July 1943
245 Squadron diary
Report by 38 and 46 Group RAF on the British Airborne Effort in Operation Neptune, HQ 38 Group, October 1944
Report by 38 Group RAF on Operation Market Garden, 1 January 1945
Airborne Operations: A German Appraisal, Office of the Chief of Military History, Department of the Army (US Army Foreign Military Studies Series, 1950)
Air Historical Branch, *The Liberation of North West Europe Vol. 4, The Breakout and the Advance to the Lower Rhine, 12 June to 30 September 1944* (unpublished official narrative, first draft)
Air Historical Branch, *The Liberation of North West Europe Vol. 5, From the Rhine to the Baltic, 1 October 1944 to 8 May 1945* (unpublished official narrative)
Notes on the Planning and Preparation of the Allied Expeditionary Air Force for the Invasion of North West France in June 1944, appendices
Notes on the Planning and Preparation of the Allied Expeditionary Air Force for the Invasion of North West France in June 1944, by PS to Air C-in-C, AEAF
Report by First Allied Airborne Army, Operations in Holland, September to November 1944, 22 December 1944
Report by Luftflotte 4, The Invasion of Crete, 28 November 1941
Royal Air Force Airborne Assault Operations, 1940–45, Vol. 1

US Army Air Forces Board Project (T) 27, Long Range Study of Airborne Operations, 29 April 1944
US Strategic Air Forces in Europe Air Intelligence Summaries
War Cabinet Summary of Operations by Bomber Command (WP series)
War Diary of Luftflotte 3, September 1944

Miscellaneous

AHB Casualty Archive
The Times
US Army Military History Institute Papers, Supreme Command, Forrest Pogue Interviews

UK National Archives Classes

AIR 20. Air Ministry and Ministry of Defence, papers accumulated by the Air Historical Branch
AIR 25. Air Ministry and Ministry of Defence: Operations Record Books, Groups
AIR 26. Air Ministry: Operations Record Books, Wings
AIR 27. Air Ministry and successors: Operations Record Books, Squadrons
AIR 37. Air Ministry: Allied Expeditionary Air Force, later Supreme Headquarters Allied Expeditionary Force (Air), and 2nd Tactical Air Force: Registered Files and Reports
CAB 44. Committee of Imperial Defence, Historical Branch and Cabinet Office, Historical Section: War Histories: Draft Chapters and Narratives, Military
CAB 106. War Cabinet and Cabinet Office: Historical Section: Archivist and Librarian Files (AL Series)
DEFE 3. Admiralty: Operational Intelligence Centre: Intelligence from Intercepted German, Italian and Japanese Radio Communications, WWII
WO 171. War Office: Allied Expeditionary Force, North West Europe (British Element): War Diaries, Second World War
WO 205. War Office: 21 Army Group: Military Headquarters Papers, Second World War
WO 219. War Office: Supreme Headquarters Allied Expeditionary Force: Military Headquarters Papers, Second World War
WO 285. War Office: General Miles Christopher Dempsey: Papers

Hollinghurst Papers, Royal Air Force Museum, Hendon

AC 73/23/49, comments on AHB monograph on the history of the airborne forces
AC 73/23/67, lecture entitled 'Air Aspect of an Airborne Operation'

Websites

www.bbc.co.uk
www.pegasusarchive.org
www.wikipedia.org

Index

MILITARY INDEX

in Market Garden, 128, 152, 209, 250, 251
and Market Garden plan, 120, 168, 184-185
3 Parachute Brigade, 67, 68, 75, 76
4 Parachute Brigade, 107, 177, 185, 205
and Market Garden plan, 129, 181, 193, 250
6 Air Landing Brigade, 72, 73
Irish Guards Brigade Group, 235-242 *passim*
64 Medium Regiment, 243, 244, 245
Glider Pilot Regiment, 49, 68, 154, 157, 208, 255
1 Parachute Battalion, 45, 184, 186
2 Parachute Battalion, 45-46, 152, 153, 184-189 *passim*
3 Parachute Battalion, 44, 184, 186-187
9 Parachute Battalion, 68, 73
1st Airborne Division Reconnaissance Squadron, 120, 184, 186, 208

German Army
Fifteenth Army, 97, 255
II SS Panzer Corps 126-141 *passim*, 143, 148, 181, 239, 259
5th Mountain Division, 31, 33
9th SS Panzer Division, 126-143 *passim*, 165, 187, 259
10th SS Panzer Division, 126-142 *passim*, 189
22nd Infantry Division, 25-27
406 Division, 127
Von Tettau Division, 127, 189

Luftwaffe
General references, 24, 30, 154, 176, 204, 225
Allied protection from, 114, 160, 201, 215
in Market Garden, 229-235 *passim*, 241, 252
7th Air Division, 25-27, 31, 34
Luftflotte 3, 230, 234
Fliegerkorps IX, 233
Hermann Goering Parachute Panzer Training and Replacement Regiment, 134-136

Royal Air Force
General references, 39, 41, 101, 107, 154, 207
and air support, 212, 213, 218, 235, 242, 252
and Arnhem landing areas, 151, 153, 161, 178-179, 180, 257
in Market Garden, 15, 176, 232, 233
and Market Garden plan, 87, 249
and Normandy, 67, 68, 159
Air Defence Great Britain, 201, 217, 222, 231, 261
Second Tactical Air Force, 102, 116, 201, 213-235 *passim*, 251-252, 253
Bomber Command, 164, 201, 213, 243, 261
assignment to First Canadian Army, 216-217, 252
2 Group, 213, 217, 235
38 Group, 15, 198, 207
and 'Comet' operation, 109-110
in Market Garden, 177, 182, 184, 193, 202, 232
and Market Garden plan, 175
and Normandy, 67, 68, 70, 74, 76, 158
46 Group, 59, 91, 207
and Arnhem landing areas, 157, 175
in Market Garden, 177, 184, 193, 232
in Normandy, 68, 110
83 Group, 213-220 *passim*
in Market Garden, 222, 230, 235-244 *passim*, 251-252
84 Group, 213, 216, 221, 252
541 Squadron, 133-134

United States Army
General references, 15, 53
First (US) Army, 91, 114, 129, 130
British operations in conjunction with, 113, 121, 259
VII Corps, 65, 67
XVIII Corps, 90, 121, 180
82nd Airborne Division, 48, 50, 51, 93, 255
in Market Garden, 127, 129, 231, 234, 259, 260
and Market Garden plan, 100, 116, 157, 180, 205, 207
and Normandy, 60-67 *passim*, 155-156, 184

GENERAL INDEX